The Moon Cottage Cats

VOLUME ONE

This omnibus edition includes:

The Cats of Moon Cottage

More Cat Tales from Moon Cottage

The first two books from the Moon Cottage Quartet

The Moon Cottage
Cats

VOLUME ONE

MARILYN EDWARDS

WITH ILLUSTRATIONS BY

PETER WARNER

HODDER

The extract on page 36 of 'The Cats of Moon Cottage' from
Norman Nicholson's poem 'The Tame Hare' has been reproduced
with kind permission of Faber & Faber Ltd.

This omnibus edition first published in Great Britain in 2007

The right of Marilyn Edwards and Peter Warner to be identified
as the Author and Illustrator respectively of the Work
has been asserted by them in accordance with the Copyright,
Designs and Patents Act 1988.

3

British Library Cataloguing in Publication Data
A record for this book is available from the British Library

ISBN 978 0 340 95452 2

Typeset in Goudy by Avon DataSet Ltd,
Bidford-on-Avon, Warwickshire

Printed and bound in Great Britain by
Clays Ltd, St Ives plc, Bungay, Suffolk

The paper used in this book is a natural recyclable product
made from wood grown in sustainable forests.
The hard coverboard is recycled.

Hodder & Stoughton
A Division of Hodder Headline Ltd
338 Euston Road
London NW1 3BH
www.madaboutbooks.com

The Cats
of Moon Cottage

MARILYN EDWARDS

ILLUSTRATED BY

PETER WARNER

HODDER

For Michael,
who grins and bears it.

CHAPTER 1

This tale starts with an email. As emails go, this is not the most obviously momentous, but, put simply, it changed my life. It also had a marked effect on my husband, Michael, and his son John and, to a lesser extent, on his other two sons, Damian and Oliver. Here it is:

From:	Mitzi
To:	Broadcast everyone in office
Subject:	Kittens
Date:	22 May 15:23

Our author, Susan Hill, has two seven-week-old kittens, one boy and one girl. She's looking for a home for them, and would rather they stay together. If anybody's interested, please give Caroline a buzz.

From:	Marilyn
To:	Mitzi
Subject:	RE: Kittens
Date:	22 May 15:36

Mitzi, I have just talked to Michael and he says we can take them, which is wonderful.

We have an old cat but I presume that won't
be a problem. But of course someone might
have got there first.
  Marilyn

From:	Mitzi
To:	Marilyn
Subject:	RE: Kittens
Date:	22 May 15:50

As far as I know, no one else has asked
about them, so I think they're all yours.
I'll let you know the details on Tuesday.

From:	Marilyn
To:	Michael
Subject:	FW: Kittens
Date:	22 May 16:14

Hey, Michael - we are parents!
  Love M

From:	Michael
Sent:	22 May 16:46
To:	Marilyn
Subject:	RE: Kittens

Now you can't shout at me for calling you
Mam!
  Hope Septi takes to them!
  Will you tell him or shall I?

And so it came to pass – well, nearly. But Michael's percipient question about Septi is to haunt me soon enough.

Meanwhile, back at the office, in the early evening of that same day, there is a sudden frenzy of activity as arrangements are made for a small drinks party to celebrate the engagement of one of our team to her young man. Just a quarter of an hour into the party, I'm unable to contain my excitement a second longer and find myself stepping forward. It is with only the smallest intent of wickedness, and with truly no aim of upstaging anyone – but more because my mind is full of whiskers and kittens – that I hear myself declaring loudly that Michael and I also have an announcement to make. Michael stares across the room at me, radiating apprehension, because he cannot second-guess what I am about to say and everyone falls disarmingly silent.

Now embarrassed, I raise my glass and mumble coyly: 'Michael and I would like to tell you all that we are about to become parents.' I will remember that silence for the rest of my life, heightened as it was by the exquisite expression of confusion and incredulity on the face of our boss. Pregnancies abound in our office, and while they are naturally supported, the ensuing need for maternity leave always creates a wake of problems. At fifty-plus years of age, I, and therefore Michael, had for some time been considered to be safely beyond all that sort of thing.

Shamefully unable to maintain the suspense any longer, I explain prosaically that this is more by way of an adoption, and a feline one at that, and with visible relief our boss rallies and offers us warm congratulations and all happiness with our new offspring.

CHAPTER 2

May

On returning to our cottage in Hertfordshire that weekend, however, Michael and I seriously begin to contemplate how the resident aged cat, Septi, might react to a kitten in his life. It is now to be one kitten, not two; as the second one had already been given a home before my email reached Susan Hill.

By this time Septi, named in full 'September' after the month in which he was acquired, has been a member of Michael's household from his late kittenhood until the full maturity of his now seventeen years.

During those years he has endured many moves and tiresome disruptions to his fiercely guarded routines. He has survived any number of unintentional shutting-ins and shutting-outs, uncounted numbers of fights, several road accidents – of which one, certainly, would have killed any lesser cat – and has generally just been left to get on with it, through times of love and also of neglect. So Septi, now in his later years, has developed an independence and aloofness that Kipling would recognise immediately. He does indeed walk by himself on the 'wet wild roofs, waving his wild tail and walking by his wild lone'. In short, he is his own cat. He patrols his domain, the cottage, the garden and the immediate environs, with *brio* and immaculate attention to detail, which, among other things, entails seeing off no end of neighbouring cats.

Septi deserves a proper introduction. He is a neutered, male, short-haired, tabby moggy. Long bodied, he has ebony-dark shiny fur, which is exceptionally silky to the touch. He sports a smart white waistcoat and a full set of matching socks. Septi has a slightly haughty expression, and can look down his nose as no other cat of my acquaintance. He has a nick in one ear, acquired in a long-distant battle, magnificent fierce white whiskers, and penetrating large, greeny-brown eyes. He also has slightly broken, yellowing teeth but manages to eat perfectly well with them.

One unusual feature of Septi is his oddly strangulated voice. Miaowing, for him, always appears to take a considerable effort, and the sound that he emits suggests nothing less than that a pair of hands might be clamped around his throat. Notwithstanding that, he can yowl loudly enough to wake me, although not always Michael, when locked out in the rain in the yard under our bedroom window. But, and this is gloriously his, he has a mellifluous and deep purr, which he can sustain for astonishingly long periods. His purr is special; he can fill the whole cottage with it. It thrums through you. It is an operatic purr.

He is a loving cat, for all his aloofness, and bestows his affection on each household member in turn. When he is in the mood, he will especially seek out all three of the boys and, in particular, John. Who, precisely, in the family *is* his guardian continues to be robustly debated and remains unresolved. John thinks he probably took charge of Septi by default when he was still a small kitten. His brothers, Damian and Oliver, both wanted dogs and John was the only one who declared an interest in possessing a cat. Damian, on the other hand, believes that Septi was introduced as just the house cat, pure and simple.

In our household at the time that this story begins, John, of the three brothers, is the one who lives with us permanently; the other two make spasmodic weekend raids, and Damian is in fact currently domiciled in South Africa. Septi had, however, lived with Damian for six months, four or five years earlier, which seems to have resulted in mutual respect, as well as a reciprocal love.

What else about Septi?

He has a pronounced and morbid fear of thunderstorms, and if I know he is outside when a storm is brewing and I am not there to let him in, I become anxious on his behalf. As for finding himself near fireworks, he would rather be buried alive I believe. His one physical weakness, I sometimes think, is that a small lump on his back possibly hurts him, as I have noticed that occasionally, if he is stroked too firmly along his back, he will bite the hand that strokes, more warningly than penetratingly; but disconcerting for the stroker, nonetheless.

Over the span of his life, Septi has been a rapacious hunter and able to kill all manner of animals with quick efficiency, but by the time I entered his life, his hunting, for the most part, is over. There is an oft-repeated story of an occasion in his youth, when Michael's youngest son, Oliver, circa five years old, embarked upon an experiment with profound results. Early one morning when all other human members of the household were soundly asleep, the young boy, awake and bored, took it upon himself to entertain Septi by introducing him to his hamster. Oliver was in fact the proud owner of a pair of hamsters, but on this particular morning he restricted the formalities to just one of them. To his delight, the cat and the hamster had a most lively game together.

When John rose from his bed a short time later, however, he was saddened to find the small corpse of the very same hamster and a faraway look in Septi's eyes. Perhaps, in order to protect Oliver's sensibilities, not enough emphasis was laid upon the mortal dangers inherent in such play and, in the tradition of Greek tragedy, the following day the same terrible scene unfolded with the remaining hamster.

Septi never had it so good.

CHAPTER 3

June

So now the moment has arrived.

'Will you tell him, or shall I?'

We both try. I open the batting.

'Septi, come over here. There's a good fellow. Look, there's something I need to say to you. I do know that just at the beginning, you will hate it and you will feel really iffy about it, but I promise you, it will be all right, really, eventually. Trust me.'

Michael watches this performance from me with an incredulous grin. He leans down and scoops Septi up in his arms, holding him close, and the great cat purr revs up, increasing in volume as Michael strokes him in all his favourite places. Septi rubs his cheek against Michael's and then glances across at me, down his nose, with an expression on his face that I cannot fail to interpret as 'eat your heart out'.

Michael murmurs into the top of his head almost, but not quite inaudibly: 'She wants to bring a horrid little kitten into your life and ruin your peace and destroy everything

9

that you are used to, and all that you enjoy most. So what do you think to that, boy? How does that grab you then?'

Out for a duck.

What is this male bonding stuff, this total resistance to change, I wonder crossly, but not without feeling a twinge of guilt. Michael winks at me and I flap a tea towel at him, in frustration. Septi continues to purr obliviously.

I hear myself pleading pathetically: 'Why don't you support me, Michael? If you don't help me with this, then I might just as well phone Susan Hill, now, and say it's off!'

Michael shrugs and observes: 'Don't think Septi really got what I said, anyway.'

'Yes, he did. I reckon he clocks much more than you think. There is an essence of understanding that I'm sure he has.'

'Don't think so, but all right. Listen, Septi. A kitten is coming and you will enjoy, OK? Acceptable, Marilyn? Does that fit the bill?'

Having exhausted the supply of tea towels, I stomp off upstairs and run myself a diverting bath. As I lie down in the water and watch it rise up the sides, I find myself smirking as I realise I'm taking part in the activity of displacement in more than just one sense.

5 June

At last the day I have been yearning for dawns and we are in Solihull for a meeting. This day was nominated as our day for collection as Solihull is close to the home of the kittens, but the waiting time has stretched out endlessly.

By mid-afternoon the meeting has drawn to a close and

we are free to go in search of the longed-for kitten, and after a thirty-minute car journey we find the village. Michael navigates the car down a long winding driveway and we pass between several fields and beside a large pond and, finally, after several twists and turns we pull up in the yard and are greeted, with great warmth, by Susan Hill, who walks towards us, accompanied by a lean red and white shorthaired cat. Having exchanged greetings with our hostess, Michael and I both bend down to say hello to this fit-looking feline, but in a very businesslike way and with no sign of embarrassment, the cat turns away, fully occupied with making her toilet in an old horse trough, now filled with soil. She completes her task and we are introduced. She is Tallulah, the mother of the kittens. I ask Susan who the father might be and she reckons that the dad is a regular consort from the nearby housing estate.

Susan invites us to follow her into a fine, rambling, limestone farmhouse and we find ourselves in a large light kitchen, which is magnificently dominated by a long wooden table. And there, on this table, is pure joy. Pure Joy is the most beautiful kitten in the world. Of course, Michael and I were bound to fall in love with the kitten whatever she looked like, but this kitten is breathtakingly lovely. What greets our eyes is a small curled-up fur-ball who, as we enter, looks up and presents to us a tiny triangular heart-shaped face, animated by two enormous, penetrating *amber* eyes, surrounded by fabulous almond-shaped, geisha-stripes and finished off with large pert ears. Her overall colouring is predominantly stripy grey and black and white, with ginger slashes, and could properly be described as 'torbie', being a dark tabby tortoiseshell colour. She stands up unsteadily, on extraordinarily long and elegant legs, and sashays towards us – and before she reaches us, we are goners. Hook, line and sinker.

I nervously ask if this is to be our kitten, for love at first sight is what has happened. Susan, smilingly, reassures us. This is indeed the sole remaining kitten. Someone, locally, took the other one.

Because the kitten has been part of Susan's household for so long, Susan warns us that she has been named already, as she could not remain anonymous for all that time. Susan looks across at me, and says, in a level tone: 'Her name is Ottoline.'

I gasp. 'You mean as in Morrell?'

Now, laughing, she nods emphatically.

I dare not look across at Michael, but as I hold my head down, in my mind's eye I see images of Lady Ottoline's fierce, determined chin and recall her legendary death from cancer of the jaw, which had always seemed so ironic. Immediately all manner of other non-sequiturs float through my head, her untiring courtship of the artistic glitterati of her day, her intense relationships and arguments with Bertrand Russell and Augustus John, and those endless soirees. She had, at one time, lived in and around Bedford Square, and I had left not only part of my soul there, but also a chunk of my heart, having, coincidentally, worked and played in that same square for many years. Although anomalous to label a tiny fluff-ball with such a grave name, it has a curiously right feel to it.

Anyway it is a done deed. 'OK. Ottoline then,' I murmur compliantly.

CHAPTER 4

Having carefully placed our precious nine-week-old bundle into a carrying cage, which we jam, for safety, on to the back seat of the car, we set off down the long drive in the direction of home. As we call out our farewells to Susan, we make a promise that we will keep in touch with a kitten-progress report.

At first, from the back of the car, we hear a series of tiny miaows, but then, as we continue to ignore the pleas, the small noises steadfastly develop into a crescendo. It is hard to believe that such a tiny animal is capable of generating the ear-shattering cries that are now emanating from the Lady Ottoline. They are heart-rending. I acknowledge my caddishness. I also cannot put out of my mind the thought that her mother will probably be experiencing a similar anguish. The look on Tallulah's face as we had bundled Ottoline into the cat carrier had not escaped me. But now, suddenly, there is silence; and soon we are on the motorway and the silence continues.

After a long but uneventful journey, we arrive home and carefully transfer the cage and its tiny occupant into the house. The front door of our ancient cottage opens straight into the low-beamed sitting room, which is where most of our lives are lived and where Septi reigns supreme. As we enter the room, with cat cage in hand, Septi, who has been asleep on his usual chair, stares across at us apprehensively, possibly speculating whether an impending visit to the vet, which he hates, is on the agenda. Why else the cat carrier?

At exactly this moment, from the depths of the cage, we all hear a small but distinct 'miaow'. Septi looks as if he has been electrified. On top of the aural assault, he has now picked up the feline scent. I cannot easily remember the last time I saw a cat with such a cross expression on its face. He looks furious. His mouth has pulled into that small governessy 'o' that cats effect so powerfully – his whisker pads are puffed out – and the tabby 'worry' lines above his eyes are even more drawn together. He is seriously put out and showing it.

We both feel concerned about letting the kitten out, but she has just endured a long and tiring journey and she really needs her freedom, and on the principle of 'in for a penny', we decide to release her and see what happens. Fumblingly, we open the cage door and one small, nervous kitten tumbles out into the room. Septi utters a deep growl of rage, glares at her, then quickly turns tail and runs from the room. Michael follows him and finds him by the back door, demanding to be let out. Septi's need to get away is so absolute that we have no option but to comply. Also, we are shocked by his growl; cats seldom growl, and it is always serious when they do.

Meanwhile, the innocent instigator of this agitation is busy investigating everything. Initially hesitant, her courage seems to increase by the second, and this small predatory creature, so recently torn away from her mother and uprooted from the only home she has ever known, quickly establishes her own familiarity with these new surroundings with growing confidence. We give her some Carnation Milk (Susan suggested this as being most like cats' milk), which she drinks, and soon she is eating a small mouthful of wet kitten food. We show her a cat-litter tray and wait; she uses it within half an hour of arriving. Ottoline has made a new home.

Meanwhile, we have the problem of Septi and his own concerns. A couple of weeks earlier I had taken Septi to the vet for the treatment of some minor ailment, but also to have him checked out, and he had been given a clean bill of health. But when I had asked my vet, a man in his sixties, on the brink of retirement and with all the experience that those years had yielded to him, what he thought might happen when I introduced a kitten into Septi's life, he had looked thoughtful and said:

'You do realise that this cat is a considerable age. And what you are doing is a major disruption to his well-organised life? He will accept it, or alternatively, I'm afraid, he might leave home. There is no knowing – it could go either way.' He then chuckled merrily: 'I'm darned certain that if it were me, *I* would leave home.'

I did not find this as amusing as he did, but laughed feebly all the same. Alarmed though I was at the time by this conjecture, on balance I reckoned that Septi liked his home comforts too much to do 'a runner', but I now recall this with increasing concern.

Eventually I manage to cajole Septi back into the cottage, and he enters with what seems to be an optimistic caution, hoping, perhaps, that the kitten has gone as rapidly as it had arrived. He walks, slowly, through the kitchen, towards the sitting room. The sight that greets him is an outrage. What he sees is one small kitten, who having made herself completely at home in the eating, drinking and cat-litter tray departments, is now snuggled up securely and comfortably on Michael's shoulder, as if she belongs there. He utters a long, low, guttural groan. So despairing, but also primeval, is this sound that it makes me worry and laugh all at the same time. Our immediate concerns are unfounded, in that no attack is forthcoming from Septi, although he is undoubtedly deeply unhappy. He lies stiffly and ill at ease on the edge of the sofa, sometimes staring at her, but mainly glaring morosely at the floor.

Suddenly Ottoline stirs herself from the reassuring warmth of Michael's shoulder, stretches her long elegant limbs in the manner of a completely mature cat, and jumps down on to the floor. She walks across the room until she is just under the cushion on which Septi is lying; she then lies down in an echo posture of his and looks coyly up at him. To begin with, he ignores her, then he stares down at her. She looks back at him very sweetly, at that moment oblivious to anything or anyone else.

And thus begins the beguiling of Septi.

Shortly after this first flirtatious endeavour by Ottoline, however, Septi firmly requests 'out' and spends the remaining part of the evening waving his wild tail on his wild own, somewhere in his private hiding places and when, finally, we do persuade him to come back inside the cottage, it is achieved only by the deceit of temporarily concealing Ottoline upstairs, where Septi tends to visit, rather than inhabit, so that he is persuaded that he has regained the mastery of his realm.

Within the confines of the cottage, Ottoline, during Septi's moody egress, has been displaying all her charms to us on full voltage and we have become completely captivated. She jumps from chair to desk and from desk to sofa; she runs with impeccable balance, as if it had been her lifelong habit, along the back of the sofa, and leaps fearlessly on to the mantelpiece. From there she springs straight on to another chair and up on to the high windowsill. She rests on her newly discovered ledge for a heady fifteen seconds, before descending into the first armchair and on to the floor. She then, languorously, rolls over on to her back and, revealing the soft snow-white fur of her belly, she daintily bends over the tips of each of her front paws and coquettishly tips her head on one side, assessing the effect of all this on her attendant audience with the one eye that is visible.

As Michael and I watch her admiringly, she changes her mood abruptly and springs up – first on to me and then on to Michael – brushes herself against our faces, and curls up on to our shoulders and then halfway round the back of our necks, that especial position seeming to be the most pleasing to her. She is wonderfully democratic with her favours, notwithstanding that each demonstration of affection never exceeds three minutes. John is away on holiday and, selfishly, in my infatuation, I'm grateful that on this first night I need only share her with Michael, although I am longing to see John's pleasure in her on his return.

By this time we have decided that Otto is the name. And Otto is what she becomes from now on. Otto the beautiful. Otto the brave. Otto the curious.

Having persuaded Septi to come back into the cottage, we find that Otto has, inevitably, emerged from her temporary concealment and followed us downstairs again where she continues with her all-important investigations of this new home. Septi, on seeing her, stalks off into the dining room. His mouth remains drawn together in that 'o'.

Reluctantly we tear ourselves away from the pleasures of kitten worship and prepare to head for the bed-room above. As we leave, we murmur gentle words of comfort to the old cat, stroking him lovingly but guiltily. We turn back and watch him walk, uncertainly, into the sitting room, his face bearing his newly permanent 'disgusted' expression. Finding a kitten-free zone, he curls up on the sofa, sighs deeply and buries his nose under his paw.

By the time we get upstairs, whence we have smuggled Otto, we have one very tired kitten on our hands and we place her carefully on the bed between us where she immediately falls soundly asleep, and so rests the household on this first night in Otto's new home.

CHAPTER 5

Andrew and Jane, much-loved stepchildren from my other family, are visiting England from their New Zealand home, and the following day come to stay with us for the weekend. They have shared their living with cats many times over and Jane, while watching Andrew manifestly falling in love with Otto, laughingly cautions us that there is no contest between a newly minted kitten and a mature old cat. I recognise the truth of this and make a silent vow to myself that we must take pains to prevent Septi from feeling eclipsed in any way by the feline usurper in our midst.

John returns from his holiday this same weekend and is bowled over by Otto as soon as he walks through the door. I watch his growing enchantment with the daft pride and pleasure of the newly besotted lover, but again become achingly aware that we must be mindful of Septi and his needs.

Meanwhile life continues and Michael, John and I all return to our respective jobs, leaving Septi and Otto to work out their *modus vivendi* in their own way. There is no cat flap on the cottage door and we have, until this time, let Septi out on demand. Otto is awaiting her injections against viral flu and feline leukaemia, so cannot yet be allowed out into the garden and beyond, and Septi seems to want to be out more than usual, so sometimes, when we leave for the office at our customary time of 6.50 a.m., he is out and resists all pleas to come back into the cottage. We are philosophical. It is summer and warm, and there is a shed and a greenhouse for him to shelter in if he needs protection from the sun or the rain.

From:	Marilyn
To:	Susan Hill
Subject:	Ottoline and other things
Date:	11 June 11:33

Dear Susan

It was really good to speak to you this morning. Please assure Clemency that Ottoline is well and happy and staggeringly bouncy and very much loved and cared for. I had to leave early last night in fact to take her to the vet for her jabs, and she was very brave and seems to have suffered no lasting side effects!! I was reassured too that you think Septi will come round – vet thinks so too.

I do feel for the sadness of her mum though – hope she recovers soon. If only one could reassure her that kitten is OK.

But thank you all for allowing such a wonderful bundle of joy into our lives – we are all soppy about her.

This email is generated by a phone call I had from Susan, who explains that Tallulah, Otto's mum, has, contrary to their expectations, spent long hours repeatedly searching for her last remaining offspring who had been at her side until Michael and I came raiding, and that Clemency, Susan's resident daughter, is spending much time necessarily comforting her. I'm instantly mortified, of course, even though I know that someone, somewhere, would have had to have taken Otto away from her mum, had it not been us.

Before Michael and I started to share our life together, I had lived many years in the Yorkshire Dales, and had spent as many hours messing about playing at farming, outside normal working hours, as I was able to persuade the long-suffering local farmers to allow me. I kept my own flock of hens and I used to help at haytime and with milking, and also with calving, and sometimes sheep shearing, and always, when possible, lambing.

One of the annual rituals of sheep farming, however, against which I was never able to harden myself sufficiently, was 'spaining'. The ewes give birth to their lambs mainly through April, and even just into May in the Dales, and they live side by side contentedly enough – apart, that is, from the repetitive, neurotic bleating of the ewes for their young to return to their sides. The greatest disruption to their daily tranquillity during this time comes in the form of being shepherded from one pasture to another, or even up on to the high hills, until the end of July. (At least, in normal years when the farms are not in thrall to the dreaded Foot and Mouth disease.)

Then one day in early August, triggered by the auction

mart's calendar, it appears as if every Dales farmer who has any lambs at all decides that this is the week for spaining. This involves each individual farmer gathering up all of his sheep, and now substantially growing lambs, from his probably widely scattered pastures into one huge flock, separating out the lambs from the ewes, and containing the ewes in a field with fencing and a gate. The lambs are then removed to an equivalent pasture out of earshot of the ewes. This is a necessary exercise so that when the lambs go to market as 'store' lambs in the early autumn, they will have regained the weight that the trauma of separation will have caused them to lose, and the ones that are to go to market as 'fat' lambs will go within the next few days.

Because many different farmers will be doing this over a period of ten days or so, it means that the hills ring out, day and night, with the unceasing cries of ewes and lambs yearning to be with one another again. When it has been raining, if you go near the gate of spained ewes you will see by the churned-up mud exactly how many hundreds of times every single sheep has stamped back and forth, back and forth, at the gate where they last saw their young taken away. Many a Dales farmer finds it a difficult time too, and they will tell you that they know that the crying and the marching go on right through the night as well as during the daytime. The sound always brings tears to my eyes.

Tallulah, I salute thee and apologise.

～

A few weeks have passed and Otto has now received both lots of injections, and the time has come, we feel, to let her out into the garden. It is hard, too, domestically, keeping the back door shut through a warm summer. Septi has evidently become captivated by Otto, but we are yet to discover quite how much. He spends much of his time with her in the cottage, and I have found them both, upstairs on a sofa in John's room which gets the warm morning sun, fast asleep and clearly content in each other's company.

One fine Saturday morning in late June we let little, long-legged Otto out into the sunshine for the first time in her life and stand back to watch. She is fearful at the very beginning, as the sounds alone must be truly shocking to her 'protected' indoor ears, and she runs out and then runs back indoors again very fast. Finding the back door remains open she cautiously ventures out, but this time she stops, and looks about her with intense curiosity and starts, slowly, tentatively, to walk up the five red-brick steps into the main part of the garden, which is surrounded by a wooden pergola bearing a profusion of climbing roses.

Suddenly, as she is halfway up the steps, over her head but way out of her reach, a large Cabbage White butterfly flutters past her, and from a stand-ing start, using the muscles in her hind legs, Otto springs many feet high into the air in a reared-up 'standing' position and briefly catches it between her front paws. Elvira Madigan take a bow. On this occasion the butterfly escapes to fly off safely, high into the sky. It is a remarkable display of the speed of her reactions.

Within seconds of her losing her butterfly we watch, impressed, as she springs up the pergola as if it were a main thoroughfare, and we see her disappear into the thorn-covered tunnel of the rose bower atop the highest arches. I gaze after her nervously and Michael gently mocks me: 'You will learn. You have to let them go. She will be all right.' And indeed, on that day, she is.

The very next day, however, she is climbing again amid all the roses when the calm of the afternoon is pierced by high, squeaky distress calls. We both rush out and quickly discover that the source of the sound is Otto, who is apparently jammed on a crossbar of the pergola over on the far side of the garden. Michael manages to ease her down from among the roses and we both inspect her, closely. Sticking out of the top of her eye, just above her eyelid, is an exceptionally long, menacing-looking thorn. I rush inside for tweezers and manage to extract it in one piece.

She whimpers dramatically as it is pulled out but then, forgivingly, licks my hand with her delicate, sandpapery tongue. We gently put her down on the lawn and she bounds across it in great leaps, for the pure joy of being young and female, and having the whole huge world in front of her to explore – and finding that it just gets better and better.

As we are watching her we are joined by Septi, lately emerged from the cottage, who has a remarkably sergeant-majorish expression on his face. His whiskers are very bristly and standing out, and he looks slightly cross and a bit ruffled. He sits in the middle of the lawn and miaows in a disgruntled-sounding way. Otto, indifferent to his chiding, bounds across the lawn and up towards the fence near the main road. Septi now, most emphatically, miaows something at her – and only at her – in his funny strangled-sounding voice. Michael touches my arm.

'Hey – Mo – do you realise what he is up to? He is protecting her. He is trying to warn her not to go there.'

'No – don't be daft. 'Course he isn't,' I retort insistently.

But again, as Otto continues to walk along the fence towards the road, Septi makes his miaowing noise, and then he turns towards us, away from the road, and runs back into the depths of the garden and the far corner, which is without roads on either side. She is now watching him and, as he moves across the garden, she slowly turns and follows him.

Septi knows about roads; Septi has already lost some of his nine lives on roads. He did what he did with full knowledge. 'Oh Septi – you angel,' I whisper.

Michael puts his arm across my shoulders as we walk back into the house. 'Septi will be her guardian. It will be fine, you'll see.'

CHAPTER 6

Septi and Otto, day by day, seem to become closer. We are both relieved, and amused, by the definite spring in Septi's step – and even detect a sparkle in his eye.

The old boy, truth to tell, had been whiling away most of his days, before Otto came upon the scene, in unremitting slumber. He would eat; he would sleep, for hours and hours, changing his favourite chair with the seasons – this being dictated by the desirability for either cooling summer breezes or which chair was closest to a radiator in the months the central heating was on. Just occasionally he would take the minimum amount of exercise a cat needs to take to stay in full working order. This would entail slowly rising, shaking each of his stiff old limbs in turn, and then, with enviable languor, drawing his body out to its fullest length, first pushing out his front legs long and low with his backside high in the air; and then leaning forward with his shoulders high he would stretch out his back legs in turn, giving each one a determined shake for good measure. And always, while he did this, he would open his mouth wide in that head-splitting yawn that is singular to cats of all sizes from tiger to tabby. Following this huge effort, he would then saunter out into the garden to do what a cat has to do and to see off the enemy should there be any around, but even in the height of summer it was pretty rare for him to stay out all night, and never in winter.

Slowly and graciously Septi had seemed to be slipping down into a peaceful and ever more dormant old age. And now Otto is here and everything is different, for ever.

Otto bounds down the stairs and rushes around the room, greets everyone exuberantly and demands to be let out. As she hurls herself around the place, Septi watches her incessantly. At least one of his eyes seems always to be upon her. If she goes out, he goes out. If she demands food, he demands food. When she sleeps, he sleeps near her. The beguiling of Septi is now thoroughly under-way.

One sunny day the cottage seems very still. The menfolk are out and about pursuing their various hobbies and I have been involved in some downstairs activity. I come up the stairs very quietly, wondering where the two cats have hidden themselves, and walk into John's bedroom. There on the sofa, under the window, the most extraordinary sight greets me. Septi is lying on his side and, at right angles to him, purring quietly, is Otto, who is clearly 'milk treading' with slow deliberation. She has her mouth clamped to one of his nipples. He too is purring loudly. As I stand there he looks across at me and shifts his body slightly with what, it seems to me, is a trace of embarrassment or perhaps discomfort. He stands up and the moment has passed. I pick him up to examine him and, with a little consternation, discover that two of his nipples are significantly inflamed. This worries me.

A couple of hours later I look in the room again and find that they are both fast asleep, curled around each other, with what appears to be the greatest trust that two cats who are not litter mates could possibly achieve. I'm hugely moved by Septi's compassion, although thrown by his maternal role-playing. But why not? Many male animals are outstandingly conscientious parents and, if this is what the lady wants, he was going to comply. Dear Septi.

I am also concerned that he is going to be very sore, but shortly after this I observe that he turns his back on Otto whenever she comes with kneading motions anywhere near him, just as a mother cat would when it's time to wean the kittens from her. They remain very close, and sleep near each other more often than not.

CHAPTER 7

July

Otto has won yet another heart in our household. Damian has returned home from South Africa and, animal lover that he always was, he has succumbed, fully, to her considerable charms. He remains, of course, loyal to old Septi, but it's very clear that Otto has bewitched him.

Otto has, indeed, powerfully imprinted herself upon all of us and it is not easy any more to imagine life in the cottage without her. Tiny, graceful, elfin creature that she is, she is irrevocably intertwined in the way we live now.

One warm night, as I'm lying on my back, head buried deep in the pillows, on the very edge of sleep, Otto creeps across the top of the pillow and gently licks my eyelids. The sensations of that rough tongue and the tickling of her whiskers are both wonderful and unbearable; eventually she moves away and I fall asleep. I start to dream. I see things somehow differently, my sense of smell is profoundly increased and my hearing strangely acute, but as well as these things my overall awareness is heightened to a point of near pain. In my dream I cannot see myself but I know that I'm a cat. I wake up and my metamorphosis dissolves but the recollection of it is disturbing:

> She came to him in dreams – her ears
> Diddering like antennae, and her eyes
> Wide as dark flowers where the dew
> Holds and dissolves a purple hoard of shadow.[1]

Otto has developed many rituals, some lovable and some strange. Every morning, when I'm bathing, she 'miaows' to come in the bathroom for a morning cuddle. She waits outside the door and calls at the moment she considers to be the appropriate one to be let in. This more often than not means that I, her slave, have to get out of the bath, as she just shouts louder and louder if ignored. By now I will have compliantly wrapped myself in a bath sheet so that she may sit on my knee. I stroke her gently and she purrs. Her purr is very quiet. You can hardly hear it, but you can feel it vibrating within her like a small engine. Sometimes she snuggles up on to my shoulder and licks my hair.

She is fabulously generous in her loving and will spend minutes on end cheek-rubbing and nestling into her chosen person of the moment. She will perform all of these things with Michael, John and Damian too. One of the rituals of the bathroom that she taunts me with is to run around the edge of the bath, almost kidding me she is going to slip, but

---

[1] 'The Tame Hare' by Norman Nicholson, taken from 'The Rockface' in *Collected Poems* of Norman Nicholson, ed. Neil Curry (Faber & Faber, 1994).

doesn't – quite. So often she seems to just miss falling in by a whisker, but that feline sense of balance is truly remarkable. She adores the running of the tap and often requests to be lifted up to the basin where she both watches and plays, obsessively, with the running water.

One thing that she does, which disconcerts me terribly, is to wee in the basin; not regularly, just occasionally, but certainly unnecessarily, as there is a litter tray downstairs always available. She still uses the litter tray even when she has been let out, which Michael finds infuriating, but I know that it's my fault because I continue to keep one going inside the cottage, and I presume a ready-made litter tray is easier to use than soil that needs digging up.

She regularly makes me laugh by pausing very dramatically and, as she slowly raises her head, opening her mouth wide into a big but controlled 'O', which she holds, as if trans-fixed, for several moments. This is a completely different gesture from the small 'o' that is used when cats are cross. I am amused as it's a carbon copy of the mock shock-horror expression that my father used to adopt when I told him some snippet of information that he needed to allow himself time to react to. This gesture when adopted by cats has a different genesis. My mentor in so much to do with animal behaviour, Desmond Morris, indicates that this grimace – in Otto's case that is, not my father's – is known technically as the *flehmen* response, and is in fact the cat exercising its sixth sense or, more technically, its vomero-nasal organ.[2] She is taste-smelling the delicious aromas that are borne on

<hr>

[2] *Catwatching* by Desmond Morris (Cape, 1986).

the air or are embedded in the carpet in our fragrant bathroom. I think I would rather not dwell on why it is so richly delicious for her.

A further endearing habit she has is to 'forget' that the very tip of her pointy pink tongue is still sticking out of her mouth, and she will hold this slightly daft – but oddly appealing – expression for up to a couple of minutes before 'remembering' to withdraw her tongue.

One day as I'm lying in the bath, dreamily pondering these things, I'm struck by the slightly unnerving thought that Otto's gestures mimic some quite specific habits that both my father and my mother had formed when they were alive. It would appear, merely from the dearth of evidence, that there are strict rules in force preventing the dead from communicating with the living, but if people who have died were to try to communicate, would it not be logical that they might adopt the channel of a favourite pet of the one with whom they sought contact as an obvious conduit?

I suddenly, quite badly, want to believe this. It would be so comforting and, as further fuel to the idea, it would surely be mistaken to 'block' an attempt by the beloved dead at communication. On the other hand, this way madness lies? I rise from the now shiver-inducingly cool bath and determine, once and for all, to rid myself of these nonsensical musings.

~

The month of July passes in a hot dreamy haze of sunlight, and one long golden day seems to slide into another, sustained by evenings of apparently endless twilight: the great solace of those who live in the northern hemisphere and know they must, in turn, suffer the rigour of short sharp winter days, leaving for work before sunrise and returning home long after sunset for weeks on end.

Otto, in this her first summer and with no possible anticipation of winter, explores every part of her expanding territory. She has now perfected her hunting skills in the butterfly department, the forensic proof of which we discover all too frequently in the confetti of broken wings on the steps leading up to the lawn.

Septi, still besotted, follows her around when she is on the ground, or even up into the pergola, but Otto frequently takes flight, too. She has a passion for heights – some cats do and some don't. If it is there and it can be climbed, climb it she does and, crucially, the higher the better. Our cottage has an exceptionally steeply pitched tiled roof and she has taken to walking along the very spine of this roof in an alarmingly vertiginous manner. She will also part-walk and part-slide down the steep sloping sides of the roof which are made up of tiny ancient (and irreplaceable) red tiles, some of which she regularly dislodges, so that at frequent intervals we have to rehang them. She frightens me so much when she does this, and if I'm around when she embarks upon her roof climbing, I cannot fail to be aware of it as it is usually heralded by the raucous calls of territorially jealous magpies.

Early one morning, just as I'm about to leave for work, I hear the all too familiar jeering of the magpies around the side of the cottage by the back gate. Having called Otto and

Septi for some minutes and having failed to get a response from Otto, I trudge out into the garden and look up at the roof. There I see, high up on the tiles, the pathetically tiny outline of a small cat. As I screw up my eyes against the sun to see better, I can distinguish the dark red of Otto's mouth wide open and the sight is accompanied, above the hubbub of the magpies, by the plaintive mewling of a truly scared cat.

'Don't worry, Otto. I'm coming to get you,' I call reassuringly, to myself at least.

She cries out, yet more pitifully, and the magpies flap closer. They are big and they appear to be quite vicious. She is young and inexperienced. I have no idea whether she would be able to hold her own against them and keep her position on that roof. I go off to look for a stepladder and realise that the only one that will get me high enough is the very long, hard to carry, painter's ladder in the greenhouse. With great difficulty I haul the ladder across the garden and manage to lodge it against the wall, but unfortunately in order to position it so I can reach Otto, I have to rest the foot of it on a high flowerbed with very soft soil and a lot of low-lying bushes. I'm wearing a straight skirt and tights, and as I start my ascent I ask myself if more than just a day in tatters lies before me. Otto continues to cry out but, as I ascend the ladder to its topmost rung and she first sees my head rising up above the edge of the guttering, she falls silent and edges backwards, higher up the roof. She moves over to the left and I stretch out my arm as far as it will go. The ends of my fingers are within a couple of hands' breadths of her.

At this point the magpies, who have been in full squawk hitherto, start to jump up and down in a semi-circle around her, making aggressive guttural noises, and I feel my mouth go dry as I realise I appear to be witnessing an ornithological haka. I shout out and flap my arms around to try to disturb them. This, of course, makes Otto back away even further, and as I stretch out to my fullest extent towards her, two things happen in quick succession. I twist round and find myself with a view that is completely new to me, over the end of the roof, over the high fence and gate, and down into the road, where I see a man walking by who waves merrily up at me and walks on. As I sadly register his misplaced jolliness, I feel the ladder, imperceptibly, start to lean to the left, as first it sinks deep into the soft soil on that side, and then from the sheer imbalance of weight continue its inexorably sinister journey. It happens in excruciatingly slow motion, and the sound of the clattering of tiles, the snagging of wisteria leaves, the cracking of rhododendron branches – as I, and my errant ladder, continue on our way – seems to last for five minutes.

When the descent is finally over and I am able to disentangle myself from the ladder and the bushes, I find, although bruised and slightly cut, I'm otherwise intact – albeit the owner of beribboned tights and a skirt split from stem to stern.

I start, a bit shakily, to ascend the ladder again and, once more, am fiercely resisted by Otto. 'For goodness' sake come down, Otto. This is stupid. Come on *now*. At once!' I hear myself shouting, crossly.

But for the complication of being up a ladder, my feet would definitely be stamping in crossness. 'Oh Otto, please come. Please? Sweetie, come on! Please, please, please.'

No movement. She sits, hunched, staring, and then looks away. I hate her. 'Michael, where are you when I need you?' I mutter unreasonably.

I begin to feel sorry for myself and to care a great deal less for Otto. I climb down the ladder, having checked to see if the jolly gentleman of the street is anywhere in sight so that I might ask him if he could assist me, but the road is empty of all pedestrians. While I was diverting myself by falling in slow motion, a phrase (other than the standard expletives) had been eluding me, but now, as I scan the deserted street,

I recall the words with taunting clarity: 'I was much further out than you thought. And not waving but drowning.'[3]

I go inside and make a strong cup of coffee. I can still hear the magpies. By this time I am hopelessly late for work and aware that my excuse for not making an appearance is fairly feeble. I go out, torn clothes flapping about me, and climb up the ladder for one last rescue attempt. She is now right up on the ridge of the roof, by the chimney stack, and the magpies are about a yard away from her. 'Otto. This is your last go. Come on.'

She looks down at me with her owl's amber eyes. She miaows quietly and starts to come towards me; she edges towards the guttering and within reach of my hand. I grab her by the scruff of the neck and carry her down the ladder in one hand. Her body hangs kitten-limply and I transport her into the cottage where I manage, just, to resist shaking her.

As soon as we are both inside and the door is shut, she goes across to her food bowl and eats as if she has been without food for days. I make a guess that her voracious appetite is in reality a trauma displacement activity and, thus encouraged, I decide to enact my own displacement – or at any rate replacement – activity, and retire upstairs to get into fresh clothes.

And so to work.

---

[3] 'Not Waving But Drowning' by Stevie Smith, taken from *The Collected Poems of Stevie Smith* (Penguin, 1985).

CHAPTER 8

August

From:	Marilyn
To:	Everyone
Subject:	BROADCAST: Kittens
Date:	27 July 14:02

Susan Hill has a cat, Tallulah, who has just this week given birth to seven kittens, five of which Susan needs to find a home or homes for. I am doing this email on Susan's behalf, as Michael and I have adopted one from an earlier litter, by the same parents, who is completely adorable, and very brave with a most emphatic character – and if I was allowed, I would have all five!

They need to be found homes by mid-September – they are mixed gender and mixed colour, some tabby, some ginger, some tortoiseshell.

Can you initially email me back if you are interested? Thank you.

Marilyn

From:	Beth
To:	Marilyn
Subject:	BROADCAST: Kittens
Date:	27 July 16:22

```
I'd be interested in a ginger one - keep me
posted.
  Beth
```

From:	Kevin
To:	Marilyn
Cc:	Michael
Subject:	RE: Kittens
Date:	27 July 17:40

```
I think Michael should let you have them
all.
  Kevin
```

From:	Michael
To:	Marilyn
Cc:	Kevin
Subject:	RE: Kittens
Date:	27 July 18:24

```
Puss . . . off!
  Michael
```

Shortly after this I receive an email on work matters from
Susan, in which she signs off, philosophically: 'Love
from Susan and Seven Kittens like the man going to
St Ives'.

～

On 14 August John and Kathy come to stay for a weekend. John, an old and very dear friend from my distant past, has had a rough passage of health and is frail and wheelchair bound, but he is fortunate in having a tender and compassionate carer in his young partner, Kathy, and together they make it work.

From the moment that they enter the cottage, they are captivated by Otto. John, especially, is taken with her looks and her geisha eyes, but Kathy is not immune to her charms either and I watch the germination of the idea of having a cat in their life together grow in Kathy's mind. We discover that Kathy misses her old cat, Biggles, terribly and she knows that a dog would be too much for John to handle. I had never thought of John as a cat man, but then before his family had acquired their dog, Maggie, he always swore, very much in the manner of Professor Higgins, that he would never let a dog in his life, but he ended up being completely besotted by her, so I do know all things are possible.

As the weekend gently advances, punctuated by meals washed down with lots of wine, the conversation turns around on itself and, it slowly evolves, we are talking about Kathy and John taking on one of Tallulah's kittens. From this moment the die is cast.

∼

Since late July and well into August there has been a steady drought and the atmosphere has become stifling and intense. For some days now the sound of distant thunder, rumbling away in the background, has created a sense of impending menace but the storm has failed to come to fruition.

During the heat of these several weeks, Septi has wandered around the place in a listless manner, seeking his favourite shady places. Mainly he has flopped out under the garden bench and the big picnic table. In the last few days, as the storm has come closer, his concern is increasingly perceptible; his head comes up at every distant rumble of thunder and his whiskers shoot forward in concentration. Now the air is electric with tension; it feels muggy and heavy. Today there has been an eerie grey light from early dawn, as the cloudbanks have built up to completely hide the distant sun. The sky is seething and rumbling, and contains within it all the plum, brown and black shades of dark bruising. The erstwhile dark edges of the great rain clouds are now engorged and have come together overhead to form an unrelenting black covering.

I rush outside to bring in the washing as the first thunder peals out and the great rain is released. At that first roar I'm aware of Septi racing past my legs and into the cottage. As I tear the clothes off the washing line I become drenched through to the skin within seconds. The rain is so solid that the strands of water appear to be motionless diagonals stretched out like harp strings. The force of the rain really hurts as it strikes my head, arms and back. The heat remains tremendous in spite of the downpour, and inside the cottage it's like standing in a warm oven. There is another massive clap of thunder followed, this time only seconds later, by a shaft of lightning so brilliant that everything within the cottage is illuminated starkly white.

I rush from room to room trying to find Septi, and keep shouting out for him, but he has completely vanished. I now call Otto. I'm unsure how she reacts to storms, and consider that this may well be her first truly spectacular one. I have not seen her for most of the morning. Because the rain is so violent I have shut the door, but can now discern through the hissing of the rain a plaintive miaowing from the other side. I open it and a small, protesting, drowned rat of a cat bursts into the kitchen, shaking herself for all the world as if she were a large retriever. Otto is saturated, but does not seem especially frightened or alarmed, merely outraged by the utter wetness of the rain.

I go back upstairs to find Septi and eventually track him down under John's bed. He is cowering with his head pointing away from the window, facing the wall. He is shaking with fear.

'Oh Septi, what dreadful trauma in your youth has caused this awful horror?' I enquire solicitously, but pointlessly. I try to stroke him but he is at that middle distance under a large bed where he is unreachable. I do not want to upset him further by poking him out with some pole, so for the moment I leave him be.

As I go downstairs there is another loud crash of thunder, and the lightning, with an extraordinary intensity, momentarily etches everything into strange monochromatic colours and then dies away. The rain is torrential and splatteringly noisy.

Otto, having managed to lick herself dry, in that paradoxical manner of cats, shakes each of her back legs in turn and saunters upstairs, apparently unaffected by all or any of it.

I look through the windows in the hope that the impenetrable black might have shifted but it remains, ominously, directly above us. I'm standing at the sink when a seemingly endless roll of thunder, accompanied by simultaneous and jagged lightning, coincides with the electricity cutting out.

Finally, the time has come when I must comfort that poor old Septi, I reckon, so slowly I walk upstairs. As I do so I find myself wondering whether our old cottage has lightning conductors and asking myself why I had never thought of this before.

I walk into John's room and see that Otto has somehow, remarkably, cajoled Septi out of his hiding place under the bed and has got him to lie on the sofa next to her where, in true maternal fashion, she is washing him, meticulously, from head to foot. Although he is not quite purring, he is definitely not trembling, as he was when last I laid eyes on him.

As I turn and quietly tiptoe from the room, I know that I leave the old cat in far better care than ever I could vouchsafe.

CHAPTER 9

September

As time goes by, Otto becomes increasingly adventurous and little by little she expands her territory. Because I fear that she might get lost in her wanderings, she now sports a green velvet collar, complete with safety-elastic, with a disc on which is engraved her name and our telephone number. The collar also has a little bell which we hope will discourage her from hunting birds. She continues to climb the roofs of both our cottage and our neighbours' adjoining cottage – to our consternation, and probably the equal dismay of our neighbours, whose tiles are under threat from her vigorous callisthenics. Michael and I go into the garden and look up at the high-pitched spine and see her etched against the skyline as a tiny black silhouette. We are mesmerised by her audacity, but we do also fear for her safety. In the end we leave her be, consoling ourselves with the ineffable truism that 'cats will be cats'.

She has, however, acquired another ill-behaved habit. When she climbs on to the roof of our neighbours' house, she will sit up on the tiles and, by her sheer presence, tease their big black labrador, Dante. We often hear him barking up at her in frustration and know that she is on his roof, taunting him with the feline equivalent of that human juvenile insult which consists of thumbs in ears and waving fingers while sticking the tongue out. What primeval instinct has made dogs and cats such enemies of each other? I know well that dogs and cats can be the best of friends if they are introduced to each other from birth, but their natural reaction, if not raised in a mixed feline/canine environment, seems invariably a hostile one.

My sister Margot and her family come out to spend a day with us around this time and she brings with them her much-loved Westie terrier, Snowy. Two things of note happen almost immediately. As Snowy walks into the cottage, Septi, who being an old and wise warrior would normally have ignored her, is forced into a reaction by Snowy, who bounces up to him and, in a manner that can only be described as confrontational, barks repeatedly in his face. Septi stares back at Snowy, holding his ground, and Snowy then rushes forward and threatens to bite him.

We will never know whether this is intended to be just a

feint or not, as, without further ado, Septi calmly, but with dangerous speed, lashes out with claws fully extended and slashes open Snowy's black nose-leather. Snowy then squeals repeatedly in shock and pain, and I'm much relieved when Margot assures me that the damage is comparatively superficial. Septi has trouble sheathing his claws again as they seem to have locked in a spasm, and as he sits back he looks down at his right paw, which he is holding out in front of his nose in a gesture that is almost triumphant, claws fully out, with a curiously philosophical expression on his face. We put Snowy out in the garden and shut the door.

Otto comes into the room at this point, having missed the earlier fireworks, and, springing on to her cat platform, sees and hears Snowy outside the French windows. She is outraged and spits and snarls. We keep Snowy in the garden, but in spite of this Otto continues to glare at her through the window, with her back in full arch and fur erect, making the most hideous protestations in the form of growls and hissings. In the end we have to accept that the situation is irreconcilable and we shut the cats upstairs out of reach of Snowy and vice versa. Otto does not show any sign of becoming a dog lover, it would seem.

One Saturday morning I'm lying in bed, half awake, with my head turned towards the little square window. Lazily I am trying to determine what sort of a day it's going to be before I climb out of bed, when I see what appears to be a flying cat, bearing a passing resemblance to Otto, who, in mid-flight, 'hovers' on the tiny windowsill, scratches at the window pane and then continues on her earthward journey. It had been a fairly celebratory Friday night and a certain amount of red wine had been consumed, so momentarily I decide I'm hallucinating, except, as I wearily lie back, I recall that as the apparition passed the window it had been accompanied by the unmistakable tinkling of the little bell on Otto's collar.

Hastily grabbing some clothes, I tentatively go downstairs, wondering what awful sight will greet me, and slowly open the back door. Not a sign of any animal. I walk up the garden steps and round the corner and there, on the lawn, is Otto. She is sitting, rear leg pointing skywards, intent on an enthusiastic grooming session. I call her and, nonchalantly, she rises and walks across to me, completely intact. As I walk back to the cottage meditatively, I hear myself humming 'Immortal, Invisible, God Only Wise'.

As well as climbing things, and disappearing and generally being very distracting, Otto is hugely lovable. She adores to be nursed in your arms, on her back, like a baby, and a particularly affectionate habit she has is to wrap the pads of her front paw round your finger and hold it, gently, but emphatically. Many cat lovers have encountered the same gesture in their own cats and it is always curiously affecting.

Septi and Otto continue to strengthen their bond of friendship in vigorous play with each other, and an activity that enchants us greatly is their game of tag in the garden. Septi chases Otto and then Otto chases Septi. The rules are hard to work out but are clearly quite specific. Sometimes it involves Otto rushing up the pergola and sometimes, Septi. Rhododendron and laurel bushes are especially good for this wheeze, and it appears to be very important to keep hidden for very long spells of time before revealing where you are, and then when you do come out, you always have your mouth wide open in silent cat laughter.

Septi plights his troth to Otto in more ways than we will ever know. One day, however, his courtly behaviour towards her is almost more than we can bear. He appears to have concluded that if she cannot hunt birds for herself, as her hunting has been hitherto restricted, by size of conquest, to beetles, wasps, butterflies and frogs, then he had better do it for her. So, this old cat, having not hunted in many a long month, even in years, returns to the cottage one morning, proudly bearing in his mouth a three-quarters-grown blackbird, freshly killed, which he deposits before her. She, little madam, disdains his kind offer and hightails it off in the opposite direction, leaving the mess of body and feathers for us to clear up. I fervently hope that this is not a new pattern of behaviour developing within the old boy, and, for the most part, it would seem it is not.

And then, suddenly, the serious business of kitten collection is upon us. I have been busily trying to find homes for some of the seven kittens that Tallulah had given birth to on 18 July, and who are now ready to go to their new homes.

One, a tortoiseshell girl, is to go to John and Kathy. Two ginger boys are to go to Beth in our office. Two more, a girl and a boy, are to go to someone with whom Susan has been in touch, and who I have offered to meet on the A40 to do the handover.

I buy three luridly coloured cat carriers, they being the only ones available locally, and Michael and I stuff them in the back of the car and drive up to the Cotswolds to collect the five kittens. We get there to find that the other two kittens have, happily, already been homed locally. Susan is away but Stanley, her husband, helps us round up the remaining five kittens, and we finally get them into the carriers, two and two and one.

This time it's not good. As we turn round and head out of the drive, the kittens, probably each one inspiring the other, cry out persistently. By the time we have reached the main road and driven out of the village, the smell rather more than the sound of upset kittens is overwhelming and Michael and I begin to falter. We stop the car and remove the sodden newspapers in the bottom of the cat carriers and start again. The trauma, for them and for us, is then repeated, and again we stop to clean up. After we have been travelling for about half an hour, with the windows half open and trying to talk to each other loudly to blank out the heartbreaking sounds behind us, we realise that for five minutes now there has been a complete silence.

We look at each other.

'You thinking what I'm thinking?' Michael asks.

'They must be alive. They could not all just die like that!' I protest. I climb over the back of the seat and, by turning the cat carriers this way and that, am able to account for five kittens, all variously curled up and asleep in rather damp-looking little balls.

'Keep driving and please don't spare the horses. It's going to be rotten doing the handover because they look so ghastly, and they were so pretty and fluffy when we picked them up,' I wail.

As we near the outskirts of London, and employ the stop/start motion that is necessitated by the sheer volume of traffic on the A40, known locally as 'Leadville' due to the outpourings from the exhausts of the commuters grinding their way in and out of the city from and to Oxford and the north-west, the kittens wake up and become upset, anew. Finally, we see the BP garage, which is our first point of handover, and pull in and wait for the two girls who are to meet us to take the first pair of kittens. They arrive, late, having been held up on the equally tiresome North Circular Road. Gratefully, but also shamefacedly due to their condition, we hand the kittens over.

The girls peer into the bright mauve cat carrier and see a tortie and a ginger kitten cowering together, peering back at them. The kittens are bedraggled, and although we have tried really hard to clean them up, they still, all too clearly, reek of the expelled contents of their stomachs. One of the girls asks me, in a worried voice, if I'm sure that we are not handing over sickly kittens, and I try to explain that travel sickness is altogether different from any other illness and, that once they are home and cleaned up, they will be fine. I show her the other kittens, looking equally unkempt, but I have a suspicion that she thinks I have palmed her off with the 'B' team. They put the kittens into the back of their car and drive away, and I say a small prayer for both the girls and the kittens.

'Two down, three to go,' I say cheerfully. And Michael mumbles something that sounds suspiciously like 'Never again'.

We arrive at John's and Kathy's house in West London, where Beth has kindly agreed to meet us, so that we can hand over all three kittens in one go. After joyous introductions and a glass of much needed wine, we feel the time has come to liberate the kittens from their malodorous prisons.

Beth's kittens are two ginger boys, with adorable, erect, ringed tails, whom she has named Malachy and Oisin. She is charmed by them and graciously forgives the condition that she finds them in. The kittens busily start to investigate every corner of the large room they now find themselves in, and we sit back and relax.

We have also released John's and Kathy's dramatically coloured tortoiseshell kitten, Delilah. Delilah – with her rich ginger, black and brown body and snow-white legs and white chest, and a glorious multi-coloured head, half black and half ginger, and the cutest pink nose with ginger 'pollen' splodge marks on either side of it. Delilah was probably her mother's favourite, as she is definitely the best nourished of the kittens that we have seen. She, of the three of them, most vehemently asserts herself and struts off towards the saucers that contain milk and food, travel sickness notwithstanding. She seems to know that this is now her home, but surely that is too whimsical? How could she?

At some point we all lose sight of one of the ginger boy kittens; he just disappears. There is an almighty scramble as those of us who are agile enough get down on our hands and knees to look for the young fugitive. Kathy races up the many flights of stairs in this tall house, searching for him, but he cannot be found anywhere. Eventually he is discovered, curled up asleep and looking wonderfully peaceful, on a low-slung bookshelf, atop a pile of venerable military history titles, no doubt grateful for the sheer immobility of his new bed. Beth, and her accompanying friend, are gratefully reunited with her pair of kittens. Meanwhile, John and Kathy coo blissfully over the audacious Delilah.

I adore this moment as I watch this little group of human beings falling, by degrees, in love with their respective pets. This minute is worth all of the cries and the smells (and the guilt) of the previous hours, three times over.

CHAPTER 10

Michael and I had booked our annual holiday for mid-September and it is now imminent. We have been going, for some years, to a house in a village nestling in the foothills of the Garrigues, hidden deep in the Vallée de l'Herault in the heart of Languedoc, where we return year after year and which feels to us like our 'home in France', but in fact it's owned by friends of ours who kindly rent it out to us.

We decide that it's not fair to ask John to look after Otto for the full fortnight that we will be away, as she is wild and hard to keep under control. Septi, on the other hand, is streetwise and could manage the odd twenty-four hours left to fend for himself. Also, he is uninjected, so no cattery will take him anyway, and the vet has advised us against injecting him at his great age.

The morning approaches that we must take Otto to the cattery and I dread it more than I had dreamt possible. Suddenly the longed-for escape down to our beloved retreat in the South of France is flawed.

Michael and I take her to the cattery together and I

behave absurdly badly. I complain that the perfectly adequate cages are far too small, and when I hear the distressed cries of some of the other cats I get completely angst-ridden. I leave her special tins of food and try to explain to the staff why they have to be rotated etc., and am convinced that this won't happen. I make the mistake of turning round and seeing her face pressed against the door and her mouth open miaowing; an image that haunts me, repeatedly, while we are away.

The holiday passes uneventfully enough, and Michael is happily distracted by the fact that the last of the grape harvest is coming in all around us, and this is the best time of year for the locals if the weather has been kind. This year it's an excellent grape harvest. I feel unable to admit to Michael how completely bereft I feel by the absence of our small fluff-ball. My sense of loss is made worse by the fact that a family of feral cats, scrawny mother and half-grown kittens (one of which is undoubtedly brain-damaged), continually call upon the garden of our house. Linda, our hostess, has firmly requested that there should be no feeding of the cats so that they might be discouraged from visiting, but clearly the occupants before us have been feeding them anyway, so they cry out plaintively for the first few days of our stay. It is a mighty test of a cat lover's resolve not to feed them, but with difficulty we resist the temptation.

Two weeks later we return home and rush to the cattery to collect Milady Ottoline. She eyes us without any sign of evident pleasure; she turns away from us and pretends she has never met us before in her life. Always on the slim side, we note that she is a little thinner. I try to find out from two of the attendants how she has fared while we have been away.

'Fine, fine. No problem at all,' a young member of staff responds cheerily enough, but with the thoughtless ease of someone chanting a mantra, which curiously fails to reassure me.

Life, however, appears to return to normal on our homecoming and Otto is soon seen waving her wild tail from the rooftops in her familiar and mad way. Septi, at the first return of us all, does seem to be slightly put out, so it might be that he had relished being Lord of the Domain again. It's several days before any of us sees the two cats obviously interacting, and nearly a week before I find them lying near each other. Who knows what interpretation Septi has given to Otto's involuntary absence?

Soon after we are back I hear from Susan Hill that poor Tallulah has suffered dreadfully this time from the uplifting of the bulk of her litter. She has had to call the vet, who thinks, probably, too many of the kittens were taken at one time and he has administered hormones to stop her flow of milk and to help her to come to terms with the loss of her progeny.

From:	Beth
To:	Marilyn
Subject:	Oisin and Malachy
Date:	28 September 16:32

Any signs of shyness have now completely worn off! Susan said they had never tried kitten food – but the boys are eating it like pros. Their appetites are growing daily. I'm feeding them the Carnation Milk, which is still an obvious favourite. The litter tray is another, less appealing, favourite. They play in it and scatter the sand everywhere.

I had a trolley next to the litter tray that had tea towels on it – big mistake. I've come home each evening to find my tea towels covered in cat litter, lying limp, half-in, half-out, of the tray. They use the trolley as a climbing frame. Found Malachy asleep in the frying pan that I keep on one of the trolley shelves.

Got to find a new location for the trolley. How's Delilah?

Lots of funny stories to tell.

TTFN. Beth

In early October my friend Annie comes to stay the night. Annie had made a bid for a kitten on behalf of her brother when I had been soliciting requests from would-be cat owners for kittens from Tallulah's most recent litter. In the event, he and his partner had decided against it, but Annie has always adored cats, and especially kittens, and is ready to fall for the charms of Otto, which it pleasures me to witness she does, wholeheartedly.

We have a long glorious night of reminiscences about life, death and the universe, and finally go to our various beds happy, but somewhat the worse for wear. In the morning, in spite of my self-induced frailty, I find myself smiling when I hear Annie's soft, pretty laughter rippling all round the cottage as she plays with Otto in our bedroom. After a less than robust breakfast, Annie makes her way home – and that would have been that but for a curious footnote to her visit.

In 1996 Michael had given me an engraved gold crucifix at the end of the Easter Vigil Mass, when I was formally confirmed as a member of the Catholic Church, and which turned out to be the last church service my father ever attended as he died suddenly and unexpectedly less than a month later. The crucifix had gained all the more emotional significance for us both, as, on one particular occasion, it had brought comfort to Michael's father, as he lay dying only a few weeks following my own father's death.

I am therefore distraught, on the Monday following Annie's visit, to discover that the crucifix cannot be found anywhere, and for several days I have not known how to bring myself to mention it to Michael. His mother is a firm believer in praying to St Anthony, the Patron-Saint-Who-Finds-Things, so I pray to St Anthony big time. Finally, I pluck up the courage and tell Michael. He is, naturally, very upset, but we both fervently believe that it will turn up. A couple of weeks go by, and then one day Annie phones me and we talk about all sorts of things to do with work, and also personal matters, and arrange to meet. Eventually we are about to hang up when Annie says, in a slightly discomfited voice:

'Marilyn, was there any special reason why you wanted me to have that gold crucifix?'

'Annie – oh Annie. Are you serious?' I squawk.

'Well, I'm serious I have a gold crucifix,' she chuckles.

'That is just so wonderful. I cannot tell you how I have been in agony looking for it.' We laugh and talk for some minutes and, although she never says it to me, I suspect she too is glad that it has been an accident. What sort of clumsy proselyte must I, otherwise, have seemed to her?

As I come off the phone I wonder how the crucifix and chain could possibly have got in among Annie's possessions, and then I remember that Otto plays with it all the time when I have lain it down on my desk. She picks it up, with her claws extended to the minutest degree, very delicately, and then throws it around, and on this occasion I had left it on the desk in our bedroom, and in the course of Otto's play it obviously just landed in Annie's basket.

Otto, the scamp, but olé for St Anthony and Annie.

CHAPTER 11

November and December

John and Kathy come for a long-planned weekend and naturally we invite them to bring Delilah, Otto's younger half-sister. In fact, if the father is the same one who sired Ottoline, which Susan believes is the case, the same parentage (albeit from Tallulah's next litter along) should, technically, make them sisters, although not litter sisters. Either way, sisters or not, the weekend is not entirely the feline success that we are anticipating.

Septi – although initially assuming a shocked expression on his face when yet again a cat carrier is brought into his sitting room and into his peaceful old age, and out steps another young female cat – appears on reflection to be graciously resigned about the intrusion. Otto, on the other hand, behaves disgracefully. That is, of course, in human terms. I presume that for her, as an adolescent, full female cat, now aged seven months, to suddenly find herself confronted by, on her own territory, another entire female cat, albeit much younger, must seem a highly threatening situation. The noise levels of spitting, and especially hissing, are considerable. I believe that Delilah with Septi alone would have been all right, but when she is faced with the dynamic of Otto, back arched and piloerect (managing single-handedly to look and sound like *both* of the fighting cats in Goya's classic painting *Riña de Gatos*), it's all simply too much for her to take.

After initially turning tail and escaping upstairs, Delilah does return to hold her own, however, and hisses back as good as she gets, but she appears, not surprisingly, intimidated by the combination of strange surroundings and hostile hosts. Who would not be? On this occasion Septi does not lend his support to Otto in her aggression, and by the end of the weekend a mainly peaceful stand-off has been accomplished by the three cats, with Septi able to discreetly communicate from time to time with Delilah, while Otto maintains her distance, but continues to stare unrelentingly at the visiting cat, who might be from Mars for all the kinship she displays. Otto, at least, now restricts her hissing to *close* encounters only with Delilah. The latter is clearly confused by the antagonism but welcomes Septi's tacit gestures of friendship.

It is wonderful, however, to see the way that Delilah is a constant delight in equal measure to both John and Kathy, and how plainly they dote upon their beloved companion. She is growing into a very beautiful, silky-haired, tortoiseshell cat, although slightly sturdier in build than the willowy Otto.

Christmas approaches and we have to decide quite soon now whether to allow Otto to have one litter of kittens, or whether to neuter her before she has her first oestrus, which is likely to be any time from January onwards. Susan Hill has recently told me that she is going to have Tallulah neutered, and this knowledge is creating within me a strong yearning to carry on this fantastic line of cats. Tallulah's line seems to produce especially pretty cats who are, by all accounts, very loving too, and there is also the literary lineage that must be considered in the tradition of 'Ottoline Morrell'. I would not want Otto to have more than one litter, but perhaps just one? Each time I have sought homes for kittens, there have been more people who want kittens than there are kittens to go round, and I'm confident that we would find willing and responsible volunteers, on top of which I would like to keep one, or perhaps even two, for myself.

All my life I have wanted to have animals around me who would be allowed to have their own offspring, and it has never before been possible. That desire is probably why I have the adolescent need to play at farming whenever it's possible. I have, too, a strong wish to see how kittens who have been socialised from birth, who have been born in the house that they grow up in, will develop.

Michael and I talk round the houses on this one. 'Have you thought what poor old Septi might feel?' he asks me, ever loyal to his elderly companion.

'It'll be all right. It was all right with Otto, and you were doubtful about that one.'

'Umm – yes. But kittens, plural, is different. And who is going to look after them during the day?'

'They don't need looking after in that way,' I plead. 'Otto will make a wonderful mother, you will see.'

'Hey, what has happened to the conditional tense then? Where has "would" gone to? This is beginning to sound like a *fait accompli.*' He rolls his eyes in a martyred sort of way.

'No, no. It must be a joint decision. And also we should consult the boys too.'

But finally I perceive that Michael, himself, is quite keen on the idea anyway. John and Damian are both, in their chic parlance, 'cool', too.

The green for GO glows on the horizon.

～

Christmas arrives and it is crisp and frosty white but there is no snow. There is almost never snow on Christmas Day now, certainly not in the south of England. But, notwithstanding, Michael and I adore Christmas. I love the family gathering in and coming to stay. Sleeping bags everywhere. Heaven. It is always difficult, when working full time, to be properly organised, and I have now given up making real Christmas puddings in advance, but I love the sending and receiving of the cards, the buying of the Christmas tree, and the ritual decorating to Christmas carols from King's College Cambridge played on our old vinyl-playing record player, which must never happen before Christmas Eve.

For some years now I have used just tiny white lights on the tree and only silver decorations, so that the effect is monochromatically simple, and this year I managed to find a large number of multi-faceted silver balls, which we have added to the other silver decorations. On Christmas Day, after the slumbering lads have folded away their sleeping bags and just as we are about to depart for church, we go into the sitting room, letting in the cats for the first time that morning, and Otto runs amok.

Her frenzy is not for the toy mice or the cat-balls we bought for her and Septi, or even the catnip stocking (although she did rather like that – nothing like a fix on Christmas Day), but because the sun is shining through the French windows, hitting the countless facets of the silver balls hanging from the tree. As a small breeze gently turns the balls in circles, a myriad shafts of sparkling light dance up and down and across the ceiling, along the thick oak beams, over the tops of the armchairs, the curtains, the walls and all around the floor. Otto is lost to the enchantment of choosing where to leap next. She dances everywhere; round and round like a little dervish, pushing her paws out quickly by turn, trying to catch the tiny sunbeams. Septi sits motionless on the arm of the sofa. His expression is disdainful but he watches Otto all the same, just as we all do.

'Happy Christmas, darling cats,' I murmur.

Two days later we have snow, and I'm childishly thrilled because it makes it almost a white Christmas. There is a covering of about three inches, enough to change the landscape outside beyond immediate recognition, and presumably also to alter the familiar scents.

Michael and I let the cats out, wanting to enjoy their reaction to the snow. Septi, of course, has seen it all before, and does not, on the whole, appear to enjoy it very much. He goes out through the back door only as far as the bottom steps, raises his head, sniffs the air, then turns round and comes back into the cottage. Otto, on the other hand, is apparently dumbstruck. She bears the expression of one who is outraged because SOMEONE took the garden away and changed it. Having rushed out, she stops dead and looks around her in surprise.

By this time, she can feel the cold of the snow on her feet. She lifts up her two front paws in turn and licks them frantically. She shakes all four feet repeatedly. She bends her head down and snuffles the snow and then sneezes protestingly. She makes a very small miaowing noise, which sounds like a muffled question. She comes back inside but within seconds wants to go out again. This time she runs around a little but, we assume, the pain of the cold snow takes its toll on her feet and she comes back inside to the warmth of the cottage and to embark upon a mega-grooming session and also, possibly, to mull it over with the older and wiser Septi. As the snow outside hardens in the cold air, we can just distinguish the sculpted imprint of Otto's delicate footmarks, which stop halfway across the lawn and retreat back towards the house.

The following day it has all gone. So that was snow?

CHAPTER 12

New Year

January creeps up on us and brings with it its baggage of gales, rain and a series of iron-hard frosts, the latter of which kills off all of the wild Irish fuchsias that we had, over-optimistically, left out in the garden. We had hoped that they were rooted deeply enough to survive a winter outside, but it was not to be. We do not get much more snow, however, and what we do get is only a smattering.

I was always heartened when one or another Dalesman would say, regular as clockwork on or around 26 December, 'Aye, well – the days are drawing out now.' Trouble is that they also used to say, on or about 26 June every year, 'Aye, well – nights are pulling in now', which I always found deeply disheartening. I can never bear to consider that summer might be on the wane, but most especially in June when often, it seems, it has barely started. By late January the days are discernibly longer and, as all those brave bulbs start forcing their way above ground, we can smell as well as see the change in the air.

Spring is on the way. Otto too is changing. She is restless

and keeps miaowing to be let out, and then wants to come in again, and out again. She has started to follow Septi around and a couple of times I have found her rubbing herself against him. He looks perplexed by her advances. She will approach him, and then rub her head against him in greeting and roll over on the floor to play with him; she then rolls around in an amazingly sensual way, and her invitation seems quite clear. He sits very upright, front feet nearly together, and looks sternly down at her. He can look so exquisitely disapproving that he makes me laugh.

Otto's coquetry towards Septi becomes more pronounced by the day. One evening, shortly after our arrival home from work, she demands, very insistently, to be let out. Septi chooses to stay in. It is dark, but the light from the kitchen window illuminates the near garden and we watch her as she holds her head up, in a way I have never seen before, and proceeds to make a long, wailing drawn-out miaow that is astonishingly loud. She stays out for some time that evening. Much later on we hear, suddenly, the most extraordinary sound coming from the furthest corner of the garden. It's only possible to describe it as an ascending wail that then slides down into a guttural, harsh, bawl. This call, far louder than any human utterance could be, reminds me, magnified many times, of the complex scale of sounds that an adolescent boy can make, accidentally, when his voice is breaking but he can still sing soprano. Even I, with no cat language at all, recognise that primeval sound. It's the heart-stopping cry of a young animal seeking a mate. It's wild and almost shocking in its volume and intensity.

Michael and I look at each other. 'I have heard it said that there are so few complete tomcats around that queens have to travel miles to find a mate,' I volunteer.

'Don't you worry, Marilyn! Any tomcat within five miles will have heard that one. I promise you.'

Septi hears it. He raises his head and his nose quivers. He seems ill at ease.

I'm worried for my girl. We call her and finally she comes in and we shut up shop for the night.

The following evening as we enter the house, instead of the cats coming forward to greet us as they normally do, there is no sign of them, although I know that they were both inside when we left for work that morning. I walk through the sitting room doors, into the dining room and there, under the table, I see our dear, aged Septi astride Otto, making a valiant attempt to mate with her. It's clearly failing and Otto is looking back at him with what appears, at the very least, to be a questioning manner. If it is possible to interpret a feline expression in human terms, then: 'Was that it?' is the only question on Otto's face.

As Septi becomes aware of us, he shuffles down, and back away from Otto, and slinks out of the room, with the air of one embarrassed. My heart aches for them both. I wonder how many times he might have tried, or was his one go just at this very moment as we walked in? As with so much to do with animals, we will never know.

Otto, needless to say, now requests, vociferously and unrelentingly, to go outside. We open the door and she races away like a greyhound released from a trap; we watch her until she disappears into the darkness. A little later we, and most of our neighbours I imagine, hear her brazen calls for a tom. Intriguingly, although her normal territory extends much further than the boundaries of the garden, in her search for a mate she seems to want to be firmly on home ground, and so the furthest point from which she has so far signalled her needs has been at the far corner at the back, by the garden-tool shed.

Another evening passes, accompanied by spasmodic, and sometimes raucous, serenades from Otto. Eventually, when I feel we cannot inflict any more of this on our neighbours, we manage to persuade her to come in for the night.

Thursday 25 February

I wake up early and find it's still dark, and wet; a most unpromising sort of day. I open the door to let the cats out so that they might perform their toilet. In Septi's case this is necessary, as he will not use the cat-litter tray. In Otto's case, unnecessary, as she will not 'go' outside, which is the fail-safe way we always get her back at night.

As I open the door, Septi steps forward, and then stands rooted to the spot, as if electrified. I hear the low rumbling of the deepest and most aggressive growl I have ever heard him make. Still snarling, he slowly turns and sniffs each of the posts flanking the back door. His hair begins to stand on end and he looks up at me with large eyes. I feel that he wants me to help him but I do not know what to do. I return his look, but shrug my shoulders helplessly. He turns round and walks firmly back into the cottage; he passes Otto but appears to make no contact with her. She bounds out and up the steps towards the lawn, passing the doorposts without giving them a second glance. She halts abruptly and quickly returns to now sniff each of the posts in turn. She then starts to lick one of them over and over again, with her eyes almost closed. We have to go to work, so I grab her by her neck and pull her inside.

On our return that evening I open the back door, with slight apprehension, to let poor Septi out – and again he reacts aggressively and fearfully to the scent marks on the doorposts. Finally, and with unseemly haste, he performs his toilet in the gravel immediately outside the back door; a place as close as this to the house would not normally be his chosen spot, and he returns inside with alacrity. We have kept Otto in while this has been happening, but now we let her go. Michael and I return inside and watch through the window. As she careers across the lawn, she suddenly stops, dead. She is completely still. As we watch her line of vision we see, some distance in front of her, a large, fluffy, ginger cat. He, for surely one so large must be a tomcat, is sitting down quietly, facing her squarely.

'He has style, Michael, I'll give him that. But I had not wanted it to be a ginger tom.'

'He's lovely – he really is magnificent. Come on, look at him.'

'He's too big for her. She is only little and she will have

kittens that will be too big. Oh, oh, oh,' I wail.

Michael groans, long-sufferingly, at my contrariness.

Otto by now is in full flirt-mode and is rolling on the ground in front of her chosen tom. He continues to watch her – admiringly? Slowly he gets closer to her, and then, almost as if they are aware that they are being watched, they both move off into the dark of the shadows and we can see them no more. It goes very quiet and still.

A couple of hours pass with no noticeable sounds from outside, then the peace is rent asunder by a sound that makes my hair stand on end. I had heard about the post-coital scream of female cats but I had not expected it to be so completely blood-chilling.

'My baby,' I cry in anguish.

'Was that really Otto?' Michael asks.

'I'm certain. It's a really bum way to be made to ovulate, isn't it? Spiky bits on the penis pulling out rake her and make the process of fertilisation begin. But they say it's like the pain that some women experience when giving birth. Nature makes you forget quickly so that you will do it again.'

On cue, half an hour later, we hear another scream. We move towards the kitchen window and see at close quarters the same magnificent ginger tom sitting, tall and haughtily, to one side of Otto, who is looking somewhat dishevelled and uncertain.

'Mo, he's smiling.'

'Oh, typical man. 'Course he isn't.'

'He is. Look!' Michael insists.

I stare closely. He *is* smiling. I have never seen a cat smiling before – perhaps he always smiles. He is wearing a red collar and a disc is clearly visible, which somehow reassures me. He has a home and someone who cares for him; no alley cat this one.

As we watch them, Otto gets up and shakes herself and comes towards the cottage and asks to be let in, so we open the door. She is covered in mud and her fur is every which-way. As I bend down to stroke her, I find that the fur all along her neck is soaking wet, so her tom has clearly held her in check, as they have to do for their own protection.

She goes over towards the fire and sits down, then starts an intense and seemingly unending grooming session, which involves licking her vulva repeatedly, almost obsessively. Septi comes into the room, observes her quietly for a few moments, and walks out.

The following morning Michael is up very early and he lets Otto out as soon as he is up. I hear him calling me down to the kitchen. 'Look at him. He is like the Lion King. So proud and tall.' I look out of the window and see Otto rolling languorously on the ground, and a few feet away is the tall majestic fluffy ginger tom of the night before, watching her, from a respectful and safe distance, still smiling. We open the door to call her in before we go to work and she shoots back into the cottage.

The next night she goes out again. We hear her calling. We watch. But we see nothing nor, other than her calls, do we hear anything. She is out until very late and only comes back after repeated pleadings from me.

The following night it is the same, and for roughly a week Septi becomes a self-enforced prisoner within the cottage, and makes only the briefest of forays into the outside world.

For all that, though, we never see her ginger tomcat again. He came at her bidding, did what cats do and has now left for ever.

CHAPTER 13

Spring

March rolls out, wild, windy and wet. The sporadic sunshine floods across the garden in waves, and as the moving
shafts of light touch the daffodils and narcissi, that English
frontline of spring flowers, the bright yellows are transformed into pure gold. In our garden this brash little army
is then quickly supplemented by the shadowy purple of
the crocuses and anemones and, shortly afterwards, by
the lovely delicate misty blue of forget-me-nots, the pinks
and whites of the early clematises and the glorious dark
blue of the last of the spring flowers, the bluebells. Spring
is such a beautiful and burgeoning period and it is over so
very soon. Too soon.

We watch Otto for some small sign of pregnancy but any
change in her size is so slight that it is indiscernible. She is
due, soon, for booster injections, so I decide to take her to
the vet, so that he may ascertain if she is indeed pregnant
and, if so, forgo the injections.

In late March I make a veterinary appointment and when
I arrive at the surgery I'm assigned a young man who is

clearly not at all at ease when handling cats, and I embark upon the consultation with some trepidation.

The outcome is that he hasn't got a clue whether she is pregnant or not, and has to consult another vet in the practice about the dangers or otherwise of injecting her. I assure them that I think she is pregnant, not least because she has not come into oestrus again since her noisy serenades in February, and so the older vet recommends holding off the boosters until she has given birth. The young man says if I really want to know if she is pregnant I would need to get her scanned, and he hardly thinks it's worth it with, he sniffs, her 'being just a moggy'. I leave the surgery, mumbling crossly to myself: 'Might just be a moggy to you, mate, but to me she's everything.'

On 10 April John, Kathy and Delilah come to stay. We have a very enjoyable weekend in human terms, but it's even less successful than the first occasion for the felines gathered together. Otto is very disturbed by Delilah, her younger half-sister, who is in fact now neutered and no threat to her in any way.

Otto is just beginning to show a slight swelling on either side of her belly and, conspicuously, she is finding it more difficult to balance and jump and walk on the tops of doors, so we reckon her pregnancy is pretty unambiguous. I have also noticed that her nipples seem more pronounced and pinker, which is a further indication that there are hormonal changes taking place. For most of the weekend she lies on the top of a chest in the dining room and hisses repeatedly at poor Delilah, who although irresistibly attracted by this termagant above her, is doing her no harm whatsoever. Septi lies next to Otto, somewhat protectively it would appear, but at least he forbears to hiss at the glamorous visitor. I find myself constantly apologising for Otto's behaviour, but Kathy and John generously forgive her as they recognise that she has much to distract her.

After John and Kathy return home I start to monitor Otto's progress more carefully, and become increasingly fearful that she might do herself or her kittens harm, as she continues to leap about outside as madly as ever. I'm aware that professional cat breeders would never allow their pregnant queens unconditional access to the dangers that lie out of doors when carrying kittens. I talk to Michael about it but we conclude that once she becomes a mother she will be tied down well enough, and for now she should have her freedom. So free she remains but, as the kittens she is carrying develop, she curtails her own wanderings and stays close to the cottage and its environs, and – to our great relief – seems to lose her taste for roof walking and other mountaineering exploits. She also seems to distance herself from Septi. They certainly spend less and less time together.

I know that the pregnancy of a cat lies somewhere between sixty-one days and seventy days in length from conception, and that the average is sixty-five days, so I start the countdown. I discover that sixty-five days would make it 30 April, which is arrestingly significant for me as it's not only my own birthday, but also, much more significantly, the day of the death of my adored father. I'm a little disturbed by the coincidence of this.

As the days go by, Otto starts to visibly balloon out larger and larger, and although she is clearly ravenous, the kittens inside her make it difficult for her to eat more than a little at each meal, so we are, and have been for some time, free-feeding her. I am amazed at how much such a little cat can consume. Septi is very gentle with her and in fact keeps his distance as if he in some way understands that she needs her space. He constantly checks her rear end, which presumably tells him some hormonal story. Otto makes little mewling noises from time to time, which I imagine are the noises of discomfort, but perhaps she is communicating to the young within her. She has, for days now, been scratching away on bedding stored inside the linen cupboard, jumping up on to the top of the wardrobe and trying to get into every single cupboard in the house. The instinct for a nesting place is very powerful.

I make arrangements to take holiday for the week that the kittens are due so that I will be with Otto in her moment of need. The one hitch to these well-laid plans is that, as part of my job, twice a year I organise major presentations which are held outside London, to which I may take several of the key directors within my company. Persuading my colleagues to agree to a date that suits all parties is normally a logistical nightmare, and the date for one of the biggest presentations is currently hotly under debate.

As the week of the due date for the birth of the kittens approaches, the date for the presentation is changed yet again and I discover that the newly agreed dates are to be 27 and 28 April.

'I can't bear it,' I moan to Michael when I get home.

'Well, you should just tell them, and say why,' he retorts.

'Oh sure. It's going to look wonderful, isn't it, if everything comes to a grinding halt and we are unable to do the presentation, and our excuse is it's because I was having kittens!'

He laughs, but his face alters rapidly when I continue: 'So you are going to have to make contingency plans because it's too close to her due date for us to leave her on her own.' So Michael, who is saintly and indulges me sometimes, does make plans, but it's awkward for him too and the cottage is filled with constrained sighs. He also keeps repeating, somewhat manically: 'But what am I supposed to do if she does give birth when I'm on my own with her? Do I have to boil water? And what do I do with it once I have boiled it?'

I reassure him that water is for human diversionary purposes only and he is very unlikely to need it, but that anyway I will be there, by hook or by crook.

I have set up a huge cardboard box on its side which I have lined with newspapers covered with an old soft white sheet and have put it down in a corner at the foot of our bed. I choose this site as Otto most often seems to be looking in this room for a birthing place, perhaps because Septi comes in here least often and she seems a little wary of him now.

Tuesday 27 April

I wake up this day, with all the material prepared for our presentation, praying that I will get down and back before

Otto gives birth, for now, somewhat belatedly, I am beginning to feel frightened that something will go wrong and that she will be harmed in some way. I am filled with the foreboding that things will happen in the next twenty-four hours. I load the car up with projector, screen, laptop and display kits and come back inside one more time. I stroke her gently; her stomach is now heavily swollen and she seems very tired. She lifts up her head before I go and nuzzles me.

'Oh, little one. I wish I could explain what is happening to you. Does your instinct tell you or does it not? You will be fine, you are one big brave girl and I will be back to look after you.'

She blinks and turns away.

CHAPTER 14

It's 5.20 a.m. on 28 April when my mobile phone rings, and I wake immediately from a fitful slumber in a hotel room far away in the West Country.

'It's all happening this end, I tell you,' I hear Michael whispering.

'Why are you whispering? What is happening?' I shout.

'Well, she doesn't look very happy right now. And I think she has had a dead kitten.'

'Tell me what is going on, please, please.'

'Well, she had one at about 5 a.m. I was fast asleep and I just heard this really loud squeaking and then Otto miaowing and running around. And I opened my eyes and there was a small black lump on the carpet and loads of gunge and the black lump was squeaking and it frightened Otto, so she ran away from it.'

'And now?' I ask, heart pounding. At which point my mobile signal fails. I bang the mobile against the bedside table, which doesn't seem to make it any better. I grab the hotel phone and dial 9, then our number, and discover thankfully that I do have a line and I hear the home phone ringing.

'She's had a second kitten but it doesn't seem to be moving,' Michael says as he picks up the phone.

'What does it look like?'

'I don't want to get too close in case it puts her off,' he replies. 'It seems to have a sac over its head,' he adds. 'And it's ginger.'

I frantically try to remember what the books say about removing the amniotic sac and towelling the kittens down and swinging them round, and how careful you must be because they are very slippery.

'Try to get it in front of her face,' I urge him. 'Just push it under her nose.'

'Oh, she is licking it. She's licking and licking.'

'That's good. That's really good. Is there any movement yet?'

'Hang on. I'll just put the phone down and have a proper look.'

He is away an age; I screw up my face to listen hard. All I can hear is Michael talking to Otto in the distance. Then suddenly, and penetratingly, there is a high-pitched squeaking. Loud and protesting, and strong-sounding. Michael returns to the phone: 'It's ginger and big and fluffy and she has got the sac off him. He is nudging towards her and he has found a nipple. He's sucking – the black one's sucking too. They're both fine!'

I gurgle happily, but then he says: 'Uh oh. She has got up and left them both and is squatting down. She's straining.'

Long pause. I just hold the phone and my breath, and pray. Then I hear: 'Hey, well done. She's had another one. Otto, good girl. Good girl.' And, I hear later, with this her third – and as it turns out, her last – kitten, she now performs like a seasoned mother. She removes the sac, then eats the placenta with seeming relish, and licks her new kitten into mewling life. This one is a tiny tabby and an almost perfect replica of Otto, but with white eyeliner and no white socks and bib.

'Michael, you are a star for being there and coping with it all. I promise I will come home at the speed of light – and as soon as I can,' I sigh happily.

When I get to the presentation, Paul and Sue, to whom we are presenting, are very understanding about my distraction. Somehow we get through it, but my head is full of miniature whiskers and tiny squawks.

I hear from Michael later, however, that in the early stages of parturition Otto is not entirely happy with what is happening to her. After she had given birth to the little black kitten right in the middle of the bedroom carpet, which is when Michael must have woken up, he – the kitten – sets up a loud squawking, intended presumably to incite his mother to take care of him. But in Otto's case it so frightens her that she runs back and forth around him and then, when she sees Michael heading for the stairs to find a bucket and mop to clean up, she follows him downstairs as the preferred option.

'She kept staring up at my face and miaowing repeatedly.

She seemed to want help. I had to say to her: "Come on, Otto. You have duties. Back to your kitten," and she did go back, almost immediately.'

Reunited with her small black offspring she now starts to lick him, very roughly, with which he comes to life. He's so tiny he can hardly move, but stimulated by his mother he somehow drags his body by his front legs round to her belly and, with astonishing speed, finds and claims a nipple. This tiny creature with eyes firmly sealed (therefore totally blind), ears halfway down his head (and at this stage, stone-deaf), but with a keen sense of smell (so acute that within twelve hours he and his siblings hiss at any of us humans, the moment we are within yards of their box), displays that his instinct is 100 per cent in working order and he noisily takes in his first meal.

Michael, finding the cat and her kittens at peace, has decided that he must leave the cottage and get on with some of his own work. He leaves a message on my mobile to let me know.

I arrive back an hour after Michael has left and open the front door quietly to see Septi lying curled up in his favourite chair, apparently oblivious to the momentous happenings on the floor above him. He opens one wary eye at me and shuts it again. I pat him on the head and tiptoe upstairs, and as I go through the door into our bedroom I notice an empty food bowl and a saucer of water straight ahead of me. I look to the right, where I left the cardboard box before I went away, and there in the shadows is the beautiful Otto curled up on her side with three, tiny, sleeping kittens next to her. She opens her eyes, stands up and comes towards me; she trills a greeting at me and then, unmistakably, invites me to meet them. She looks at me, comes up to me and cheek rubs me, miaows, and then walks back to the kittens, and then comes back to me again and so on.

'Otto, you are so right to be proud of yourself and of them. They are adorable,' I assure her. And they are too, in a blind, helpless, vulnerable way. I left Otto as a singleton on Tuesday and return on Wednesday to find she is head of a family. I quickly get her more food, which she devours instantly. She obviously does not want to leave her kittens to go downstairs, so I make a mental note to keep food up here at all times.

While she is eating, I move the kittens to one side and change the bedding. I gently reposition them on top of the clean white sheet. 'There you are, Otto, complete with hospital corners.'

I sit on the floor with her by the kitten box for over an hour, enchanted by the marvel in front of me. She lets them suckle contentedly and I notice that the black one is down near her tail end, the torbie in the middle and the red one up near her head. Finally, they fall asleep and she turns over in the box on to her back. She has on her face an expression of extreme contentment, but also about her there is an air of exhaustion, which is hardly surprising. I sit by their side, quietly, for some time.

Other than moving them on to the clean bedding, I do not want to touch the kittens yet as I'm not sure what Otto will feel about it; however, when I do ultimately yield to the temptation, she is hugely generous with them. She watches carefully, but she is sweet and trusting. I swear she is feeling the pride of maternity as much as she is on guard for their safety. I pick up each one in turn, and as I do so each one opens its mouth wide and emits a strong hiss of protest, the only defence open to these tiny vulnerable creatures. Ignoring this, I look them over to find perfectly formed little pads and claws. I observe their tightly scrunched-up eyes and folded-over ears and lightly touch their impeccably stiff military whiskers. Otto has chewed off the umbilical cord from each one of her kittens to just under an inch of each of their bellies; this is as it should be and the little stalks will in due course drop off. I am in awe at the instinct that compels her to do exactly the right thing to protect her young kits.

When Michael returns from his truncated day he tells me that he has made a video of the kittens and their mother, which he started half an hour after their birth when they were still damp with the foetal fluids, and later when I have the chance I'm able to replay it and see almost how it was. Dear Michael, who at some point in the video proudly and with real excitement in his voice tells Otto: 'Brave Otto, good Otto. What a day you have had, and you are so good and clever. You just wait until Marilyn is home. Oooh, I can't wait to see her face when she sees what you have done.'

When I hear this bit of the video my eyes fill with tears. Yes, indeed, Otto; indeed, Michael.

~

While all of this is happening, Julie back in the office knows that I have a cat who is about to have, or might already have had, kittens, and she emails me as follows:

From:	Julie
To:	Marilyn
Subject:	Kittens
Date:	28 April 17:38

```
Have you got homes for all your kittens? One
of our cats was killed last week. It was
very sad - he was only one - but wasn't
marked (killed on the road), so must have
been very quick - and is now buried in the
garden.
   Julie
```

From:	Marilyn
To:	Julie
Subject:	RE: Kittens
Date:	28 April 20:38

```
Julie - how completely ghastly. You poor
thing. Oh I wish . . . we have such a small
litter, only three, and we have seven people
who want kittens. I will talk to Susan
immediately and see if she has any.
   Marilyn
```

I email Susan about Julie's plight and am delighted to hear from her that although she has just taken Tallulah to be neutered, it is not before she – Tallulah – has triumphantly given birth to a final litter (small by her standards) of three tortie girls and a ginger tom. I feel a pang of sadness that the days of breeding by the great Tallulah are now over, as she has mothered so many completely wonderful kittens. 'Down to you and Otto now, to keep the line going,' Susan teases me.

She has already arranged homes for two of them, but one of the girls, who looks much like Delilah, and the ginger tom are still to be homed. As soon as I hear the news, I quickly pass it on to Julie.

From:	Julie
To:	Marilyn
Subject:	Kittens
Date:	29 April 21:33

```
I will email her straight away - it is a
ginger tom I'm really looking for, so this
sounds ideal. Thank you very much!
  Julie
```

In fact, later in May, Julie herself collects her tom kitten from Susan's house and transports him directly to her own house in Oxford. At the same time, she also collects his litter sister for Jasmin, who works in our office at this time, and brings her into the office the next day. She is drop-dead gorgeous and is christened Millie by Jasmin. This Millie is to walk across more than five miles of London in search of a full tom, and is finally adopted by another family who look after her and her brood of hard-sought kittens.

It is anecdotally reported that full toms are so rare on the streets of London that queens have a tough time finding a mate, and the drive to breed in the female cat is an especially strong one, which is why Millie is to take such extraordinary risks.

An electrician, who lives in North London, is doing some work on our wiring one day and, as he gently fondles Septi, he quietly observes: 'I have a grand old boy like this one. He gets up to all sorts and I never quite know what's what with him.'

'Is he a battle-torn old moggy like Septi here, then?'

'Well, not exactly. He is a Burmese outcross. Very good-looking and would almost pass for the proper thing, but he is not the same as he used to be.' He looks down at the carpet, frowning slightly, and I nervously enquire what has happened.

'Well, it's not as bad as I originally thought, so perhaps what happened is all right really.' He throws me a wan smile.

'Go on!' I laugh, encouragingly.

'At the time I'm talking about, he is about three years old. Anyway, one day he just goes missing. Sometimes, before that, he would have gone walkabout for twenty-four hours, but he always came home. A couple of times he had been in a fight, you could tell, but he had a really strong homing instinct. Well anyway, on this occasion I'm talking about, he just never came back.'

'How awful. What did you do?'

'Well, I used to go out every night and call him, and put all his favourite food out and things like that, but in the end I just gave up.' He shakes his head, sadly. 'This must have gone on for a good month. And then, one morning, early, I hear his voice – well, I reckon it's him but I'm not quite sure. He is calling me and he has some voice, my boy, I'll tell you. So I belt downstairs and open the door and I can't believe my luck. There he is all fit and well, and looking up at me for all the world as if nothing has happened and it was only yesterday that he went off.'

'But that's wonderful. So why do you say he is not the same as he used to be?'

'Well, after we had said our hellos and all that, I'm just standing back and watching him walk off upstairs with his tail up, the way he does, and I notice that they're not there any more.'

Suddenly he looks embarrassed so, giggling slightly, I ask: 'You mean he's been castrated?'

'Exactly that,' he replies. 'But it's a bit of a turn-up, isn't it? I mean, your cat goes out for a walk and comes back a month later with a squeaky voice and a new mincing manner.'

We talk more, but we both conclude that probably on the night in question his cat had been making a load of noise, as courting toms do to see off the opposition, and someone decided to hand him in to the Cats Protection League, who had done what they need to do to keep the number of unwanted strays and feral cats down. He did, however, have a collar and disc round his neck when he went out, but when he returned he was without identity. It would have been good to hear that cat's version of events, or perhaps not on second thoughts.

CHAPTER 15

So Ottoline, beloved cat of the household of Moon Cottage, at exactly one year and twenty days of age, on this sixty-third day since her conjugation with the smiling ginger tom, having issue in the form of three kittens, black, ginger and tortoiseshell, proves herself to be a completely wonderful mother.

We watch entranced, and every moment that any of us is at home we pay homage to the new mother and her kittens. Otto is an exquisitely big-hearted mother as she has no concerns about us picking them up and cuddling them, although whenever they squeak or hiss, which they invariably do when they are handled, she will appear quickly, heralded by the tinkling of the bell on her collar, just to make sure they come to no harm, but she never agitates if they are being held in the arms of a loving admirer.

My birthday follows two days after the birth of the kittens and Michael and I celebrate with champagne in the garden. It is hot and sunny and the kittens are asleep upstairs, but Otto and Septi join us out on the lawn. Septi has not yet ventured upstairs, as far as we know, so we are not sure whether he is aware that this is now a household of five cats, rather than the two of less than a week ago, although the kittens squeak tellingly when being manhandled by us. As Otto passes him, he takes the inevitable quick sniff at her rear end, presumably to keep himself up to date on her condition. What it says to him it's hard to judge from his inscrutable expression, but the smell of the milk alone that she is generating must tell him a tale. As Otto passes by in front of him a minute later, she gives him a cursory, but amiable, lick on his nose. 'And that's your lot, old man. She has other things on her mind,' Michael teases him.

It is a gloriously hot day and we indulge ourselves in our little enforced holiday, made necessary by our new surrogate parentage. I glance across the garden at the now recumbent but, I notice in the bright sunlight, slightly moth-eaten Septi, who is lying stretched out on the paving flags, panting. 'John told me last night that he thinks now we have kittens they'll finish Septi off,' I confide.

At that point we hear a wonderful sequence of birdcalls, which, a little belatedly, provide me with food for thought, and I pull a face at Septi. 'Hey, listen. Now that we have five cats you may never hear that sound again. Celebrate while ye may.' In guilt at my

ornithological carelessness, I shrug my shoulders philosophically and wander upstairs to check on the kittens, where
I find their dutiful mother taking care of them.

Otto has in fact developed a fine technique of mothering.
She spends much of the time with the kittens either feeding
them, or cleaning them, but she has also established that
she must get away from them, and is quite controlled in the
time she spends with them. She does, however, stay with
them for most of each night, every night, in the box in our
room, and it is rare that I hear the gentle tinkle of her bell
move any further away than to the other side of our room,
as she seeks out food or water.

As soon as we knew that Otto was pregnant we had told
people in my office that kittens were on the way, and had
had a total of seven separate requests for a kitten, but
precedence had been granted to Eve – friend, neighbour
and cat-nanny – who very early on had asked us if she
could have one of the kittens for her daughter, Jenny, to
which request we were delighted to yield.

Tonight they come round to look at the kittens and I hear
Jenny's happy cries of pleasure as she picks up each of them in
turn. Michael has made his own bid, however, which is to
hang on to the ginger one, as he wants to own a cat who
smiles, and he hopes that this little ball of ginger fluff might
take after his father in this and other respects. I nervously
inquire which of the other two Jenny might like to own, but
she needs time to think about it, so I must bide my time awhile.

We now have to postpone a long-planned trip to Ireland
over the May Bank Holiday as we need to be here for this
new family.

On the eleventh day following their birth, the ginger kitten's eyes are properly open. They are that startling azure blue of cat babyhood. The tortie kitten's eyes are slightly open, and the black kitten's eyes are still firmly closed. The ears of all three are still positioned a little way down their heads but are just beginning to prick up, and their hearing is slowly increasing. They are all able to haul themselves around by their front legs, using their back legs as levers to push forward their bodies. We have built a barricade of books to keep them safely in their box (but which allows Otto to come and go at will) while we are all out at our jobs during the daytime, but in truth they are not ready yet to leave the confines of their nest. At this stage they are still firmly in the neonatal period where they are completely dependent upon Otto to care for them.

By the fourteenth day the other two have opened their eyes and all three of them are beginning to move out of the box. The transitional phase has now begun where they remain massively dependent upon their mother but are ready to start seeking other stimuli.

One evening around this time, Septi comes up to the bedroom and takes a long look at them. He seems soulful, and Otto watches him warily. One of the kittens, inspired by curiosity, starts to crawl towards him and Otto, with great alacrity but in complete silence, interposes her body between Septi and her young offspring. The moment passes and Septi moves quietly downstairs to his haven of peace. I suddenly feel this is not the first time he has inspected them, and as he walks away his body language does not convey unconditional pleasure.

Kitten adoration from the rest of us, however, is in full swing. Damian and John are both in residence, and I can always tell when they have been near the kittens as the top of each of the kitten's heads smells of one designer aftershave or another, which leads me to conclude that the big softies have been planting kisses on the kittens as they come and go. They do not, however, know that I know this. Oliver also visits us for a long weekend and is almost permanently stationed by the box. I am enchanted, though not surprised, that lads in, variously, their late teens and early to mid-twenties should be as knocked out as Michael and I are by the considerable charms of small, fluffy, endlessly curious and irresistibly pretty kittens.

The kittens, now at three weeks old, are beginning to move around with more and more energy and appear to be fearless in their efforts to investigate each other and things close by them, although they show no interest in straying outside the bedroom. They play together constantly when they are awake, and at times clearly hurt each other more than they intend, evidenced by their loud squawkings. This is an important phase in their socialisation with each other, and this is when each kitten will lash out or bite if it's hurt too much by one of its littermates, so setting the parameters of how far each one is allowed to go. Their eyesight is improving all the time, although their focus appears to be slightly soft when, for example, we hold up a pencil or a finger as their eyes wander 'drunkenly' from side to side. Their hearing is palpably more acute and strengthening, and their sense of smell remains as well defined as ever.

Michael and I and the boys play with the kittens whenever possible, almost dutifully, as we are aware that at this stage in their development being handled frequently by people is paramount. Kittens that have not been handled early on may not develop into friendly adult cats. 'The peak time for socialisation is between two and seven weeks of age, and although socialisation can continue beyond this time, it's never as effective.'[4]

I am on continual tenterhooks, however, as I'm still waiting to hear from Jenny as to which of the remaining kittens (Michael having chosen the ginger one) she wants. It is right that she should take her time but I do long to know. We reckon that the black one and the ginger ones are toms, and the tabby-tortie is her mother's daughter.

Near the end of May, Eve and Jenny tell us that they would like to take the black kitten and are unconcerned whether he is a tom or a queen. He is to be called Beetle, and they are happily certain in their choice.

Now we may undertake the all-important naming of our

---

[4] *Veterinary Notes for Cat Owners*, ed. Trevor Turner (Ebury, 1994), p. 63.

two, and endless discussions ensue. Because Susan Hill started the ball rolling with the lit-kit idea when naming Ottoline, we decide it would be only fitting that all the subsequent cats from Otto's line be named in some sort of literary tradition. Eventually we name the ginger kitten 'Titus' after Titus Groan, a favourite character of ours, and we name the torbie girl 'Fannie', in honour of Fannie Flagg, an author with a big soul who once helped me to recognise and believe in human kindness again when I was a bit down.

Although the names are initially my suggestions, the decision is reached by consensus. Actually, honesty compels me to say that John has reservations about calling out the name Fannie. I do not understand this – Fannie is such a pretty name. Young men are odd, but he accepts it as her fate with good grace.

So, in order of birth, we now formally welcome to the world Beetle, Titus and Fannie.

CHAPTER 16

For some time Septi has been out of sorts, on and off. As an old street-wise moggy, he has never used a cat-litter tray, but Otto, who was trained to use one when first she came to us, has never been 'weaned' off it. Recently, however, Septi has been 'caught short' in John's bedroom, where he sleeps every night, so we have introduced a cat-litter tray downstairs just for him, although John will not countenance it in his bedroom, unsurprisingly. The experiment has not been entirely successful, and because John is now shutting his bedroom door at night, Septi, in what seems to be some sort of defiance of both human and feline social rules, is spasmodically excreting, in both forms, outside John's door – which makes it especially exciting for John if he needs to make a sleepy barefooted foray to the bathroom in the night.

During the daytime, Septi rarely comes upstairs to visit the kittens or Otto, and instead spends most of his time on a blanket on the Ottoman downstairs next to the radiator, even though it is not giving out any heat at this time of year. I have been aware, too, that when he jumps on to the piano from the dining room table, he not infrequently misjudges it and falls off. Is this the dreaded old age now showing itself, I wonder? His eyes are showing signs of slight cataracts too. He is definitely eighteen years of age, and possibly nineteen, so it would not be surprising if these were the results of the passing years.

I do wonder, though, if he is not also upset by the loss of his friendship with Otto, who has been distracted much of the time by her kittens. Since their birth, we have seen Septi attempt to flirt gently with Otto, and we see him in the garden still playing chase with her of old; but although she will play with him a little, her concentration is severely curtailed and she will stop, halfway through the game, and suddenly retire inside.

As the kittens grow, though, Otto restricts the time she spends with them more and more noticeably, and begins to play again with Septi. Now, at five weeks old, the kittens are practised climbers and particularly like to climb legs of the human variety, although anything that touches the floor and goes straight up will do. Their claws are truly needle sharp, and they have not yet learnt the 'polite' sheathing that an adult cat adopts (if you are lucky) when climbing on bare human flesh, so all of us go to work each day covered in a network of long, thin, red scars, which are immediately recognisable to all those who have ever lived with cats as the handiwork of multiple kittens.

Their play with each other is increasingly vigorous, and the protesting squeaks ever louder and more frequent. They run round our bedroom at breakneck speed and it is dizzying merely to observe them.

One day Michael and I are watching them fool around and it's evident that Otto is also trying to play with them, but she is clearly in two minds. Michael comments: 'You know, I think she's jealous of the huge attention they are getting.'

'Yes, I think she is, but also she's still half a kitten herself. She has only just had her first birthday and she wants to play, but her instinct is telling her she has got to be responsible. Poor Otto. What a dilemma.'

In fact, she has been supremely responsible. She has fed and cleaned them impeccably. As is the way of all feline mothers, she has meticulously cleaned their faeces away, right up to the point when they started to eat a small amount of dried food. From that moment on, different rules came into play and she left them to figure out what the cat-litter tray is for. Fannie and Beetle have worked it out; Titus seems OK with the principle but a little backward in practice. Sometimes he makes it and sometimes he doesn't, but he is getting better at it. I am reminded of what many human parents say of their babies at the time of weaning: babies' nappies when the baby is milk-fed have a purity of smell that only changes the moment solids are introduced into the diet.

So already the kittens are losing their babyhood – so quickly. Otto comes to them now to feed them only perhaps three times a day, and no longer spends the night with them, although she will visit them nocturnally. In spite of this, they have never ventured out of this one room to find her. When she decides to feed them now, she comes to the open bedroom door and summons them with a special miaow that she uses just for them. Fannie, whom Michael calls 'mummy's little girl', always stops doing whatever she is about and immediately runs up to her increasingly imperious mother. Beetle and Titus may or may not stop what they are doing, depending on the mood they are in. Otto will lie down to be suckled, but for only a few minutes at a time. The kittens by now also have needle sharp teeth, which cannot be comfortable for their mother.

When they were two weeks and under, they used to swap with each other for their nipple of choice, but now they have their regular feeding positions. Beetle goes to the top end near Otto's head, Titus chooses the middle, and Fannie the tail end. In large litters, 'ownership' of a favoured nipple prevents ongoing battles between siblings. Beetle and Titus are much larger and also fluffier now than Fannie, with much larger feet, too. Of the three kittens, Fannie is the most active. She is, however, the most delicate and is very girly-looking; she is as close to a clone of her mother as it's possible to imagine from a natural birth. Beetle is pure black, from top to toe; there is not a whisper of white anywhere on him. He has black nose leather and black footpads, and just the merest hint of even blacker stripes through his shiny black fur. He is a magnificent-looking kitten. Titus is a light red marmalade cat, with white chest and tummy and socks, and remarkably long, stiff, white whiskers – much larger whiskers than the other two. Fannie and Beetle have tiny little 'o' mouths, like their mother, and Titus has the big smiley mouth of his father that Michael so yearned for. They all still have their baby-blue eyes, but these look as if they might be about to change.

Their ears are now properly up on the top of their heads and strong and pointy and stiff.

In spite of these outward signs, I do not fully appreciate exactly how fast the kittens are developing until something happens that makes me think again.

It is early evening and the kittens are now just over six weeks old. I am sitting at my desk in our bedroom reading a book and have my back to the door when I hear Otto making her special 'calling all kittens' miaow. Without turning round, I presume that they will go to her and that she is about to feed them. I hear it again and the tone has changed, but I continue to ignore it, until I hear it a third time. I then realise, suddenly, that the sound is coming from outside the bedroom, which is not at all characteristic. I get down from my chair quietly and walk across the room, and slowly open the door on to the landing. In front of me is a remarkable tableau.

Lying facing me is Otto stretched out with her back against the door of the bedroom on the other side of the landing. Between her and me are the three kittens. They are sitting bolt upright in a tiny semi-circle and all of them have their front feet placed neatly together. Each one of the kittens in turn is tipping its head from one side to the other, watching its mother in a concentrated kind of way. Otto is making the low 'chchchchch' noises of a cat who has seen a bird and, as I too watch, I'm horrified to see that she is batting, back and forth, between stretched-out forepaws, a tiny brown fieldmouse who, probably from pure fear, seems now close to catatonic paralysis. I glance down the stairs and see Septi looking up, watching every move with the impassive attentiveness of a long-serving umpire on Centre Court.

'Hey, this sure isn't the moment for a killing lesson. Not here, not now, not nohow,' I protest. I scoop the now almost motionless mouse, who is himself not much older than the kittens, judging by his size, into an empty tooth mug and take him across the road and gently tip him out on to an enclosed bit of wild land where Otto and Septi are unlikely to go. He doesn't move, so I fear he may already be dead from fright, although he is still warm.

When I come back and tell Michael about the lesson on the landing that I have just witnessed, he says: 'So that was what the commotion was about. I reckon that Septi hunted that mouse down for Otto as some sort of offering.'

'It's true that recently Otto and Septi seem to have bonded

again and are spending much more time out and about together, so no doubt the old boy did think it would be helpful. Perhaps she put in a special request?' I wonder aloud.

Ironically, shortly after this event I received the following email:

From:	Beth
To:	Marilyn
Subject:	Birds
Date:	8 June 11:40

```
Oisin and Malachy have killed! They caught a
blackbird this morning, brought it through
the cat flap, then lost control of it,
blackbird started to fly around my bedroom
until it was trapped behind the curtain. In
the meantime, I opened the front door, then
threw a sweatshirt over Oisin. The bird flew
out of the door. Malachy went after it and
caught it again. I finally got them off the
bird and put it in a box and took it away to
die in peace. Ugh.
  Of course, they both think they're hot
stuff. I was left cleaning birdshit off my
bedroom window and curtains.
  Beth
```

The very next day, following the hunting lesson, Otto and Septi spend hours playing their complicated game of chase round the garden. Septi has always been a strong climber, but Otto can out-climb him with ease, so when the game is finally called to a halt it's usually because Otto has disappeared into the thorny tangle of the roses which have twisted their way up through the pergola, and Septi gives up the chase. This day, however, I see Otto veering off after Septi, through two sides of the tunnel formed by the roses on the pergola, round under the wall of the greenhouse, up over the compost heap, and down by the bike shed – where she called for her tom to come to her – back under the laurel bush and out into the open garden right in the middle of the lupin beds. A little while later I go out and see that Septi is now chasing Otto. He is still more skilful at hiding himself than she is, and as I watch he waits down below the steps, and then he sneaks across and crouches under the lavender bushes from which vantage point he jumps out, surprising her. They play for what seems like hours. Finally, they both flop down on to the cooling stone flags and lie with their mouths open in the silent laughing way they have together.

I am so glad that they have not lost that special companion-ship that they have established.

CHAPTER 17

Midsummer's Day – Monday 21 June

Shortly before 8 p.m. the telephone rings. I answer it and a woman's voice says: 'Do you have a cat called Otto?'

There is a slight pause on her end of the telephone, and then I hear: 'Rather, I should say, *did* you have a cat called Otto?'

My world slides on its axis. I feel sick with fear. Shortly after she finishes her second sentence, I hear my own disembodied voice, shouting, pointlessly:

'No. No. No. No. No.'

I fight for control. 'What happened?' I ask.

'She was run over.'

'Where are you?' I finally manage.

'Outside your front door,' she replies.

I call for Michael out of the window, but he has heard my agitated voice and knows beyond doubt, in the way that a loved one always does know, that something terrible has happened. We open the door together and a young man is standing there with a black bin liner in his arms.

'I'll bring her in and you can bury her in the garden,' he

says. He then adds: 'The lady who rang you has had to go home.'

We go out through the sitting room where Septi is asleep on the sofa and out into the back garden.

'I need to see her,' I whisper.

'She doesn't look very nice.'

Michael and I carefully unwrap her from her prosaic shroud. She is warm and soft and, as I put my nose to her fur, I'm overwhelmed by the singular sweet smell that is special to her. Her mouth and nose are bashed, but otherwise her body seems intact. She is deceptively pliable. I swear I can see her breathing.

I look up at Michael. He has tears in his eyes. 'Oh Otto. Poor Otto, why this?' he chokes.

'Are you sure she's dead?' I plead. 'She looks as if she might just be unconscious.'

'I promise you she is dead,' the young man replies.

I lay her gently on the ground and put my hands all over her, trying to find a heartbeat. It's completely impossible to accept that this life has just been snuffed out. As I'm touching her and watching, hope against hope, for some sign of life, I see a small trickle of milk leaking out from one of her nipples. Upstairs there are three kittens that are waiting for their mother. I pick her up in my arms and bury my face in her fur.

'Otto, you are the best cat in all the world. You are so brilliant and so lovely. How can we live without you? Any of us? Why, why, why, did you have to go and get yourself killed? Otto, come back.'

I gently stroke her poor flat lifeless body, willing life to come back into it, but in reality saying farewell. I fondle her pert ears, the way she likes it best. I stroke her soft shiny still warm fur and imagine that I hear the thrum of her little purr. I touch her four white socks in memory of the giddy dances that she danced, and finally I pick her up and snuggle her head down on my shoulder in the hope that she might lick my neck, like she does, just one last time. 'You never said goodbye.'

Michael disappears inside to find John and tell him what has happened. John comes out shortly afterwards because he wants to be the one to dig her grave. He starts to dig a hole under the rhododendron bush where she used to play hide and seek so often with Septi. As he digs, with the apparent determination of an escapee who knows he has only one bid for freedom and this is it, I see the tears running down off the end of his chin. He later claims this was sweat, but all the same my heart goes out to him for the pain he feels, as it does to Michael, who is being strong for all of us, but who is patently shattered by the loss of our little cat. As John covers her body with the final layer of soil over her hugely deep grave, Michael and I whisper a prayer to send her on her way.

The young man stays for a drink and we talk about Otto. He says: 'She was a remarkably beautiful cat.'

I cannot bear it. I cannot bear her being *was* and not *is*. I am suddenly overwhelmed with a sense of how very wicked I must have been to need to be punished in this manner and to this degree. This is a very egocentric thought, as others are hurt by Otto's death as well as me, but it haunts me.

We open another bottle. The young man tells me that the woman who phoned me is from the Cats Protection League, and that she had said to him that anyone living on our road and keeping cats needed their heads examining. So that is comforting, but she may well be right. The woman had rung him because he lives on one of the boats on the canal nearby and she had thought it was his cat. He came out with his heart in his mouth, but found that it was not his cat after all. I ask him exactly where it happened. He tells us that Otto's body was found five yards away from our front door on the other side of the road opposite our neighbours' house. Impossible to tell which way Otto was going, but she must have been hit just once at high speed and flung into the gutter by the force of the car.

'Cats are fantastically fragile, you know. It really does not take much to kill them, and if they are hit by a car, that is pretty much that,' he said.

The driver had driven on, but maybe without even knowing that a cat had been killed. The young man leaves shortly afterwards, but I am touched by his consideration and feel deeply sorry for him in having to cope with us at this time.

Michael's brother, John, has been staying with us for the weekend. Today he has been out visiting friends and arrives back amid this scene of deep mourning. As a priest he is used to comforting the bereaved and as soon as he walks through the door, we take him round the garden and tell him every detail of what has happened for the umpteenth time, and Michael points out where the dogs of the previous owner are buried, under the apple tree, and then where we have just buried Otto across the other side of the lawn, and John murmurs: 'Ah, cats on one side, and prods, sorry, dogs, on the other.'

Bless him for the gift of giving us laughter.

CHAPTER 18

Later on in the evening we realise that Septi has gone missing and we go out in search of him. We look everywhere, and eventually we find him on the wasteland across the other side of the hateful main road that killed Otto.

'Michael, I'm sure he's looking for her.'

'Do you reckon? Don't you think he saw us burying her?'

'I think all that went over his head, and she was in a bin liner when she came into the house so he may possibly not have smelt her.' Finally, we persuade Septi to come back inside and we close up for the night.

Never has the 'longest day' seemed truer.

At regular intervals through the night the kittens in turn squeak out. I presume they are calling for Otto as they have never made this noise before, certainly not at repeated intervals. I hear them get up and go across to the food and water again and again. They have all been eating solids for a few weeks now and they are fortunate, as orphans go, that they have at least had their mother for the first seven and a half weeks of their life, and have even had one hunting lesson, so they are of an age where they can now live independently. A few weeks back and the story would have been very different. It is startlingly painful, however, to hear them suffer this first night of life without a mother.

In the morning Septi is restless, so Michael lets him out early. I rise shortly afterwards, and as I enter the bathroom I hear a noise that arouses my curiosity. I open the window and the sight that greets me breaks my heart anew.

Outside the bathroom window, in a little alley that leads out on to the main road, we have placed a very tall water butt, and sitting on top of this water butt is Septi. He has his head turned away from the cottage and is staring straight down the road towards the distant traffic lights. He is making his strangulated 'miaow' over and over and over again. I feel certain, from observation, that miaowing is for him a huge effort, but at this moment it seems as if he will never give up. He is calling Otto. I'm sure of it.

So poor Septi. No one knows how to tell him that his beloved kitten, his playmate, his queen, the beguiling elfin creature who has filled his old age with sunlight and laughter, is never coming back, however hard he calls. I burst into tears and Michael comes running up and hugs me. I helplessly indicate what I can see. Michael looks out and nods compassionately. He goes straight down and out through the front door and picks Septi up in his arms and, talking gently to him the while, he carries him back inside.

While all of this has been going on another phase is also beginning. Miserably I'm trying to get us some breakfast, before leaving for work, when I hear a bump and a couple of scuffles. I walk into the dining room and see the tiny figure of Fannie appearing round the corner from the bottom of the stairs, followed by a plopping, falling sound, and then Titus appears. I stick my head up the stairs and, sure enough, two stairs higher up Beetle is suspended half on one stair and half on the other.

Although the flight of stairs in the cottage is short, only ten steps in all, because the cottage is very old, the steps are fiercesomely steep. Some time in the 1600s this cottage would have been a farm labourer's dwelling place and the

upper floor would have been the hayloft. This is what has deterred the kittens from venturing further than the bedroom and the landing, but possibly they now think that their mother is playing another training game on them and, if they show enough enterprise, they will be rewarded by seeing her.

I groan. 'Now what do we do?'

Michael, with savvy, suggests: 'While we are out, can't you just keep them shut in our bedroom, and then when we are here we can just let them be?'

And so that is how it is for the first day after Otto's death.

That night when we get back, we let Septi out and we open the bedroom door and see what the kittens will do. Septi returns to the water butt and calls for his ladylove. In all the time we have lived here, he has never sat on that water butt and miaowed until now. It's so hard hearing it, but Michael thinks we should just let him do it.

'He needs to be allowed to grieve just as we all do.'

'But he's calling for her?'

'Same sort of thing.'

Septi continues to call for Otto for nearly ten days, but eventually he becomes dispirited and gives it up. He now spends much of his time outside. The weather is hot, and also the kittens now have the run of the house.

The kittens, meantime, are displaying the astounding resilience of extreme youth, bordering on apparent insensitivity, even. They jump exuberantly over the furniture, they fight roly-poly tussles with each other, they throw cat litter around everywhere, they start climbing up the curtains, they discover the mantelpiece. A whole new world opens up to them. I am sure that they do miss Otto, but young fit animals have a hugely strong sense of survival and that is where their energies are being spent.

It is strange, however, that for days on end I can hear in the far distance the tinkling of the bell on the collar of that little cat. Somehow she is still coming to me in dreams . . . her eyes wide as dark flowers.

CHAPTER 19

Going into the office the next day is as all right as it could be and my boss, rather endearingly, manages to make me laugh by his reaction to my tale of the unforgettable tense change of the woman on the phone, as she switches her question so brutally from current ownership to past ownership of a cat called Otto. 'Ah! A member of the Sensitive School of Counselling!' he suggests.

Friends and colleagues are sympathetic, and I am aware that it's unreasonable of me to mind when one says: 'Anyway, you have the kittens to take her place.'

True, but Otto is irreplaceable. The death of a loved one is an annihilation beyond just the existence of that being. Death kills something inside of oneself too. There is a marvellous observation by one of Anne Tyler's characters, Poppy, about his long-dead wife:

> 'People imagine that missing a loved one works kind
> of like missing cigarettes,' he said. 'The first day is
> really hard but the next day is less hard and so forth,
> easier and easier the longer you go on. But instead it's

like missing water. Every day you notice the person's absence more.'[5]

However, because I know that animal bereavement is an embarrassment for anyone who has not experienced it, rightly or wrongly I have decided that I need to be 'grown up' about it and not talk about it to anyone.

My self-enforced regime of stiff upper lip might, just might, therefore be the reason why, when some days later I am sitting at a long, linen-clad, inexpressibly elegant dining table in a garden of supreme beauty in the grounds of a manor house in the depths of Wiltshire, I find myself, suddenly, behaving badly or, at the least, questionably. It is a gloriously hot summer's day and the long table in question is set out under the especially welcome shade of a group of trees. An atmosphere of well-being and tranquillity is enhanced by the steady flow of gentle conversation and sporadic ripples of laughter among the fourteen or so guests around the table, aided by the copious refills of fine wines supplied by an immaculately clad *sommelier*. A luncheon party of sumptuous proportions is under way and, as part of my job, I have been included in the guest list.

Our very kind hostess is on fine form and I am fortunate to be seated near her. I'm much taken with her superb Irish wolfhound who is the finest I have ever seen, and who is called Gideon. He spends much of the lunch gently nudging those of us sitting at his end of the table with his warm, wet nose, and even though all his four feet are firmly on the

[5] *Back When We Were Grown-ups* by Anne Tyler (Vintage, 2002).

ground, he nevertheless towers above us. Our hostess, confidingly, informs us that they have had a visit from a vet only the week before who had collected sperm from Gideon to be stored on their behalf.

'Twice within the hour,' she boasts, triggering a round of applause and cries of admiration (from those of us who are within earshot and to the lasting mystification of those further up the table) at Gideon's prowess. The purpose of this exercise is that because the magnificent Gideon is now of some age, she would hate something to happen to him and so, by default, for his line to cease to exist; therefore, with his sperm being held, there is just a chance, with the benefit of AI, that they would be able to have his puppy at some point in the future.

Probably because the day is so glorious, the food wonderful, the company stimulating and she herself is such a sympathetic person, I find myself, unforgivably, starting to talk about Otto and my eyes fill with tears. This sweet woman rushes round from her place at the head of the table to the side of my chair. She flings her arms around me comfortingly and cries: 'Oh Marilyn, please. You can take home some of Gideon's sperm.'

Laughingly, I turn down her kind offer, but am compelled to say: 'Never could anyone have tried to comfort another person in their loss with such gracious generosity and such truly lateral thinking. Thank you, thank you, and you too, Gideon.' He puts his head on one side but makes no remark.

That lunch is a truly cathartic one for me. The pain resulting from the bereavement of an animal who has been much loved can be every bit as sharp and sickening and long-lasting as human bereavement. It is not always so, but if compassion can be shown to those who are suffering it, who may, God forbid, want even to talk about it, it might help them tremendously.

~

I have made an appointment to attend my local veterinary clinic as the time has now come for the official sexing of the kittens and for them to have the first of their two lots of injections. I talk to the receptionist about what makes a good 'cat vet' as I discover that the young man who was unable to tell me whether Otto was pregnant or not has also written her up in his notes as 'dangerous' – and a less dangerous cat than Otto is hard to imagine. We are assigned Pat, who is indeed first class with the feline species.

First, though, I need to get the kittens there. A simple task, I think. I'm so wrong. I have recently acquired a large mesh cat cage, which means that the captive travellers can have a fine view of all that is around them, and which I hope may make them less panicky than the enclosed carriers that I had used to transport Otto and her various half-sisters and brothers. I duly place the three kittens into the cage and carry it out across the main road to put it in the car. From the very moment that I place the cage in the car, the most terrible caterwauling starts up. At first it is Fannie rendering an ear-shattering solo. I start the engine and ease the car out on to the road. Now Titus and Beetle join in lustily, but the sound is wholly lacking any harmony; it's an indescribably dreadful noise.

As I turn the car from the first roundabout down towards the second, I can see out of the corner of my eye a small tabby body squeeze its way straight through the mesh on the corner of the cage and jump down into the footwell where my feet are pumping the clutch and brake pedals. Terrified lest she get under the brake pedal and I crush her tiny body, I go round the roundabout twice before finally daring to brake enough to bring the car to a halt, half on the road, half on the pavement. By this time Beetle has climbed through too, and is now walking up and down the back seat howling; Titus alone, the plumpest of the three, remains in the cage, wailing in protest. In desperation I put the cage on the back seat and firmly shove Beetle and Fannie back inside it. I proceed with the journey, and in less than fifteen seconds Fannie reappears under my feet. I bend down and grab her by her scruff and lift her on to my lap where I hold her firmly with one hand and attempt to drive with the other. Eventually I reach my destination and take them into the vet's reception area. As I'm standing at the desk I realise that the front of both my thighs are seeping blood through my jeans where Fannie has repeatedly buried her claws into me in terror, but there is nothing to be done. We pass the time, noisily, as other people accompanied by their animals, waiting for their own appointments, coo obligingly at the kittens and I smile affably, while trying to ignore my smarting legs.

Our turn finally comes and we go in to see Pat. She confirms immediately that the squeaking Fannie is all girl, which I knew; and that the now silent Beetle is all boy, which I had expected. But she confounds me totally over

Titus, whom she declares to be female. When I query it, she calls in someone else for a second opinion and they both confirm Titus is female. They admit it's hard to sex a kitten that young, but finally – on demonstration – I accept their diagnosis.

'Help, because she's now registered as Titus and it's a boy's name,' I agonise.

'Well, give me a girl's name then.'

'But she's so much Titus already.'

'Then that's fine. She is a female Titus. OK, Titus?' and she pats Titus affectionately; and so she is, and always will be, Titus.

All three of them are injected, resulting in varying degrees of protest. Fannie most, Titus least, and Beetle in between. They are otherwise declared to be in good health, and have all the bits that a healthy kitten requires.

With some dread, I contemplate the journey back home. The receptionist manages to find me a bin liner, which I gratefully tie over the cage – and although Fannie gets out of the cage and into the bin liner on the way home, at least she stays out of the footwell. As I arrive back at the cottage, I realise with a sickening sensation in the pit of my stomach that they could so easily have got out of the cage as I was carrying them across the main road. I drive the car on to the pavement immediately outside the cottage and bundle the black-covered cage firmly in through the front door.

Now that they have been injected, we face another crisis. The time is fast approaching for Eve and Jenny (and John and Matthew) to take delivery of Beetle. Eve has suggested a Friday, so that Jenny will have the treat of a whole weekend to bond with Beetle immediately following his arrival at his new home. Beetle is in fact a very lucky boy, for he is going to a home where he will be well loved and which must be close to cat-heaven. Eve and John live beside a nearby lock, where John is the lockkeeper, and their cottage is in the middle of open countryside and as far away from a main road as it's possible to be. Fields, woodland and huge gravel pit lakes surround them. The possibilities for hunting for little Beetle are just infinite. Also, in the cat world the boys in the family appear always to be sent away or choose to go away of their own volition, so Beetle, if left to his own devices in our household, would probably have upped sticks and moved away anyway even if we had kept him.

Knowing all of this, however, does not make the pain easier and I approach the Friday of his departure with melancholy. Eve and Jenny are coming round at 8 p.m., and I return from work so late on this particular day, the traffic out of London being at its horrendous Friday worst, that at the very moment I get back and slip the key into the lock they arrive, as arranged. I literally just have time to grab him and bundle him into their cat carrier and that is that.

After they have gone, I sit down and whisper behind the closed door: 'Goodbye, Beetle. Be a good boy and remember to write sometime.'

CHAPTER 20

I watch the two remaining sisters anxiously for any indication that they might be missing Beetle, but there is no
discernible change in their behaviour that could be con-
strued as pining. They play even more manically, if
anything, than they did when there were three of them.
When I ask Eve how Beetle has settled in, she reports that
they have all been in stitches at his antics and that he is
either at full tilt or flat out, fast asleep. He is still being kept
inside, for the moment, as he has not yet had his second
course of injections. The next time I see Eve, she laughingly
says: 'We all think he's mad. Mad as a hatter – but completely gorgeous.'

As July advances, hot and dry for the most part, Septi still
keeps his own counsel and spends the majority of his waking
hours out in the garden and beyond. He comes into the
cottage to eat and sometimes to sleep, but he is back on his
lone patrols. I suspect he continues to mourn Otto.

By this time we have, with much sadness, made the very
hard decision to keep the kittens confined within the cottage
as the main road outside is simply too treacherous. I talk to

a friend, who is also a vet, and she shrugs, saying: 'I always feel you need to let cats take their chances outside, but I grant that a year is not much of a life-span. I do warn you, though, that if you keep them inside you must be firm at all times and not weaken, so they are used to the indoor life only. It must be one or the other.' I am in an agony of indecision, but Michael has no such qualms. 'Mo, let them go free and it's only a matter of how long. We *must* keep them inside. As long as we live in this house, you are going to have to get used to the idea.'

I do, however, spend many hours thinking about it, and trying to find a way round the problem. The garden is impossible to make cat proof and no cat understands that a standard garden fence should be considered to be its perimeter. I find a site on the Internet, which supplies cat-containment fencing, but it's American and they cannot send the materials to me because of the prodigious costs. For the moment I am beaten, and have to accept that the kittens will be interned.

Septi appears to relish his sole right of exeat and saunters out with his tail up, sometimes throwing an inscrutable glance over his shoulder as he sets off. The kittens watch him go, possibly bemused, but they do not especially show any sign of wishing to follow him. They are fully occupied by the distractions of their own making within the boundaries of the cottage itself.

Titus and Fannie have become inseparable. They sleep together, they fight together, they play together, they eat together, and they groom each other. They are developing rapidly and their eyes have changed from the baby-blue to what will be their adult colouring. Fannie, who is now a replica of her mother, has the same tiny, pointy, heart-shaped face and almond-shaped geisha stripes round her eyes. Her eye colour is more greeny than the striking amber of her mother's, but she is as near a clone as it's possible to imagine.

Titus is developing into a smaller version of her father, with dramatically large whiskers and a smiley mouth. Her ginger (or, more properly, red) coat is thick and fluffy and stripy throughout; she has a white bib with socks to match. Most arrestingly, she has dark golden eyes, the exact colour of her fur. Titus is more easy-going and languorous than Fannie, and lies on her back and schmoozes with one and all. She's especially fond of John and spends as much time with him as possible. He spends a lot of time lying still watching television and Titus likes that. It means she can lie on him, also being still and watching television. She eats more than Fannie and has a tiny potbelly.

Fannie is a much fussier eater and has a tendency to have a bit of this, and a bit of that. Mostly she likes to eat Septi's food when he is there, and surprisingly he lets her do that. I find her heartbreakingly cute because she is so like her mother. She loves dripping taps, just as Otto did. She is very wary, quite nervous, and I suspect more intelligent than Titus – but this is just assumption. She licks my eyelids just before I am going to sleep, and always sleeps in our room. At night the kittens both find separate sleeping places, although they sleep curled up together during the daytime.

By the beginning of August, Septi's relationship with the kittens has changed very slightly and he now sometimes plays with them a little. One of the things that Michael and I find extraordinary about his play with the kittens, which was not the case when he played with Otto, is that he stops playing with them the moment he thinks we are watching him.

The powerful sense of dignity, which all cats possess, never ceases to impress me. Sometimes, although it never seems to last for very long, he will allow one or other of the kittens to lie in the armchair next to him. If, however, both of them climb up to be with him then, invariably, he will grunt discouragingly in the manner of an old man and, rising stiffly, he will abandon his resting place and ask one of us to let him go outside to his private wide-open spaces. It's hard to determine whether Septi is indulging the kittens, whether he really likes them, or what he feels about them at all. I long for him to respond to them as he did to Otto, but that may be hoping for too much.

Halfway through August, John and Kathy and Delilah come to visit us once again. This is the first time since the kittens were born, and I am hoping for good things as the kittens are comparatively young, so surely they will be more adaptable. Wrong. Fannie is every bit her mother's daughter, and behaves equally disgracefully as Otto did, spitting neurotically at every turn at poor Delilah. Titus is much more phlegmatic and once or twice she and Delilah rub noses. We conclude that were Titus and Delilah to be left alone they would become the best of friends, but poor Fannie has a long distance to go yet awhiles.

Although Michael and I try to conceal which cat or kitten might be our favourite at any one time, Damian has no doubts at all, and does not attempt to conceal it. Without any question, Fannie is his. Damian has now provided Fannie especially (Titus is not as interested) with a source of endless amusement. In early August he wins a large goldfish at a visiting local funfair, which mysteriously enters the cottage under the cover of darkness, and the first I know of this aquatic addition to our family is when I go searching for my large yellow pastry-making bowl and find it complete with fish, water and pebbles in Damian's bedroom. Disarmingly formally, he introduces his fish to me as 'Bertie'. I remember all too clearly how many fish I inflicted upon my own parents, for my mother to clean out on a weekly basis, to be able to make any remark other than, 'Er, welcome, Bertie.' Shortly after this, Damian invests in a sizeable fish tank complete with pump and lid to house Bertie more comfortably on a permanent basis, which provides all of us with a greater peace of mind.

Since the introduction of Bertie into our home, Fannie in particular has developed a special welcoming ceremony for him, which involves complicated gymnastics. Having persuaded Damian to allow her into his room (she is the only one allowed free access), she then jumps up on to the cupboard, which is the platform for Bertie's tank. The first part of her greeting is, very delicately but repeatedly, to pat the side of the tank with her paw. This always has an electric, and presumably from Fannie's perspective, desirable, effect on Bertie, who charges full tilt round the tank, making waves. This is now the cue for her to jump up higher on to the top of the bookcase, which stands on top of the cupboard, behind the tank. From there, she diligently studies Bertie, head turning from side to side, and then proceeds to hang down from above to get an even closer view of him and to see if there is the slightest chance that he might be persuaded to leave his watery cell and jump out and join her. She appears fascinated by him and watches him for huge amounts of time.

In late August Annie comes to visit us again and is enraptured by the kittens, as I knew she would be. We have another 'epic' night and in the morning, when all of us discover we are rather the worse for wear, I invite Annie who, because John and Damian are both at home, has been exiled to the sofa bed in the sitting room for the night, to use the sanctuary of our bedroom to dress and spruce herself up. As an echo of less than a year ago, when Otto was alive, Annie is playing with both Fannie and Titus in our bedroom, and yet again I hear that enchanting laughter of hers as she talks quietly to them both.

She has to go early as she has things she must do at home. Damian, with great courtesy, and somewhat to my surprise, offers to escort Annie home on the convoluted tube route she must take to get to her flat and, unknown to us, that is the last we are to see of Damian for many weeks, as it seems it's not Fannie alone who has won his heart.

CHAPTER 21

As summer fades into autumn, the kittens display increasing degrees of affection for, and dependence upon, the human members of the household, and we have to be especially careful when cuddling either one of them, as each of them betrays conspicuous symptoms of jealousy. This will vary from a plaintive but artless miaowing, while staring fixedly at the human who is currently indulging in feline disloyalty, usually demonstrated by Fannie, to a more complex turning of the back and constrained sighing and then walking off disdainfully if approached – the most commonly adopted stand-off used by Titus.

As our holiday approaches, I begin to experience pre-France anxieties. We have decided not to put them in a cattery, but even though John will be at the cottage, I'm fearful that they may think that we will not come back, which they have already experienced with their mother and their brother.

Eve has very sweetly agreed to come in once a day to feed and water all three of them. Only last weekend John forgot his duties – when we came back, the water bowls were dry, which has made me panic.

We have a wonderful holiday in Languedoc, although I miss the kittens terribly – and for much of the time I find also that I am haunted by memories of the beautiful Otto, and that she stays inside my head. Much to my relief, when we finally come home we find the cats in one piece and the kittens seem totally forgiving of our abandonment of them. They are touchingly affectionate, so I conclude being left on home ground is a better option by far than a cattery, and I feel guilty for having doubted John's efficiency.

Septi, on the other hand, seems especially out of sorts with us. He refuses to be stroked or cuddled, and for several days he walks off if either Michael or I go near him. We discover from both John and Eve that he has repeatedly emptied his bowels on the bathroom carpet and outside John's bedroom. Every night now I put down Puppy Training Pads; these have plastic backings and are impregnated with a chemical that attracts animals to make use of them in this way. Septi is generally accommodating enough to avail himself of them rather than the carpet. However, if I attempt to move them away from John's door, which remains his optimum site, he continues to perform there, so we have no option but to keep the Puppy Pad routine going outside that door. I have tried using a cat-litter tray instead, but he stubbornly performs outside it rather than in it. I have heard it said that once a cat starts refusing its cat-litter tray and uses other places, it's a sign of some disturbance, so I am concerned at what is upsetting the poor old boy.

As the weather heralds autumn by rattling at the cottage windows and doors with a series of rain-filled gales, flattening all the remaining perennials in the garden, Septi spends more and more time indoors, and with some relief I observe that now at last he does seem to have established a rapport of sorts with the two girls. He seems to spend most time with Fannie; does he see her mother in her? She is the more obviously flirtatious of the two of them and will actively seek him out, in contrast to her laid-back sister who likes the world to come to her. And yet it's perhaps the laid-back nature in Titus that is at times more appealing to Septi as she is less threatening, and will lie comfortably still for hours at a time, gently purring. From time to time I find him lying on a sofa flanked by them both, but I have never seen him share with them the special companionably close proximity that he would enjoy with Otto.

Truth to tell, the things that might happen between them are not always seen by me, and catwise there may be much that goes on that I do not know. They are true to themselves and keep their own counsel.

Around this time I receive an email from my friend Sue, who has for some months been in quiet mourning at the loss of her adored Devon Rex cat Spottiswoode, and who knows that the only long-term fix is to find another Devon Rex.

From: Sue
To: Marilyn
Date: Monday 8 November 23:43

Dear Marilyn

I went to see a Devon Rex kitten today. I trailed all the way to a place near Bedford - the nearest kitten I could find.

He is a Si-Rex, so a Devon Rex with Blue Siamese points. At the moment he is eleven weeks old, and when he sits on his fat little bottom he fits in the palm of your hand. He is an outcross - his mother was a Burmese with a Rex father.

I am afraid to say I put a deposit down, and seeing him climbing up the curtains knew with dread just what I shall be letting myself in for at the end of the month.

God help me if they don't all get on, but there were four dogs in the house as well as various uncles, aunts, brothers and sisters, so hopefully he is pretty gregarious.

As I have Chatto and Cape it would make sense to have a Bodley Head, but this is not a good cat name, so I shall call him Max Reinhardt who, I believe, became part of Bodley Head through Putnam. Max Reinhardt used to publish one of my favourite British humorists - Paul Jennings - so I have always thought he must have been a good egg! He will only have to use his surname on forms and tax returns, so Max is a good cat name for everyday.

Love Sue

Because I am lucky enough to have a car and Sue does not, and because I am a complete pushover for kitten collection, I nag Sue into letting me drive her to collect her new family member. She has a lively time ahead of her, as she will be introducing her new Devon Rex into an established household of three Siamese/Burmese females. However, new kittens, for the following reasons and many others, are excellent diversions for those in mourning.

From: Sue
To: Marilyn
Subject: Progress Report
Date: 6 December 15:08

So far we have:

- been in oven (once)
- fridge (twice)
- fallen off kitchen counter bottom first into bowl of Whiskas (great shock for Nora at the time) - unfortunately this did not coincide with fall in washing up bowl
- have stood on heater (not done this again)
- stood in saucepans on cooker countless times
- reprogrammed fax machine
- have ignored all nice toys and played endlessly with piece of blue parcel binding

However, we have made up for these transgressions by being very adorable and sleeping

a lot, giving everyone a respite. Have even
managed to sleep curled up with Jonathan,
and Nora doesn't mind too much when we eat
her dinner. Chatto was not impressed by the
threat of loads more Maxes arriving, and at
least is sulking a little less spectacularly.
We do spoil things a bit by chancing our arm
(or paw) just a little too often, and things
have not got so friendly that tail chasing
is acceptable as yet. Eating continues to be
a favourite habit and we oblige by hoovering
down everything and anything including other
people's dinner - who, although tolerant,
do not like having it stood in. I think you
know to whom I refer.

  Sue

My postscript to this is that Max Reinhardt is a knockout.
He is so pretty and so naughty that he has hooked me
totally on to the breed of Devon Rex.

We make a foray into Scotland with the kittens where
we stay with Michael's brother, John, for a week. The
week we are in Scotland is splendid, but the long journey
is not a success and Michael's despair makes me ponder
seriously on the wisdom of undertaking journeys in the
car with two kittens. It is certainly a tax on a marriage,
regardless of whether or not it is healthy for the kittens in
question.

We return to the cottage in time to make all the myriad
arrangements necessary for Christmas, and happily look
forward to the company of Damian and John who will both
share it with us. Sadly, Oliver must work, so we forgo the

pleasure of his company and he remains in Wales with his mother.

Septi's 'problem', which has been a regular occurrence over the last few months, is currently in abeyance, so I'm hoping it might have 'gone away'. He continues to tolerate the kittens and even, sometimes, seems to enjoy their company, so perhaps his antisocial toilet activities were merely a temporary protest.

CHAPTER 22

December

My former husband, Geoffrey, who is a close friend to us both, invites us to stay with him in the Yorkshire Dales. He has even extended the invitation to the kittens too. He has never been a cat lover, so I'm aware of the indulgence he is affording us. He lives in a large Georgian house in the Dales, which I shared with him for many years, and I can just imagine the pleasure with which Titus and Fannie will rampage around it. We load up the car and set off on our journey, as we did before on the Great Scottish Expedition.

It is a strange fact but the memory can be curiously selective in what it retains and what it rejects. Somehow the interval of Christmas has wiped the memory of the Scottish journey from our minds. But suddenly I have total recall.

As we turn in west from the A1 to wind our way up the valley of the Ure, following that great river that never flinched at any obstacle in its way as it evolved its riverbed, but rather twisted and turned a myriad times empowered by its never-ending supply of Pennine hill water, I realise that the resulting travel sickness from the kittens is absolutely inevitable and that I should have been able to predict that this is what would happen.

I feel my own pleasure at returning 'home' being inexorably diluted by Michael's increasing horror at the smell and inconvenience of stopping every five miles to clean up, and on this occasion I do know that his foreseeable 'No, this time I mean it. This *really* is the last time. Never, ever again' is a serious, to-be-forgotten-at-my-peril, warning.

We arrive at Park House in the dark and pull up at the back door. We are met by Geoffrey, who calls out to us with his customary greeting to all visitors who approach his manse from this angle, and which on all previous occasions has made us both giggle: 'Please MIND the dog shit. There's a lot of it about.'

He has a deep horror of visitors bringing in unwanted 'calling cards' on their shoes, having suffered a seminal experience of this nature some years earlier. The little ginnel at the back of the house is a favourite short-cut of dog walkers, and also solo dogs, that, Geoffrey is adamant, particularly favour the verge outside his Reading Room window as their chosen latrine. I cannot bear to tell him that we are one travelling car full of much worse than this. I creep round the side of the car and give him a big kiss and Michael comes up the other side of him and grips him in a bear hug, and then we hush him back inside the house. I then retrace my steps and try to pile all the detritus from our sickly journey into a bin liner, and then into his dustbin, without him being especially aware of what I'm up to.

It is a bitterly cold night and there is already a heavy frost lying outside, but inside the house it's as warm as toast. The central heating is at full pitch and I can see an enormous log fire burning in the grate in the sitting room. We gratefully sink into the welcoming luxury of the warm house and let the kittens out of their cage. They scamper around in a flurry of delight. Now, at last, no sickening car movement and loads of space to move and exciting new places to investigate; what more could two young healthy cats possibly want?

Geoffrey makes some modest requests about places he would rather they did not visit, which I try to enforce, but that turns out to be more difficult than I had foreseen. Mealtimes prove to be the main stumbling block as that is when the kittens are most used to being with us. I am, however, much moved by Geoffrey's growing enchantment with them. He has always had a fondness for dogs and he and I both loved, and were loved in return, by our yellow labrador, Sam, some years earlier; but in common with many dog lovers who have not known cats closely, he has also always claimed that he does not like cats. They are selfish, scratchy and unreliable creatures in his view.

Dog-love is awesome for the recipient of it, who is given, regardless of whether they seek it or not, the most unselfish and unconditional loving they will ever encounter, and I found myself that this background ill prepares the hitherto dog-only person for the world of cats, and the love of cats, and the stoicism of cats, and the loyalty of cats – and the stubbornness of cats. And also for the courage of cats, and the elegance of cats and the humour of cats, and that these things are distinct and special to the species. All of which I'm trying to tell him now. But it's enough that for this moment he is watching Fannie and Titus with amusement and evident pleasure. They are responsive cats, and he is rewarded for his attentions to them by small gestures of affection in their typically brief, catlike way. He is also charmed by Fannie's delicate, girly, tiptoeing around the place, and Titus's more in-your-face approach of turning over on her back waiting for her tummy to be rubbed, or simply just climbing on to his knees regardless.

All in all, as always when returning to Geoffrey in Gayle, it's a tremendously enjoyable visit. Michael and I visit nearby friends, Kath and John and Doreen and Thomas, who are mildly bemused that we are indoctrinating cat lore into Park House, but all of them are cat lovers anyway, so they understand our madness.

When we take our leave, Geoffrey very generously invites the girls back again, but I know, even without discussion with Michael, that they have been allowed their last excursion, as they are such terrible travellers.

The journey home is not a good one. There has been a major pile-up on the M1 south of the point at which we join it, and we find ourselves trapped, stationary, for several hours and eventually, breaking all rules, the only way we can cope with the protesting prisoners is to let them have the run of the car until the police are able to clear the road and traffic is able to move freely again. It is the final seal on the end of journeying.

CHAPTER 23

The New Millennium

We arrive back at Moon Cottage in time for New Year's Eve and all its attendant revelry. Although we have so far resisted the extraordinary hype surrounding this occasion, both on the day and then the night itself, Michael and I, along with thousands of others, find ourselves enormously moved by the truly global nature of the televised celebrations. We watch, rapt, as New Zealand and Australia, and then China and India, see in the New Millennium. In the late evening we walk down to our local church and find that although there is no formal service underway, about fifteen local people have turned out to silently pray in the New Year; and as the midnight hour arrives, there is an enormous whoosh as nearby fireworks are let off to celebrate the moment, and the darkened windows of the church are lit up by the lurid greens and pinks of rockets and catherine wheels and we hear the distant sound of laughter and applause.

We leave the church, greeting our fellow parishioners as we go, and then start our walk home through the streets.

We suddenly find ourselves and others calling out and greeting one another with true warmth and friendship and it does seem a very special moment.

As we near the cottage the sky is lit up all around us, again and again, by the multiple dazzle of fireworks, and the air is filled with repeated explosions of variable loudness. We look at each other and speed up our walking pace, aware too late of the effect that this hubbub will be having on Septi. We put the key in the door and call him, but we are unable to find him. Fannie, followed shortly by Titus, comes forward to greet us and they both appear untroubled by the general commotion, but we cannot track down Septi. In due course, we uncover him crouching on the seat of a dining room chair, under the overhang of a tablecloth. His eyes are large and he looks unhappy. There is a discernible 'frown' on his forehead and his cheek pads are puffed out, making his whiskers bristle. His ears lie alternately flat against his head or bolt upright, and his nostrils are quivering.

'Oh Septi – it's all right, boy. I promise you it's OK. They won't hurt you.' Michael holds him in his arms, and I come across to stroke him too. 'If I could stop the beastly things, Septi, I would,' I murmur.

It has been a matter of concern to me that, certainly for the last two years and possibly longer, in a neighbouring street to ours, we have been aware of fire-works not just on 5 November, which is when they might normally be expected to be heard, but now regularly on other occasions. The winning of local football, birthdays, anniversaries, who knows what might be the reason, but now there seems to be no closed season to when they might happen. Fireworks have an awful effect on some, although not all, animals, and I would love those who use them regularly to have more awareness of how much distress they may be causing. However, having said this, I can see that the dawn of the New Year of a New Millennium might reasonably be considered to be something worth celebrating in this manner.

Michael and the boys have no knowledge of what it was that happened in Septi's youth that so frightened him, but maybe, once, he was too close to a firework as it exploded and he has never forgotten the horror of it. Is it possible, on the other hand, that some cats and dogs, and also some horses, cattle and sheep – not to mention hundreds of other small mammals and most birds – are just simply terrified of these harmful-sounding detonations, and that they may never be able to conquer their fear of them?

Spring arrives, and with it a discernible difference in the girls now. They are beginning to develop and become very 'teenaged'. Fannie, who is more and more girly all the time, and usually extraordinarily delicate in where she places her feet, or where she lies, has suddenly started to break things.

As I walk into the room early this evening I'm just in time to see her knock over my desk light and smash the light bulb. As I watch this performance with my jaw agape, she then proceeds, right in front of me, to knock over the printer and thereby pull out all the cables. She has phases of racing round as if 'Old Nick' is after her, or more accurately, as if she is after 'Old Nick'.

Titus watches her excesses with a seemingly more adult disdain, but I wonder if it's not that Titus eats more, and is carrying more weight, so simply cannot be bothered to do the running. However, the two of them do continue, regularly, to play tag with each other and they seem on this one to take it turn and turn about. It starts downstairs, it involves heavy pounding up the stairs, running the full length of the upper corridor, round and under John's bed, back into our room, up and over and behind our bed, and back down the stairs again. It is quite extraordinarily noisy, and at the end of it they are both quite breathless.

Fannie has also started to fish for Bertie with both her front legs in the water at the same time, if the lid is left off the fish tank. She sometimes squats on the top of the tank on her back legs and puts her front legs down into the water by pure balance. It's nerve-racking to watch from outside the tank, and must be terrible for Bertie, so it has to be stopped, although she is never anywhere near catching him in truth.

Titus definitely prefers men and when there is a choice of bodies will always select a man to lie on. Women are favoured only by default. Being red-haired she especially likes dark suits. Navy blue and black are best, so she can really leave her mark. She quietly climbs on to the knee of any and every man who visits the house and, given time, will slowly and insidiously climb up their shoulder, and then sit, nestled in the crook of the arm, leaning her own head against the human cheek of her choosing, purring quietly. At this moment John is her number one man, with Michael a very close second.

Fannie prefers to lie next to people rather than on them, and will usually choose me, or Damian if he's around. Her special thing with me is to wait outside the bathroom in the morning when she hears me running the shower, and when at the end I open the bathroom door she leaps in and jumps on to my knee for her morning cuddle, which is now highly ritualised. Truth to tell, I get so much peace and tranquillity out of those few moments of schmoozing before work that I could hardly bear it were it to cease. No wonder hospital patients find the company of animals healing.

Septi's toilet problems throughout this time continue and we all learn to live with stepping over the soiled Puppy Pads outside John's room on the upstairs landing, although it is of course much worse for John than for the rest of us.

On Saturday 1 April, the semi-final of the FA Cup is to be played at Wembley between Aston Villa and Bolton Wanderers, the latter being significant as the team that Geoffrey, as a son of Bolton, supports. As a consequence, Michael and Geoffrey, without much involvement on my part, engineer the purchase of a pair of tickets and Geoffrey comes to stay with us for the weekend. Knowing, of old, Geoffrey's distaste for all things associated with animal incontinence, I look forward to the weekend with minor apprehension on the cat front, but with the exception of one slight 'hiccup', and by the stealth of my early rising to destroy the evidence, Septi gets away with it.

It says much for Geoffrey's new-found affection for the kittens that in spite of the fact that Bolton gets beaten on the penalty shoot out, he is able to return to the cottage with Michael and be buoyant enough to announce that they are the only cats he has ever actively liked. Truth is, I think they are the first cats he has actively had inflicted upon him.

Less than a week after Geoffrey has returned home, I begin to be aware that Septi is not eating as he should be.

He has been sleeping more and more and spends much of his time curled up in the armchair that Michael normally sits in. I try tempting him with his favourite foods. Septi has always enjoyed the pleasures of 'real' food, while the kittens have become addicted to Hill's Science Plan dried cat food and cannot be persuaded to eat anything else, except for a shared pack once a day of Friskies Go-Cat wet cat food. Septi, on the other hand, eats sardines, ham, salmon, prawns and pretty much any brand of proprietary cat food as long as it's wet; he does not like dried food.

During this period he responds initially to salmon, and then to some ham, but very soon he leaves even these delicacies. I have begun to watch him closely, and twice have seen him turn round and, as he has moved, he has made a small, almost inaudible, moaning sound. I am worried, but do not want to say anything to Michael yet.

Eventually, though, I say: 'Michael, I think the old boy is in pain. I have been watching him and he is groaning when he moves – and you know Septi, he's a real stoic.'

'Are you sure? No – you're fine, aren't you, boy?' Michael strokes him gently. He then, with both hands, puts gentle pressure on either side of Septi's ribcage, and at that we both hear the old cat groan, which he follows with a long

159

sigh. I see a sad look pass across Michael's face like a dark cloud, and I feel a double stab of pain, for him and for Septi.

I find suffering in animals harder to bear than in adult humans. I imagine it's similar to the feeling that parents have when they see their child in hospital, frightened and in pain. It engenders an overwhelming sense of help-lessness at not being able to explain it, or alleviate it.

The following day finds me setting off in the car with, unusually, Septi in the cat carrier. Having not taken him to the vet for a long time I am not sure what to expect, and am much saddened by his outraged howls of protest and fear, which he keeps up all the way to the surgery.

On this first visit we see James, who is clearly worried by Septi's condition, but initially gives me antibiotics to clear up any infection that might be causing the problem. When I get Septi back home, he does eat a bit initially, so I hope against hope that this has sorted out his problem. Soon afterwards, though, he stops eating again and it is very clear that he is having trouble with his stomach.

We return, yet again, to the vet and once more see James. He handles Septi with great care and gentleness, and very thoroughly checks him out all over.

'Tell me again exactly how old this cat is.'

'He's either nineteen or twenty, we're not sure.'

'He has had a very good innings, you know.'

I wait, braced.

James looks at me. I know he is trying to see what he should say. It's hard being a vet, because you have to handle people, as well as their animals.

I look back at him and murmur: 'Go on. Say it.'

'You know what I'm going to say, I think. I believe that your cat has tumours and they seem to me to be pretty widespread, but . . .,' he says, as he sees my eyes fill with tears, 'I believe that he still has some quality of life ahead of him, and there is something we can do to help him as a temporary measure. Are you prepared to give it a go?'

I nod bleakly.

He rummages around in the huge drawer behind him, while I fondle Septi helplessly, and he then produces the inevitable syringe and injects Septi with a huge dose of steroids.

'You must understand that this will not cure him, but what I hope it will do is give him a new lease of life, and it may restore his appetite. I have given him a very large dose of steroids, but cats are surprisingly tolerant of them. You will be able to tell within the next seventy-two hours whether it's doing any good or not.'

When I break the news to John and Michael after returning home from that second visit, they are wretched beyond description, and I cannot find the words that will help them. Loving animals exacts its toll in pain at their weakness.

By the following day, however, Septi is eating like we cannot remember seeing him eat in years. He eats chicken, fish, and even some ham, and would, I believe, eat all manner of food if we gave him the chance.

Michael, always the optimist, keeps grinning as we watch Septi eating yet another plate full of food, and says he knows it's a miracle and that Septi will be all right after all. Oh, I so want this to be true. Certainly the old cat's eyes have a sparkle in them and it's the first time in days that he has eaten without being sick. It does appear as if his pain has been alleviated in some way.

James, during my last visit, had warned me, however, that when Septi next slips 'down' they will not be able to help me further, and that I will know instinctively when the right time to 'take action' will be. I am not so sure.

From: Marilyn
To: Sue
Date: 13 April 17:08

On Septi, don't think he has long now and the awful bit is don't know how or when to do the dreaded end bit.
  Michael is distraught because he has had him man and boy (Septi is twenty and Michael has had him since a kitten).
  Marilyn

From: Sue
To: Marilyn
Date: 13 April 200 22:03

Oh how dreadful. Having lost Spotty at nineteen years, I have some idea of how awful all this is.
  Charlotte, my first cat, had cancer, and

we called it a day as soon as she started
sitting hunched up and not eating, but you
are left with that dreadful thought of should
I? It is horrible to have to play God, but
I did feel better that I got the vet to come
to her and do it, and held her at the end,
so the slip from life to death was as
painless for her as possible. So, if it
comes to it, do insist the vet comes to you.
  In great sympathy
  Sue

Septi continues for a short time to gain strength from his
new voracious eating, but now he has stopped eating chicken
and ordinary fish. He will only eat cold ham and hot bacon,
which is strange food – but pork clearly has what it takes for
him. He is painfully thin in spite of his bingeing, but he
still walks around the house and goes outside to do the all-
important things that a cat has to do.

He seems to me, and Michael and John, fantastically
brave. We are sure he must be in pain, but his courage is
phenomenal. He lies alternately on the sofa and on the
chair, and the kittens, although they come close to him
from time to time, are keeping what seems like a respectful
distance. They walk around the room and look up at him,
but they do not jump up next to him.

I notice how both John and Michael take time to talk to
Septi gently and I ache for them. I, too, when they are not
around, find myself talking to him more than I ever did in
the past, as Septi was always so much his own cat that
somehow it would have been impertinent before.

As he loses more weight and sleeps for an increasing amount of time, I talk to Michael about what I should do about the vet. He makes a joke about Septi being a Catholic cat, and as such cannot be subjected to euthanasia. My eyes fill with tears, as I hug my man, who is simply in denial at the fact that Septi might be dying. However, joke though it is, it doesn't make it any easier to decide when or how.

CHAPTER 24

Septi barely moves from either the sofa or Michael's leather armchair. He has stopped eating, although he is still drinking a small amount of water. Hitherto, as he has been sleeping he has mostly been facing into the room, but I have noticed that now he lies with his back curled away from the room, and my father, a physician, always said that when a patient's head is turned permanently to the wall, it is of significance.

On the Wednesday before Easter I drive down to the West Country to see Paul and Sue, and when I get back that night Septi does not move. I know the moment is now. The Easter weekend is approaching and vets will be hard to get hold of, and I cannot abide to see him suffering any longer. It is truly unbearable.

Michael and I talk that evening and I know now that Michael cannot tolerate it any longer either. We both know that Septi will die anyway, whatever we do.

The following day Michael and John both leave to go to their offices and I'm upstairs when John leaves, so do not hear him say his farewell to Septi, but I know that he does and guess how much it hurts him. As Michael is about to leave, I'm not brave enough to be in the room when he says his goodbye to Septi, but shortly afterwards I hear his sob even from the room where I'm hiding. I go out to him and his desolation shatters me.

After they have left the cottage, it goes deadly quiet. I beg Septi to forgive me, but know that I am asking too much all the same. As soon as the vet's surgery is open, I phone them and ask them to send a vet to the cottage and explain the reason for the home visit. They ask me if I am sure it's necessary and I reply rather crossly: 'Yes. I'm absolutely certain.'

'A vet will be with you, hopefully within the next two hours.'

That should make it 11 a.m.

It's a terrible day. I keep going in to look at Septi and am fearful that he will feel bad vibes from me and know what is in my evil mind.

At 1 p.m. I phone the surgery again and am told that the vet has had a very full morning of emergency calls, etc.

At 2.30 I call again. Still no news of when the vet will arrive.

At 3.15 the doorbell rings and I find myself facing the vet, who is standing on the doorstep, bag in hand. By this time, I find it hard to speak. She is kind and apologetic, and says she has had a nightmare of a day, including just despatching the victim, a large dog, of an especially grisly road accident.

I introduce her to Septi who ignores her and remains steadfastly in his chair with his back to her. She asks if it should be that chair and I say yes, and shut the kittens out of the room.

She opens her bag and assembles her equipment and does the deed there and then, with gentleness and speed, but sadly the needle in the vein in his leg hurts him and he cries out and tries to move away. I hurt for him myself. She tries to hold him still, and I move across to be with him too. She injects him again. As I sit with him, with my hand on his side, his breathing stops.

The old warrior, the feisty one, is dead.

I have prepared a box with a sheet which I want to lay him out on, and I get up in order to fetch it from the adjoining room so that I might carry him away before the kittens see him.

'No, no. You must not do that,' she says. 'It's very important that they see him and understand that he is dead, otherwise they will not grieve and that is bad for them. Put him in the box, and then call them and let them smell him.'

We put him in the box and I do not cover him with the sheet; we call Fannie and Titus. They come to the box, gently, curiously. They both walk round to his head and smell his ears, his eyes and his nose. They look at each other and then they walk away, seemingly curiously detached, but also of one mind.

The vet and I talk for a while and I'm very grateful for her sympathy and understanding. She takes her leave and, after she has gone, I wrap Septi in the sheet and carry him in his box out to the greenhouse where I lay him with a candle at each end to await Michael's return. I know that

167

he's going to be upset by the candles, but I also know that if I do *not* do this he will be upset anyway.

We say prayers for Septi and bury him under the pear tree. Michael then confesses to me: 'Today is the first day in all the time we have been together when I didn't want to come home. I knew, all day long, that when I finally got home, Septi wouldn't be there any more.'

He then says that finding the candles next to Septi helped him in some way. I know exactly what he means, and I owe this one to my wise friend Sue. When my dog, Sam, who contracted an awful kidney infection, was finally put down, I made the mistake of leaving his body with the vet for him to incinerate, and my last image of Sam was of his body being dragged across a cobbled yard in a bin liner. (Although in fact that is also the last image I had of my mother, not being dragged across the cobbles of course, but the undertakers took her body out of our house in a black body bag which looked just like a bin liner, and I had to make sure that my poor father, who was distraught in his grief, did not see her passing his study window looking like that.)

From:	Sue
To:	Marilyn
Date:	15 April 22:57

I wish people [who don't have close companion animals] could sympathise more when you lose one. They, the animal, give so much for so little and it is impossible to describe what a gap they leave behind them when they go. I don't know if I should add this bit or not, but when Spotty died I felt awful that I only had an old box to put him in, and I did feel better after going out and buying a new cardboard cat carrier to take him to the vets. I laid him on a fresh pillow and gave him some flowers, which made me feel a lot better - why, I don't know, but it did.

  Best wishes,

  Sue

So not only has Sue helped on the matter of the final vet visit to Septi, but also in providing him with dignity in his death. Very sadly, a little later I then receive this email from her:

From: Sue
To: Marilyn
Date: 31 May 22:02

Just to let you know that I have also now lost my 'old stager'. Poor old Nora was going down hill rapidly, and last week I took her to the vet one last time. I was much luckier than you as he did use the sedation routine and left me with her while she fell asleep, and then he gave her the last injection so she didn't have to struggle like poor old Septi. I was quite touched by his consideration, and he even suggested I moved so that she could see me as she faded away. I knew it was coming so it didn't come as a complete blow, but it is always hard when you walk home with that empty basket.

  It has been strange without her, the others don't seem to miss her as such, but their

pattern of life has changed - and she was
obviously keeping the peace with Max as he
has got bashed more than ever without her
here.
  Life goes on . . .
  Sue

Immediately after Septi's death the kittens are very strange
indeed. For about three nights they have been leaping out
of corners and rampaging around the house. Michael and
John have both commented on it. Some of their behaviour
is a knowledge that Septi is not here any more, I'm sure of
it, and a letting-off of steam as they seemed to be on their
'best' behaviour while he was ill. Some of it, however, is
uncomfortably to me as if they are seeing something the
rest of us are not seeing? Animal grief remains a mystery.

I write an email to my friend Harriet, who has two sons,
Josh and Robbie, saying that I still feel terrible guilt for
betraying Septi's trust in me, and that on top of that the
kittens are behaving very oddly and rushing around and
running away. She replies:

From:	Harriet
To:	Marilyn
Date:	27 April 22:27

Dearest M
  So sorry to hear about Septi, but I think
you misjudge that cat. I think he did trust
you to the end to help him make that last leg
of his journey, and who are we to suppose
that what comes after death is not to be

trusted. But sad to see him go. And I'm not surprised the kittens are flexing their newfound independence – they have a whole lot of additional space to occupy now. It is amazing how, when the status quo changes, adjustments are made. You should see Robbie, with Josh away, expand in personality to take up the slack in his brother's absence.

Love Harriet

At the end of *Charles: The Story of a Friendship* by Michael Joseph, a wonderful book about the special relationship Michael Joseph had with his Siamese cat, Charles, through the war years, he quotes Carl Van Vechten writing about *his* cat, Feathers:

It is seemingly very simple, such a companionship, depending on scarcely more than mere propinquity, a few actions, a touch of the cold, moist nose, a soft paw against the cheek, a greeting at the door, a few moments of romping, a warm, soft ball of fur curled on the knee, or a long stare. It is thus that the sympathy between men and animals expresses itself, but interwoven, and collectively, these details create an emotion which it is very difficult even for time to destroy.[6]

---

[6] Taken from *Charles: The Story of a Friendship* by Michael Joseph (Michael Joseph, 1945).

And borrowing Michael Joseph's own tribute to his beloved Charles, may I say to both Otto and Septi, from all of us who loved them:

For while we live you shall not die.

More Cat Tales
from Moon Cottage

MARILYN EDWARDS

ILLUSTRATED BY
PETER WARNER

HODDER

To the memory
of
Giles Alexander Esmé Gordon
(1940–2003)

CHAPTER 1

Summer

As I march across the main road carrying the large cage and its woebegone passengers, I find myself wincing at the outlandish noises that are emanating from within. Reaching the car, I now inelegantly wrestle the cat carrier, with its outraged cargo, on to the back seat.

'How many times do I have to explain it is for your own good?' I exhort the two kittens, ineffectually, while strapping myself behind the wheel.

My pointless rhetoric is, however, obscured by even louder cries of anguish, as the two feline occupants feel the gentle motion of the car being manoeuvred out into the road to join the busy queue of traffic. We're on our way to the veterinary clinic for the annual ritual of the cats' jabs against flu and any number of other feline diseases.

We arrive in full voice. That is, some of us do. But, as I am endeavouring to appear invisible at this point, I am far from exercising any vocal chords, unlike others in my party. When it's our turn, I lift my protesting charges inside their carrier on to the examination table for Kate, the vet, to give them her full attention. She has met them before, but this is the first time she has had the chance to give them a complete appraisal. She opens the door of the cage, at which point they both fall silent, and she gently pulls out the kitten nearest to her. In her hands she is holding the red tabby shorthair with the striking amber eyes, white bib and white socks.

'And who do we have here?'

'This is Titus,' I reply.

'You are a lovely little one, but what is this I see? You have the beginnings of a very grand apron.'

'What on earth is an apron?' I ask, surprised. She laughs.

'It's this roll of fat.' She wobbles Titus's lower stomach. I had, until this moment, considered it to be merely an extra-thick clump of fur hanging down.

'Ginger – or, correctly, red – cats are especially prone to them. You have to watch them, as they get older, because they have a tendency to gain weight.'

Titus, who has up to this point been crouching down on the examination table staring into space, now gazes rapturously at Kate with an expression of trust, bordering on passion, on her face.

'You are a very calm cat, aren't you, my little one?' she murmurs. Titus purrs and flops over on to her back for her now contentious tummy to be rubbed.

'You call her by a boy's name. Why is that?'

'Ah! Yes! Well! We thought she was a boy and by the time we'd had her sexed, here, at your clinic, it was too late. We were too used to her name. So Titus it's remained.' I shrug, adding:

'She is named after Titus Groan.'

'Oh not Titus Andronicus?' she enquires, a touch sardonically, I feel. Hesitating, now braced for the inevitable question as to the name of her sister, I decide to retaliate first.

'Both the kittens are named after either writers or characters in books,' I announce portentously. 'The woman from whom I acquired their mother is a writer whom I greatly admire and it seemed to make sense.'

What I forbear to tell her is that the mother of these two kittens had already been burdened, by the time I met her, with the rather weighty name of Ottoline Morrell, which had so perturbed a former vet in this same practice that he had point-blank refused to enter the full name on the inoculation certificate, so Titus as a name by comparison, even if the wrong gender, is a mere trifle.

Having poked, fondled and peered at Titus from every angle, Kate finishes her examination by quickly and efficiently injecting the round purring cat, whose sole response to her assault is to blink placidly. The vet places her back inside the cat carrier and takes out her sister, a much smaller cat. In her hands now she is holding a black torbie (having predominantly silver-grey tabby markings, but which include odd patches and stripes of reddish colouring), which she gently places on the examination table. The kitten cowers down on the rubber mat of the table, trembling and making small faltering miaows. Kate picks her up and nurses her on her shoulder, crooning to her gently.

'You're all right, my sweetie, there, there, there.' After more in this vein, the little cat goes quiet and slowly retracts her claws, which up to this point have been deeply embedded in the cloth of the vet's white coat, and visibly relaxes. Her ears come forward, alert, and she pokes her whiskers inquiringly into Kate's ear.

'And what is *your* name, might I ask?'

'She is called Fannie,' I volunteer into the silence, adding, 'after Flagg, the American author. She is a wonderful writer who reassures you about human kindness.'

'Mmmmn!' Kate replies non-committally, and I deduce this is not the moment for a dissertation on the compassion of the great Fannie Flagg.

She inspects the ears, nostrils and teeth of the small cat in front of her.

'You have lovely white teeth, what a clever girl. No problems there then.' And so, in due time, Fannie too is declared to have a clean bill of health. She is now injected and squawks loudly in protest as she feels the needle penetrate the flesh on the back of her neck.

'There, there. You are making a big fuss about nothing.'

Kate rubs the place where the needle has entered and puts Fannie back in the carrier along with her sister. They lick each other's noses for comfort.

'Remind me, how old are they?'

'They were born at the end of April last year, so they are now just over a year old, fourteen months in fact.'

'Should you not be bringing them in for neutering? Normally females are done at six to eight months.'

'I would like each of them to have the chance of having one litter and I will then neuter them immediately after that.'

We discuss the risks involved in the pregnancy and birthing for a cat as opposed to the safer route of neutering. I know myself how I have yearned to have children and I wish for these young queens not to suffer that same frustration.

'I have a long list of people, friends and colleagues, who have shared their lives with cats in the past, all of whom would care for them wonderfully, who've put their names down for kittens from this particular stock, so I know I would find good homes for them. I really will be a responsible kitten owner, and I'm doing this with my eyes open. At the office I'm the official finder-of-homes-for-kittens-in-trouble!' Kate smiles as I say this, and I feel gently reassured.

'And we would keep one from each litter ourselves anyway,' I add. I feel a twinge of guilt as I say this, knowing that I have not exactly spelt this out to Michael, my long-suffering husband. He has agreed to us keeping one kitten, but I am uncertain whether I have even proposed the idea of two.

'If you *really* want to do this, allow your cats to become pregnant that is, you should not leave it longer than two and a half years, or three, maximum.' She pauses and then adds warily:

'If you don't have them spayed and they don't have kittens, then there's a really strong possibility that they will have womb problems.'

I swallow hard but decide to say nothing more about kittens, as I have the next hurdle to cross, which manifests itself in her very next question. She produces a worming powder from the drawer.

'Now the cats both go outside, don't they? When did you last worm them?'

'Well, actually they are inside cats and I haven't wormed them since they were first born.' We talk on. I remind her (she had been the one who had had the unenviable task of having to despatch our aged cat in the last painful stages of his terminal cancer, and so had met the kittens then) that their mother, Otto, was killed by a car on the road directly outside Moon Cottage, leaving her kittens orphaned in the bedroom above, where they had been born a mere seven weeks earlier, and that it broke our hearts, not to mention the heart of Michael's venerable old cat Septi, and that on balance we knew it would only be a matter of time, and not much of that, before the kittens would go the way of their mother. She nods her assent to my point of view, but says that she always feels cats need to take their chance even if it is a short life. I counter that selfishly I couldn't bear that grief again so quickly, and the two kittens are all that I now have of Otto.

Having persuaded me that the kittens still need worming, with laughter in her voice she finally asks me how the pregnancy is to be achieved with the strictures I have in place, and I say that at the moment I don't know. I haven't worked it out, but I will let her know in due course. I bundle the cats up and take them, protesting the while, back to home, sweet home.

CHAPTER 2

The two kittens completely dominate Moon Cottage and all who dwell within its walls. At this time the human residents are Michael, his son John, and yours truly, the cat-chronicler, with occasional visits from John's brothers, Damian and Oliver.

The cats are beginning to grow up and their kittenish ways are noticeably changing. They still love to play, both with each other and also with their human companions, but already the way they amuse themselves is markedly different from their former clambering, climbing, clawing, biting, fighting, kicking, tumbling play, which was some-times destructive and always totally exhausting. A play that would quite suddenly finish with the kittens falling asleep in spent heaps, and one that, if witnessed by an uninitiated visitor, especially one who had just had their legs severely scarred by being used as a climbing post, would leave them sadly shaking their heads and saying, at best:

'Will they ever grow up?' and more than likely any manner of less indulgent other things that I know not of, because they have simply been too tactful to say what they really think!

The truth is that all too soon kittens shed their one-time seemingly endless appetite for tomfoolery and change into the serious, skilled, streamlined, hunting-machine that is an adult cat, although they never totally lose their sense of fun. Cats who grow up with their own family members, especially their siblings or mother, can maintain strong elements of that early playfulness with each other which will recur throughout their lives, while cats who are the lone feline occupant of a household often maintain that same playful bond with their humans, but there is a distinct turning point when kittenhood proper has passed and the playfulness becomes occasional and the initiation of it harder to stimulate. When the friskiness of kittenhood starts to wane it would appear that growing cats develop other routines in order to assert their presence upon others.

All three of us human residents are liable, very early in the morning, to be woken by Titus who has developed an especially menacing habit of summoning us from deep sleep to instant consciousness. Usually she selects just one person per morning for this treatment, but on bad days she will inflict it on all of us in turn. Her method is this. At around 5 a.m. (our alarm is set to go off at 5.30 a.m. and an extra half-hour of sleep at this time in the morning is very precious) she jumps on to the bed of her chosen victim, heavily, and clambers over them until she is at their head level. She now patrols behind the pillow until she reaches the optimum position for her greeting and then, with great delicacy and skill, she extends her left paw – it is always her left paw, although she is not a 'south-paw' in all that she does – and touches their upper lip. So far, so cute, and her touch is wondrously gentle. But if no response is forthcoming, she then, with equal delicacy but complete deliberation, unsheathes her claws and with one of the longer middle claws will gently scratch the upper lip of her chosen human. At this stage of the assault the victim will be aware of the merest hint of a prickle but, should the chosen subject be foolish enough to try to sleep on, the second stage of the assault turns into a penetrative stab inflicted with serious intent and has on occasion even drawn blood. The sensation of injection-by-claw is completely impossible to ignore for even the heaviest sleeper.

'No – Titus. Stop! Stop! Please stop! That really hurts.'

'Miaow, miaow. Miaow. Miaow. Miaow.'

When I am the target I will stroke her briefly to divert her and turn over and pull the duvet over my head. Slowly I will sink back into slumber. She waits, for probably five minutes, when sleep and a false sense of security have enveloped me again by which time, in order to breathe, I have opened up the duvet bunker slightly. And then it comes again. Stab, stab, stab.

'Titus – I mean it. Dammit. Stop . . . pleeeeease. It's not even as if you need feeding 'cos there's food down all the time.' Michael groans in protestation at the mingled noises of cat and human interchange and I know that sleep is a lost battle and that the beastly clock is going to go now, anyway. The difference is that cats don't have a 'snooze' button! John, Michael and I, having all cursed her in turn, admit to finding her habit bizarrely endearing even though it is quite appalling when it's actually happening.

Fannie does not act so invasively. Fannie loves her humans from a greater distance on the whole. She will stare across at her chosen person for hours, sometimes even when they are asleep. She, herself, sleeps on top of the highest bookcase in our bedroom which she has to reach by jumping on to clothes hanging on a hook on the back of the bedroom door from which point she climbs on to the top edge of the door and from there she leaps up on to the bookcase. Sometimes she sleeps on her back with her legs up in the air, sometimes curled up in a ball with her nose under her front paw, and most often stretched out on one side. She has one habit at night time of the close encounter variety, which is not put into practice every night, and there is no telling what triggers it. She will slowly patrol across the pillows behind our heads, and as I lie there I can feel her very slowly and meticulously groom my hair with her tongue. Sometimes she will add a cursory lick to the eyelids too, which because of the roughness of a cat's tongue, is almost unbearably tickly. This is only ever carried out while the bedside light remains switched on; once the light is extinguished, she jumps down on to the floor. It would seem that this is her unique form of greeting, or perhaps the intention is more that of grooming, as each of the cats will only groom her sister if she is awake. She will occasionally lavish the same attentions upon Michael, but again only if he is awake and he tends to fall asleep before me usually. Her mother, too, sometimes did this, but Fannie was too young ever to witness it. Odd that such a trait should be hereditary.

∾

It is amazing how two adolescent cats can pervade a dwelling place so completely with their presence and their personality. In the morning when we go down for breakfast we are welcomed vociferously and insistently, as if we had been absent in spite of the fact that we have all shared the same space through the night; well, truth to tell, some of the night. The cats come and go as they please and we leave our door open so that they might have that freedom of movement. John tends to keep his door shut more often than not so he is often beyond their reach. As the three of us prepare to leave for work in the mornings it is possible to distinguish the body language of sorrow in each of the cats, as they recognise in our behaviour the signs of our impending departure. They both pull stern mouths and stare long and unblinkingly across the room, and more often than not they will lie on our bed with their backs to us as we say goodbye to them. Titus is the most dramatic at the big sulk. She has developed it into an art form.

Conversely, when we return home from work the welcome from each of them seems to me surprisingly enthusiastic, as our former cats sometimes only lifted an eyelid in greeting. Fannie is always the first to race down the stairs as she hears the key in the front door, so that by the time the front door is open she has leapt up on to the music centre speaker behind the door – the highest point from which she can receive us – from whence she issues her little miaows of greeting, short, repetitive, staccato sounds that she reserves entirely for human interchanges. This she will do to all three of us with varying degrees of intensity depending upon her mood. She allows the interaction of stroking from us all.

Titus saunters in much more slowly, usually half a minute or so behind her smaller more agile sister, and to Michael and me her greeting is a silent one, which is, as it were, simply the showing of her body. If either of us bends down to stroke her she walks away, shunning the hand that is proffered. When John comes in, however, she issues repetitive short harsh miaows, which increase until he acknowledges her presence. She has a particular fondness for John and a special voice for him too.

It is at this point when we return from work that they both demand more play. The play requires human participation, but now the cats will quickly reject screwed-up paper and pieces of string, which they had loved in their younger months. It is more active exchanges that they seek and for the moment, at least, they most like to chase small light plastic balls with bells inside them, with holes, although Michael as a long-term serious soccer supporter is appalled at the way they 'cheat' and pick the balls up in their claws and carry them quite long distances. Myself, I just reckon it is the rules of rugby that are being employed. There is a complex game of paw ball that they play in which each of them allows the other complete domination over the ball until a given moment when the other may move in. I am in awe of this game as no dog, no untrained dog that is, would ever hold back in the way each of these cats does for the other. They require that things be thrown for them a great deal and will sometimes retrieve them, but more often they will play with them but finally expect you to retrieve them, and because one becomes a well-trained human, in the end you do. My friend, Sue, has a Devon Rex called Max who retrieves things himself, but Devon Rexes are special and more dog-like in their responses. They have the gift of eternal kittenhood.

Although both Titus and Fannie are growing away from their kittenish qualities, they still play a fierce spring and slash game with each other. It is as if they still need to test each other for the level of endurance that each of them has to pain and also where the line should be drawn between play and real fighting. Another game that they play repeatedly, and which I believe is common to all cats confined to a house, is what we call 'chase and gallop'. They take it in turns to chase each other upstairs, under the beds, then downstairs again; round and round the sitting room, the dining room and the kitchen and then up the stairs again, thunderously. The rules of this one are quite hard to determine, but the cats definitely take it in turns to be either the chased one or the chaser. When they are at this at full pelt it is astonishingly noisy and they can sound surprisingly heavy footed.

Recently Fannie has started to climb the curtains, and this is something that dear podgy Titus cannot do. But Fannie, who is not only more agile than her sister, also has

what seems to be a driven need
to get as high as possible, always.
Her mother was the same and used
to climb along the ridge of the roof
of the cottage, on top of the rose pergola
and wherever else was the highest point
that could be climbed. Fannie has the
same torbie colouring as her mother and
a similar temperament, although if anything she is more nervous and more timid
of more things than ever her mother was.
Fannie's fearfulness is strange, as these cats
have had a completely protected existence inside
the cottage where they were born and, other
than losing their mother before they were
two months of age, nothing horrible has ever
happened to them.

Titus, on the other hand, endears herself to anyone and
everyone who comes to the cottage, which she achieves by
employing copious cheek rubbing followed by climbing up,
with or without invitation, on to their knee or shoulder
where she will then purr quietly but seductively. She also
beguilingly rolls over on her back for her white fluffy tummy
to be rubbed by absolutely anyone, and although Fannie
also sometimes does this, Titus is the one with no
inhibitions. She prefers men on whom to bestow her favours
and of course the cat cliché is true in her case – the more
the person does not like cats, the more likely he is to be the
target of Titus's favours. She especially loves dark trousers
and navy blue and black suits, and although she is

technically a domestic shorthair, she has long 'short' hairs of a very light ginger hue, which cling tenaciously to the clothes of those with whom she flirts, much like their begetter.

~

It has been a dull sort of summer without much sun, but very warm and dry, and I am finding it increasingly tiresome and sweaty cooking in the kitchen with the door closed. I am able to open all the cottage windows by dint of using white-squared plastic mesh, the sort that a garden centre might supply for climbing plants, which are screwed over the window frames and which allow for the little cottage windows to be slid backwards and forwards behind them so that we and the cats can breathe in fresh air without incurring the incidence of flat cat on the treacherous main road outside. However, I cannot resolve the problem of the door.

We have about a third of an acre of cottage garden, but try as I might I cannot find a way of making it cat safe in terms of containment. Cats are amazingly skilful at finding ways out of places; they need to be because they are such strongly predatory but fragile animals, and these skills are what make them able to survive at all. I find a website on the internet advertising very clever containment fencing that might do the job, but when I contact them I discover that they are American and are simply not prepared to ship the material across the Atlantic. Probably if they had been prepared to, I would not have been able to afford the shipping costs in any case. Fellow cat lover, writer and friend

Karin, who is incidentally one of the few women who Titus simply swoons upon when she sees her, when I tell her about the lengths I am taking in my attempts to make the cats happy, tells me with glee about an extraordinary house somewhere in San Diego where the owners of the house have made small cat-sized holes right up at ceiling level in the majority of the rooms in their house, so that the cats can travel from ground to ceiling throughout the house, with the assistance of slides and ramps and further aided by little perches strategically cemented into the walls; this means they need never remain imprisoned in one room or, if they are truly skilful, even touch the ground. But, as she adds wryly: 'Could make resale of the property a tad difficult.' I realise I am only just beginning and it could be a long road ahead of me.

In frustration I have combed every garden centre and DIY place I can think of and finally I've purchased a combination of two sorts of wooden trellis fencing, which I have turned into a six-foot-high fence with a narrow gate which opens into the outer garden, which, by utilising our neighbour's side wall, has now transformed an area outside the back door into a small contained suntrap the size of a large room. We have furnished it with our wooden garden table and chairs, a small tiled Moroccan stand, a cat scratching post and platform, the hanging baskets containing our fuchsias and tubs of scarlet geraniums, and a dramatic purple bougainvillea to remind us of France. At last we can have the back door open and eat outside and the cats can come and go.

When the moment arrives to let the cats outside I thrill

to their evident tension and sense of excitement as they cross the threshold of the door with great nervousness. By the time they reach the centre of the yard their confidence visibly increases. Their noses work overtime as they are assailed by a multitude of new smells and their ears twitch in harmony with the whole host of fresh sounds they are experiencing. They quickly gain self-assurance. Within minutes they have both jumped up on to the cat platform and from there to the little Moroccan table in order to watch assorted birds and bees and butterflies through the fencing. From time to time, all three, birds, bees and butterflies, venture into the inner yard to the unutterable delight of the cats, although the birds alone learn quickly to avoid repeating this behaviour.

For the next few weeks it is rewarding to observe the two cats relishing the sunshine when we get it; they lie stretched out on the garden table, tails twitching gently. Watching, *really* watching, cats lie prone in the sunshine is both cathartic and a potent lesson in the true art of sensual relaxation. However, I know that many cats can suffer quite severe sunburn to their ears, so initially I am mildly wary, but so long as the kitchen door remains open they seem to come inside if it really does get too hot. I am experiencing a new liberation in being able to open the kitchen door and let out the cooking smells and heat.

CHAPTER 3

Through the many dry days of this long summer the cats spend much of their time outside in their little yard. At the beginning they make several stalwart attempts at escape by climbing up the trellis and hanging upside down off the overhang, but fortunately the angle of the overhang seems to defeat them and eventually they drop, disheartened, to the ground. Now, after some weeks, such attempts have ceased and we reassure ourselves that they can't get out. Sadly, however, frogs can get in and because the yard contains a tap flanked by several watering cans, and because hanging baskets with geraniums and trailing fuchsias abound and are constantly being watered, the frogs squeeze themselves through the trellis in their perpetual quest for nourishment.

For a couple of months now, although it has been dull and overcast, there has been no rain and it is very warm, so Michael and I are sharing the chore of watering the garden regularly each evening on our return from work. This acts like a food-gong to the frogs, who gather in to harvest the slugs and snails emerging from the dried-out cracks in the soil to the newly dampened surfaces. Like all cats, I find that the kittens are hunters and, without any training at all except for a brief encounter with a near-dead baby mouse – which was all that their young mother, Otto, had time to teach them before her untimely death – they still manage to corral the frogs into the kitchen with meticulous efficiency.

Michael and I find ourselves regularly rescuing screaming frogs from all corners of the ground floor of the cottage. (It is most disconcerting, to me at any rate, to see and hear a frog 'scream' when grasped by a predator such as a cat, which they do with their mouths wide open and which sounds completely human. It's something I had never witnessed until the kittens were born in Moon Cottage, although, in my youth, I had reared many a tadpole to full frog status.) One morning I am dismayed to find a very stiff, cold, white (belly-up) slightly-flecked-with-blood frog lying in one of the cat-litter trays and, thinking him dead, I take him out into the garden, respectfully removing the polystyrene beads that bedeck his little body, and lay him under a plant in the middle of a sun-baked flowerbed. I return half an hour later to bestow upon him his funeral rites and find that he has disappeared. Has he resurrected or did a bird eat him?

∾

Before the summer has run its course we are determined to host a long-overdue lunch party for a special group of friends and colleagues and my ambition is that it should be in the garden on the lawn where there is more room to put two dining tables end to end rather than cram them together inside our little cottage.

Plans are finalised, invitations issued, and preparations underway. The chosen day is a Saturday in the first half of August; the barometer is steady, the weather set fair, and there has not been so much as a wisp of cloud for days. Much of the food that I am to cook is to be done on the day and I cannot prepare in advance, guaranteeing the greatest amount of culinary pandemonium possible; but one gorgeous concoction designed by Nigella Lawson, whose passion about how food should *taste* is compelling, can be prepared the day before. It is called, humbly enough, 'Strawberries in Dark Syrup',* but being steeped in balsamic vinegar it has garnet depths of a gorgeous intensity. In Nigella's own words, the red of the strawberries 'shine with the clarity of stained-glass windows. And it tastes as it looks: deep and light at the same time.' This pudding, glinting in a large glass mixing bowl in the depths of the fridge, begins to assume the significance of a holy chalice and its contents, while I attempt to grapple with objective reality as presented by the challenge of the feast I am preparing in the rest of the kitchen.

Saturday dawns, and as I rise and throw back the curtains I am mightily gladdened to see a full sun blazing away in an azure sky, early though it is.

Michael and I together manhandle all the furniture out of the dining room into the garden to the increasing bemusement of the two cats, who find acres of space where before there was a forest of wooden legs. For two days they have both been behaving slightly oddly around the dining

---

*From *How to Eat* by Nigella Lawson (Chatto & Windus, 1998).

room in particular and on some sort of private cat alert, and I have feared that yet again there is some entrapped frog somewhere, but we have all searched repeatedly and found nothing. As I start to wind up towards cookery frenzy shortly before our guests are due, Michael calls me.

'Have you had a good look under the piano? That is certainly where *they* seem to be looking!'

The piano is now one of the few remaining pieces of furniture in the room and the two cats are sitting in front of it, staring, with their ears pricked forward, vibrating minutely, indicating a concentration I have rarely observed in them before.

'Michael, this isn't the moment! I can't deal with this *and* with the food. We'll just have to ignore it. Whatever it is will get away, I'm sure.'

'I think I agree with you,' he replies phlegmatically. I race back to the kitchen to carry on cooking. Distantly I think I hear him say:

'Come on, Titus, come on, Fannie. This is your chance. You can do better than just looking.' But I may have imagined it. The door bell rings and our guests start to arrive. We shush them through the empty dining room and out into the garden where the happy sound of corks being pulled and subdued merriment echoes around the garden. The lunch party is now well on track.

The first two courses have been presented and consumed without a hitch and I am just beginning to relax, but I cannot fail to be aware that each time I come back into the cottage again the kittens are still fixedly staring at the piano. I am concerned that any one of our guests, who may well be made anxious by cats, may be even more phobic about 'wildlife', or more likely 'vermin', or whatever else may be hiding under the piano. The kittens are seriously unsubtle in their watch. Other than walking round with sandwich boards proclaiming 'Here Be Dragons' they could not be doing a more sterling job of advertising that a living creature lurks beneath the piano.

However, the time has now arrived for the Ruby Pudding, and Michael, who has taken pity on my trailing back and forth, has elected to take on the kitchen/garden run himself. I am sitting back, being soothed but also stimulated by the animated talk around the table, when out of the corner of my eye I see him bring to the table the strawberries still in the scratched thick-glass Pyrex mixing bowl rather than in the elegant cut-glass dish with its own pedestal, which was set aside in the kitchen to display this creation in all its glory and richness of colour. The oversight is entirely my fault of course. How would he, or could he, know as I had not told him, but this does not stop my squawk of anguish.

'No, no, no. Oh Michael! How could you?'

I scuttle back to the kitchen and return clutching the dish I had intended should be used. Michael and I together now attempt, with indecent haste, to decant the strawberries in their luscious syrup into the crystal bowl on its fragile stem, as if by this act we will magically eradicate all visual memory that our guests will have had of the crude vessel in use hitherto. But now we both stand back horrified as we watch the bowl slowly and inexorably tilt over on to its side, tipping its contents in a huge scarlet puddle into the middle of the heavy white lace tablecloths that shroud the long 'banqueting' table at which we are all eating. Without thinking twice – after all, these are the contents of a chalice – I scoop the crimson mess up off the cloth and back into the bowl and start to serve out portions to our somewhat bemused guests. To my surprise and embarrassment, they are generous enough to applaud this bravado.

Flustered by this unexpected acclaim I retire to the kitchen to check that the cheese is up to room temperature and to start the process of percolating coffee. I walk into the dining room and there I see a triangular tableau. The two cats are crouching at right angles to each other, staring down at a small brown mouse, who is sitting up staring straight back at them. Nothing is moving. As I watch them, I suddenly become aware of a hand touching my arm and a deep gentle American voice in my ear, saying:

'Marilyn, I think our little friend needs some help, don't you?' and, without more ado, Bob gets down on his knees and reaches out for the small mouse. This is, of course, the trigger for the mouse to unfreeze from his catatonic trance and scamper off to hide under the adjacent Welsh dresser which, besides the piano, is the only other remaining piece of furniture in the room.

'Don't you worry. The cats will flush him out,' Bob murmurs.

'I know, but eventually they will kill him.'

'Yes, but it will be OK, we will get him when they get him out – and before he is dead, I promise you,' and somehow, miraculously, and quite quickly, that tall gentle man does capture the mouse. As he is holding it in his cupped hands, he says:

'Hey, wouldn't it be fun if we just took him up into the garden and put him down in the middle of the table. Think of their faces!'

'No, Bob, please. He is already frightened half to death – it would kill him.'

'Yes, I guess you are right,' he laughs and, shrugging philosophically, he agrees to let him go across the other side of the road in the wild scrubby bit of vegetation by the trees close to the canal.

My real fear, however, is that I am not sure this lunch party can take a mouse in the middle of the proceedings on top of the sticky mess that is still up there on those once white tablecloths. Soon after, though, I hear the rich, warm laughter of Bob's partner, Patti, and I hear Klaus's voice booming out:

'A *what*? And where did you say it was?' So I reckon that the truth is out, but at least they did not have to share their table with what I from now shall choose to call 'Bob's mouse'.

Meanwhile I take note of the two kittens. In my mind, this was their first hunting expedition, as for some reason I don't count frogs, as frogs feel like substitute cat-prey. They both look inscrutable and cat-like and I cannot tell whether not having killed is a disappointment for them, or whether the chase was all.

Hunters, generally, have mixed feelings on this subject.

CHAPTER 4

Autumn

The long, dry summer finally burns itself out and develops into a rather wild autumn. Initially there is much celebrating, as we badly need the rain, but it continues to blow. One blustery Friday night in mid-autumn we have got the back door open, as we often do, to amuse the cats, who particularly enjoy sitting out in their little yard in the dark, even in the rain, if it is not too heavy. This particular night is, however, the beginning of a terrible series of gales and torrential rain that will have the whole country in thrall for some weeks, and this night's wildness, we learn later, is to devastate homesteads throughout the land. Michael, who is sitting downstairs, is in receipt of the full blast of the wind, and having had more than enough of it he gets up and slams the door closed.

Upstairs in our bedroom, in a state of complete disregard for the elements and the draughts, I am at my desk, merrily working away. Slowly I become conscious that Fannie, in metronomic fashion, is agitatedly patrolling our bedroom, the corridor, the staircase and back again. I have registered her idiosyncratically plaintive 'miaow' several times and she is now calling with increasing intensity. Time to investigate, I reluctantly decide, and stiffly climb down the steep stairs to the dining room below. Michael, in the newly sealed-up warmth of a centrally heated cottage with doors firmly closed, is, I observe, comfortably and deeply asleep in front of a roaring log fire in the sitting room, next door. I find Fannie now staring distractedly at the back door and miaowing with a new vigour. Her message is very clear. I open it, and a sodden ginger ball that is all protesting-wet-cat bursts into the kitchen and belts upstairs to the safety and warmth of our bedroom. I run after her and find Titus, wetter than I have ever seen a cat, licking herself as if her very life depends upon it. Fannie, rather touchingly, comes tiptoeing up to lend a tongue, but Titus is focused so completely on herself – no change there – that she is impervious to sisterly comforting. I remonstrate with Michael about not 'looking' properly before shutting doors, etc. and he acknowledges the oversight with typical generosity of spirit. And that would have been that, but for the discovery the following day.

The next day is a Saturday and Michael rises early while I stay on in bed in the self-indulgent 'I-have-earned-this' tradition of the fully employed whose work routine necessitates very early rising five days a week. Hanging on to the last vestiges of sleep, lulled by the warmth and softness of my surroundings, my state of semi-consciousness is brutally arrested by Michael's voice calling urgently from outside:

'Mo, can you come out here and give me a hand.' I look blearily out of the window and see a rain-washed sky and watery sun trying to come through, and then as I look down into the yard I am horrified, as the full implications of the sight below impress themselves upon me. What I am looking at is a very large, very scruffy, long-haired black, brown and mostly white cat who is soaked to the skin and clearly terrified, almost out of it. As I watch he hurls his body – size alone makes me think it must be he – at the fence, clings on ferociously, and scrambles to the top of it, but failing to circum-navigate the over-hang at the top and unable to hold on any longer, he falls back with every sign of exhaustion and fear into the little yard. The weary desperation with which he performs this action suggests he might well have been doing it for many hours.

The scene is made more lurid because we had put out a large black bin-liner full of rubbish the night before and he has, probably in a frenzy of frustration and hunger, ripped into that and distributed its contents, including vegetable peelings, chicken carcasses and other food waste, around the yard so that it looks like an unusually untidy pig pen. Michael has by this time opened the gate, but because he is standing on the outside of it, politely inviting the cat out, the disturbed creature, getting mixed messages, obdurately remains, cowering, within the yard. In this state of advanced agitation, the cat begins to make threatening, guttural, and deep growling sounds, which, to even the untutored ear, contain the alarming notes of pure, naked aggression. I race downstairs, flinging some clothes on as I go, and find our two girls on the inside of the kitchen door in a high state of agitation, listening intensely – between their own contributions, that is – to the growling from the other side. And then all falls silent. Michael, who has by this time come back into the yard, has chased the intruder out through the gate to his freedom. And he has run for it exactly as would a cat from hell.

'Oh Michael, what have you done?' I demand, unfairly.

'What do you mean, what have *I* done?'

'That cat was clearly there all night. So what happened all the time that Titus was locked out there with him?'

'No – rubbish. Of course he wasn't there last night. He just climbed in this morning to raid the black bag.'

I long to believe him. The alternative is too horrible. Horrible for that big fierce scared cat who would have spent a totally wretched night as drenched captive in my unwitting cat-trap. But even more for little Titus, who has never encountered a predatory male cat in her life and who, in this scenario, would have been trapped with him in this tiniest of spaces, for an hour, for two hours, unable to withdraw to the sanctuary of the cottage. I become increasingly uncomfortable at the dawning possibility of the feline rape that might just have taken place.

'I think you are just saying that to keep me quiet.'

'No – I am sure that he just got in this morning, love, honestly.'

As I look across at him I see a shadow of uncertainty cross his face and I swallow hard. But – what was done was done. And so wild October blows itself to a close.

∿

Do I suddenly remember the agony of being young now? The nightmare of looking in the diary – then of counting the days – and in this case watching Titus like a hawk – sometimes prodding her plump fluffy belly and asking her earnestly how she feels? She regards me as always with that slightly haughty hooded-eyed stare that is her specialty, and I remain none the wiser. And, as ever, I have to bide my time. Until today. Today it is 23 December and 63 days since the cat was trapped. And 63 days is the gestation period for a cat. And Titus is no fatter and no thinner than she was in October, so she gets the all clear. I still feel, however, that the old tomcat was trapped all that night and I will never know how he and Titus passed the time together in their enclosure. Did they or did they not? One assumes they did not.

All of this has focused our minds wonderfully – well, mine at any rate! I long to find the girls a mate. I have spoken to the local pet shop, I have looked at notices in all the local shops, I have contacted Cats' Protection and although fully grown, neutered, rescued tomcats can be found easily, and many of my friends have given them homes, kittens are hard to come by. I so want these two cats to have one litter each, after which I pledge that I will have them neutered. Having talked to the vet and to friends who are long-term cat owners, I reckon that a tom kitten is going to be the easiest way to introduce a new cat into their environment. When we first introduced their mother, Otto, to Michael's old crotchety tom, Septi, it was the difference in gender and her youth and her instinctive skill as a coquette that won him over* and I am sure the kitten route is the right one to follow. I now am much taken with the idea of finding the girls a Russian Blue husband, which breed I know are simply exquisite-looking cats with lush double pelts and sweet temperaments. We have not yet selected a breeder, but Michael is under strict instructions to provide the Russian Blue as my Christmas present – although it is now unlikely that we will find one until January or February.

25 December
Michael gives me a small pot dog, which he has been conned by the shop who sold it to him into believing it to be a small pot cat, which is supposed to symbolise a Russian Blue, but attached to the small dog is a large cheque – bless him – so I just have to wait for the tiny newsagent in our village to open again after Christmas in order to rush down and buy *Your Cat* and *Cat World* to look at the ads in the back.

New Year
I spend hours and hours combing through the cat magazines and comparing one eloquent pitch with another. Eventually

---

* As told in *The Cats of Moon Cottage* (Hodder & Stoughton, 2003).

and with great nervousness, I make contact with a couple in the Midlands who have a pregnant Russian Blue queen who is due to give birth in early spring, and my fingers are so firmly crossed that I can barely do anything. They know that I want a tom and they are looking for a home for their kittens where the toms are not used as breeding studs, as it can be a bleak existence, being kept in an enclosure and permanently required to 'perform', so they are glad to know that should they have a spare tom, this kitten will be a house cat and will run free with other cats. I don't mention that I hope he is to mate with my cats as I am confident that 'breeding' applies to a tom who may or may not mate with pure Russian Blues, and therefore whose progeny would have implications for the Russian Blue gene bank, and therefore 'breeding' is not an issue when it comes to a couple of much-loved moggies whose offspring would never be offered for sale. In any case, I long for him simply to join the community within Moon Cottage and to become a dearly loved companion to the cats and to us humans.

Knowing that a pregnant cat exists who may – who *will*, I hope – give birth to our kitten fills me with a strikingly heightened sense of anticipation. My concentration on all things worldly unconnected with this small creature who is about to join our family is completely shot to pieces. I really do experience the agony of an adopting parent waiting in a twilight world for the moment of fulfilment. After what seems an eternity (but in reality is only a few weeks), I receive a phone call from the owners of the pregnant Russian Blue to say that the kittens have been born and a boy is available. I get in the car and take off to inspect and be inspected. When I arrive I find a bundle of utterly adorable Russian Blue kittens. There are four of them and one, who is very brave and game but much smaller than his brother and sisters, totters towards me and I fall totally, hopelessly in love with him and only him. At some point during my visit I realise that I, too, have been the subject of inspection, and I suppose I must pass muster as the very sweet couple who own all these cats go on to discuss deposits and injections and the time when I can expect to bring him home. Weeks and weeks away!

I get back to the cottage full of kitten-desire, but I find myself watching the girls nervously and speculate long and hard about whether I am about to wreck their quite extra-ordinary relationship with each other. As siblings – having, I suspect, long forgotten their brother, Beetle, who is happily homed with Eve, John and Jenny a mile away – their bond is special and strong. They are wonderfully content with each other. How terrible if this self-indulgence on my part were to wreck their happiness. Well, time will tell and I shall just have to be very patient.

∽

I record the following anecdote because the emotions that cats can generate in others have a wider application than just for those who are cat-obsessed. Michael and I have maintained a close friendship with my former husband, Geoffrey Moorhouse. At this time Geoffrey comes to stay with us so that he and I might attend the funeral of a very dear friend, John Rosselli. The funeral is held at St Bene't's Church, Cambridge, and as John's two sons and his partner, Lisa, and his brother and other chief mourners proceed down the aisle of the church following John's coffin, David, his youngest son at thirty-something, draws level with the pew in which Geoffrey and I are standing. He throws us both a brave, tearful, shining smile which is in total contrast to the position of his body, which suggests that his heart is breaking, and I am overwhelmed by the sense of his vulner-ability. Later, at the graveside, he puts his arms around me and the force of his hug reminds me powerfully of Fannie at her most yearningly, hungrily, clingy. At the reception afterwards, I find myself mumbling to Geoffrey that in a special way, related to his neediness, David reminds me of Fannie. Geoffrey responds with alacrity:

'Yes – I know exactly what you mean.'

This surprises and pleases me as Geoffrey has only recently converted, due in fact to the influence of Fannie and Titus, to accepting cats as anything other than wild creatures who are sharp at both ends and who make free with his garden as a public toilet. On the other hand, he could have just been indulging a mad cat woman.

CHAPTER 5

Titus and Fannie have a complex, albeit charming, relationship. Mostly, they seem to be very fond of each other and
full of love, and then, suddenly and for no reason, other
than boredom perhaps, they will enact mock fights. These
fights, however, may generate displays of real spikiness, to
the point where they will actually hurt each other and one
will leave the room. The fights, though, never have the
savage quality of the fights of a cat on heat, or a tom in
search of a mate. These little spats sometimes occur at the
end of a long and intense period of mutual grooming, when
they will have lovingly licked each other literally from nose
to tail. Titus is the one who is inclined to lie back and let
Fannie do the work – but a lick near the throat suddenly
becomes a pretend bite which then escalates and they are
off. Legs flail and jaws open. There will be one or more
loud miaows of protest and pain. And then one of them
stomps off, tail erect. Usually the stomper is Fannie. Sometimes they compete quite strongly against each other when
playing with balls or other shared objects, and at other
times they seem to have really complicated rules as to 'whose

go' it is, and although Titus is the more pushy of the two, she will stand back for what seems more than the 'normal' time to allow Fannie to finish tossing around one of her much-loved toy mice. Each evening they play what sounds like an exhausting game of tag up and down the stairs and the full length of the cottage which, given how light and small cats are, is astonishingly loud. Standing in the kitchen, opening a bottle of wine, hearing this ear-splitting gallop above our heads, always makes Michael and me laugh out loud, however many times we have heard it.

On our bed they will lie back to back for mutual warmth, or completely separately, and more rarely but enchantingly they will lie like little spoons, one around the other. If one of them goes missing for any length of time, then the other one will become fretful. Fannie seems to need Titus more than Titus needs Fannie – although, as I write, Titus has been here on the bed on her own for a long time and Fannie is curled up on John's sofa. That seems to be their regular pattern on workdays, although some part of it will find them both together on our big bed. Titus, more often than not, at some stage during the day when I am writing, will come and insist on draping herself over my shoulder and neck. In truth it is hampering and uncomfortable for both of us, but I am flattered, of course. Fannie, if she decides to interrupt, has a totally different approach. She comes from under the desk and digs her claws into my shins and climbs up on to my knee that way. She will then sit, with a tangible intensity, waiting for me to rub her ears and whisker pads. If she is feeling passionate, she might then fold herself into a ball and tip up the underside of her chin to be tickled gently. In her case, you can feel the thrum of her purring but never really hear it. They will never both approach the same person at the same time. If any of us is engaged in stroking one of them, then the other will keep well clear – although Titus makes a distinct groan of sadness or disgust as she passes Fannie if Fannie is being caressed. Fannie is merely silently disdainful if the position is reversed.

Titus

She has unusual eyes with which she stares penetratingly, straight back into your eyes. Sometimes she holds this eye contact for a disconcerting length of time, and on occasion it can make you feel not so much that you are being regarded by one of a different species, but more that you are under the scrutiny of a creature from another planet. Her eyes are amber, the exact hue of her fur. This arresting combination caused my friend Matthew, when he very first encountered her, to do a tiny jig of pleasure at the jolliness of meeting 'an orange cat with orange eyes'.

She is a cat verging towards plumpness, in spite of still possessing her womb, and I am fearful that, when she has the inevitable hysterectomy, she is likely to really 'round up'. Her weight impedes her agility. Both Otto – in her short lifetime – and Fannie would always seek out the highest point in any room. The upper edge of doors, tops of cupboards, overcrowded mantelpieces and the highest bookshelves – all provided irresistible challenges to those two cats – but not for Titus. Titus will studiedly and almost sedately jump from floor to chair, from chair to table, and from table to piano top. (Piano top in this case means the covered keyboard or, on a bad day, plonkingly, on the keys themselves – not the dizzying heights of the upright part so beloved by Fannie and even dear Septi, in his days of seeking refuge from Otto, and also, once, in a stifling summer, in the desperate pursuit of a place which would provide him with even a faint draft.) For Titus, serious mountaineering is out of the question.

But sensual she certainly is, and vocal withal. When either Michael or John comes home she greets them with any number of complex but plaintive miaows – which are repeated and become more insistent. If she is ignored, they become short stabby sounds conveying an unmistakable sense of urgency. It is said by some that a cat's miaow can mean just about anything. It is certainly observable that those calls do seem to embrace a range of emotions from pleading, fear, anger, resentment, loneliness and hunger through to pleasure, lust, joy and, I am sure, love. I rarely receive this noisy accolade from Titus, which might be because she is inhibited by my closeness to Fannie, as she will display affection for me at other times in other ways. But that's how it is with cats.

With both Michael and John she is a complete babe. Having miaowed her greetings at them she then proceeds, with a sensuality so profound that it can seem almost theatrical, to roll her body around their shoulders, turning and twisting in abandonment. Sometimes, if she is on the back of a chair or sofa, her frenzied endeavours to imprint her scent upon the new arrival by twisting and turning her head will make her lose her sense of balance and suffer the resulting indignity of falling in a heap on to the floor, only to trot round to the front of the chair and start it all over again. She has recently started to perform this sensual body rubbing with me too, although I am still not in receipt of her vocalisation. She does, however, bite my hair, which sometimes ends up with her biting my head, and I am completely unable to determine whether this is clumsiness or intentional. Fannie regularly 'grooms' my hair and it may be something that Titus is imitating. I am tempted to say that it appears that she knows that this irritates Fannie no end, as she certainly does not attempt to hide it from Fannie, who notably always leaves the room when she sees Titus do this.

If Fannie and Titus have been apart for over a couple of hours, Fannie will seek Titus out. Her normal custom is delicately to join Titus wherever she is and lick her affectionately and at length. Titus accepts this, graciously, with her eyes closed, clearly experiencing much pleasure, and will, ostensibly to keep it coming, give the odd lick back, but not enough to dissipate her own happiness.

Fannie
Fannie is a total girl. She has all the independence of her mother, together with her looks and her grace, and if perhaps she is more timid, she makes up for this by her sublime elegance. She is slim to the point of thin and is the

quintessence of femininity. Newcomers to the house are struck by her looks – those stunning geisha eyes again, slanting up in the oriental way – but, while captivated by her appearance, they can sometimes become estranged by her aloofness.

She has the same habit that her mother had, which is that when she has been grooming herself she forgets to put her tongue away, so there will remain the tiniest tip of red tongue still showing at the front of her mouth, endearingly reminiscent of 1950s teddy bears. She will maintain this expression for several minutes and it makes me melt. When she is feeling particularly amorous she will roll around on her back, fantastically sensuously, with her head curled round and tipped up. It is hypnotically attractive – and she has a remarkably girlie way of almost completely covering her eyes with her paws, and bending her head down while watching you to see the effect it has on you and to make sure you are taking it in.

The other night she was doing this when she heard Titus jumping up the stairs preceding Michael. She turned quickly, sat upright, and curled her tail fastidiously around her front toes as if waiting for a curtain call, so that, as they entered the room, what greeted their eyes was Miss Proper, not the abandoned sensual creature of five seconds earlier.

~

But now the time is coming for the Easter bunny, in the shape of the New Boy, to enter the lives of all of us. I am feeling a heady combination of excitement and apprehension.

I continue to torture myself with a terrible sense of betrayal of the two cats in residence. It is a life-changing step to have taken, and initially they are bound not to like it. On the other hand, it is probable that they want to mate and that instinct appears to be a driving force in both of them, most clearly evinced by Titus who has no inhibitions in displaying full abandonment. Fannie has called out, on several occasions, but always runs inside before any passing tom might hear her. I am hugely worried at upsetting that balance between them. They are firmly bonded with each other, but I must remind myself that they can be competitive. I have just acquired for them a large three-tiered climbing arrangement, which in fact Titus can get to the top of, which she loves, and which Fannie initially was frightened of because of the ball hanging from it with a bell inside. But now Fannie is at ease and leaps at the topmost shelf from the ground – this must be nearly my own height. She did this today and Titus climbed more laboriously to the third stage, the one below her, and I was amused but shocked to see her bat Titus on the head with her foot, not just once but several times, until Titus reluctantly had to give up and jump down.

Michael was playing chase the 'palm' from Palm Sunday with them both on the table tonight and it gave me a very clear indication that Fannie is instinctively 'right-pawed' and Titus 'left-pawed' – although I have noticed when they play football that they both bat the ball with both front paws, though they do seem to have a serious 'leaning', and why not?

Tomorrow is the day I go to collect the New Boy and Michael has delighted in teasing them all week. He keeps saying:

'Look out. It's a nose job,' by which he means 'nose-out-of-joint' job.

Two strange things happen tonight. I get back from work at about 9 p.m. Ollie, Michael's youngest son, has been here all day so the cats have not been on their own, but he has gone to the pub with his father and brother about an hour before I get home, and as I park the car opposite and cross the road, I see the two cats' faces staring out from under the net curtain. Sometimes Fannie stares out, but it is rare for Titus to haunt passers-by in this way. Tonight here are both of them, and looking so forlorn. Why would this be? Is this feline precognition?

The second thing that happens follows my letting them out into the little yard to mess about, as they like to do, especially as it gets dark. I'm not paying particular attention to them, but casually register that Fannie has climbed on to one of the flowerpots, which is the highest point she can get to – naturally – and Titus is messing about on the ground. I retire inside to cook the meal when suddenly there is a screeching noise – a deafening, high-pitched scream – from Titus. Fannie flies into the cottage in fright and runs halfway up the stairs, but then comes down again and lurks. I rush out, expecting what? I am not sure: a small dragon breathing fire; a big brown bear baring his teeth; the Ghost of Christmas Past being 'now a pair of legs without a head, now a head without a body'?

I bundle Titus, unceremoniously, into the kitchen to protect her against whatever creature lurks outside, and shut the door. Now standing outside on my own, in the manner of the protective parent, I look out into the darkness beyond the yard and see nothing. I walk round the garden, but there is no indication of anything at all that could have caused such agitation to Titus. I go back inside and find her standing with her body fur so on end that she resembles nothing less than a large ginger porcupine. Her crowning glory is her erect tail, which, at 90 degrees to her body, is so fluffed out that it appears to be the width of a fox's brush rather than a cat's tail.

'So what is this about?' I enquire, gently. She looks up at me, clearly agitated, pupils dark and enlarged. Fannie approaches her and there is a lot of nose sniffing and smelling of each other. This is when I think they are 'speaking'. Fannie's tail is now, also, slightly fluffy, but Titus, who had evidently taken the main blast of whatever it was, maintains the full piloerection of fur along her spine and her tail stays plumped up for a further ten minutes.

In the morning I finally discover from Oliver that a black cat, whom I have seen before in the garden and have always deliberately chased back over the wall, got into the yard during the day and that when he, Oliver, opened the back door the cat climbed up the presumed cat-impregnable fencing and up and under the cat-prevention overhang and away, watched intensely by Titus. Oh surely he is not a full tom? This would be such an ironic blow right now.

CHAPTER 6

The New Arrival

The day has come for us to collect the new kitten. We are calling him Pushkin because under our self-imposed house rules all cats are called things bookish and he is, after all, a Russian Blue. We had been going to call him Tolstoy, but my friend Sue persuades me that Pushkin has a much more feline element to it.

I drive the nearly two-hundred-mile round-trip to collect Pushkin and bring him back to Moon Cottage in a state of longing. I feel nervous, excited, apprehensive and, yes, I admit it, maternal. Michael has been unable to come with me because of his work commitments, and I know he is feeling a little sad that he is to miss this important occasion. I, on the other hand, am guiltily thrilled to have these precious moments to myself. I arrive at the appointed hour and am warmly welcomed into the house where Pushkin was born. I am very grateful that I do not encounter his mother, as the last time that I came here she had looked across at me over the head of her young son, who at that time was feeding from her, with a very definite expression

of 'mine, not yours' in her eyes, which had compelled me
to turn away.

As I leave the house with Pushkin inside the carrier I
hear him give a high plaintive little mew, and on our journey
back he miaows a few times. I have his cage strapped into
the front seat with a belt holding it in position so I am able
to talk to him non-stop. From the corner of my eye I see
that he watches me, nervously, but eventually he goes quiet
and when I next look down I realise that he is curled up
fast asleep, and so he remains for the rest of the homeward
journey.

When I get him back to the house he walks out of his
cage and drinks some water as if used to his environment
from birth. I have taken the precaution of shutting the
door to the sitting room so that the two girls cannot see
him. Soon after drinking, he uses the cat-litter tray and
starts to look about him. Eventually I decide that the time
has come to let the two other cats inspect the goods. Disaster

of course! Well, certainly rudeness. Fannie hisses violently and Titus, surprisingly to me, although quiet looks a little frightened of him.

Pushkin now shows his colours. He looks back at them both in complete silence and with an apparent placidity that astonishes me. I pick him up to comfort him and he starts a loud and irresistible purring. I put him back down on the ground, at which point Fannie and Titus both back off into the dining room away from him and stare at him fixedly. Titus really does look horrified. Fannie keeps coming up to him and then moves away, but all the time she is hissing aggressively. Having initially stopped what he was doing, he then ignores her hissing with style and steadily walks right up to her. She growls deep, and long – it is very dog-like. He stops dead when he hears that. I suspect he has never heard such a hostile sound in his life before.

Oh my girls. Oh my boy. I am so sorry – what have I done?

Michael returns home. He is really glum that he has missed what he feels is the all-important intro, but in truth it really wasn't. He has kept phoning me up wanting to know exactly how all the protagonists are faring, but when he arrives he is properly charmed by Pushkin, as well he might be, and has eyes only for him. Pushkin is, after all, a remarkable boy.

Pushkin can sit completely in the palm of my hand. He is a beautiful blue-grey colour with almost invisible dark parallel stripes down his back, which will disappear shortly. His eyes are just turning from baby blue to green and he has magnificent whisker pads and dark grey whiskers and the most adorable dark grey nose leather I ever did see. And, magnificently, he has two of the largest, most perfectly triangular and upright and enormous ears in the world. He is so cute and he is just twelve weeks old.

On this first night, in deference to the girls, and for Pushkin's own safety, we shut him in the sitting room with the litter tray, food and water and his little bed, to which he has taken immediately. Is this the difference between a moggy and an aristocrat that the one chooses to sleep on anything but a made-to-measure bed and the other chooses cat bed only? The girls are upset and patrol round our room miaowing, and are generally out of sorts. Also, because of their anxiety, although they want to be with us, they will not let either of us properly stroke them or comfort them. I get up at about 2.30 a.m. and go down and find Pushkin lurking under the desk uncomfortably, so re-establish him in his bed and wait until he goes to sleep. I try not to imagine what it is like to be wrenched away from your mother, your sister and your two brothers and the only home you have ever known, and then driven miles and miles to end up in a cottage with two very cross and unfriendly female cats and everything totally strange.

~

Pushkin is astonishingly lively and gets into everything. He moves so fast. I had forgotten quite how fast kittens could go! He climbs to the top of the cat-frame, but if Fannie is on top she bats him quite hard with a right hook, and twice she has sent him spinning off and down to the ground. He has so much dignity; he just shakes himself and stands up and starts the big climb all over again. He keeps shimmying up to Titus who, being rounder, is warmer; he seems to be a real heat lover. Titus remains aloof and somehow outraged. She has also lost her miaow, although I do not properly pay it the attention that I should. Oddly enough, Fannie, normally the more nervous of the two, seems to have accepted Pushkin more easily.

Michael and I have had to spend a long time today cuddling one or other of the two girls. Eventually I manage to get both of them to do their very quiet purr, more a vibration than a purr, but it takes a long, long time to get it out of Titus. Fannie gets into Pushkin's empty bed, and so I risk finding the 'boy' and putting him in with her to see what will happen. Very slowly she starts to groom him, which makes him purr loudly. His purr is physical. She then, while still licking him, gently starts to hiss. Schizophrenic or what? Even Pushkin looks confused at this particular mixed message.

Last night we put Pushkin on his own again in the sitting room, but the girls were still restless. John was on the phone to one of his mates and as I walked into the room I heard him say that we had a new kitten whose name was Stud. His friend presumably inquired further because his next remark was:

'Oh we always call all our cats after the job they do.'

Shortly after that I found Titus briefly licking Pushkin on John's bed, but it didn't last long.

Tonight we leave him to find where he wants to sleep. He sleeps on our bed, confidently positioned between Michael and me. This cat has chutzpah. The girls radiate even stronger degrees of irritation. Oh dear.

~

One morning, about three or four days later, having had my shower and with Fannie still cradled in my arms on her back following our morning cuddle, I wander into John's bedroom, in search of the two missing cats. There I find Titus and Pushkin lying back to back on John's bed. Titus takes one look at Fannie lying in my arms and immediately turns round to Pushkin and gives him a thorough and completely uncharacteristic grooming. Pushkin, ever the opportunist, purrs happily. Fannie, who – although on her back – has absorbed the entire tableau by squinting sidelong at the two cats on the bed, appears to take umbrage at this point and leaps out of my arms and races downstairs. I walk out of the room, but peep back through the crack in the door. As soon as Fannie and I have left the room, Titus stops licking Pushkin. So it really does appear to have been a 'he's my friend, not yours' gesture aimed at Fannie because I was cuddling her. How complicated their relationships are!

This morning I walk out into the little yard with Fannie and Titus leaping on to the garden table ahead of me. Pushkin follows. This is the first time he has ventured outside. In his fear of outside, he fluffs out his baby fur and looks exactly like a tiny silver hedgehog. His little tail is not so much at 90 degrees, but more at 145 degrees over his back and the hairs are bristling out like a chimneysweep's brush all the way round.

I am busily trying to fix chicken wire to the outside of the enclosure as Pushkin could easily escape through the trellis holes when, to my surprise, Titus leaps at the gate and at surprising speed climbs deftly up and over it, apparently on the exact route of escape that Oliver had witnessed the black cat adopt – so they do watch and learn from each other. Titus has had since last July to do that and today was the first time. As I think about it, I realise that Titus has been sitting inside the enclosure staring up at the fencing for some time before her sudden onslaught. This suggests to me that cats are capable of considered thought processes and even 'planning'. Titus, having reached the outer garden, is now cowering down, not quite certain what her next action should be, and I scoop her up and return her to the enclosed yard. I now set to, for what seems like hours, fixing up more chicken wire and complicated two-way overhangs, and I am just praying that they will be enough to contain the cats and keep out strangers. Was Titus just trying to escape from the annoyance of the new member of the household?

We are now having trouble at feeding time. I have always left dried Hill's cat food down for the two girls, and it is almost the only food they will eat, but on my vet's advice I try to make sure they have one 'wet' food meal a day. Until Pushkin enters their lives, I have always put the wet food in one bowl for them to share, now though he behaves uncouthly and head butts them out of the way, so I am having to feed him in a separate room, shut away from them. This seems to solve the problem, although he does tend to attach himself to Titus whenever she feeds from a dried-food bowl, and so as self-preservation she has now taken to carrying a mouthful of dried food and taking it away to eat on her own. Pushkin loves to eat next to another cat eating. This desire for social eating is, I imagine, engendered by the memory of his mother and his siblings; when he was born he was the runt of the litter and he quickly made up his weight once allowed to feed for himself.

Easter dawns and over the Bank Holiday members of both our families come to see us and to greet the new arrival. He is, of course, at his irresistibly cuddliest at this stage and we begin seriously to fear a kidnap might take place.

A few weeks pass and the energy that Pushkin expends is astonishing. Are all kittens this bouncy? The answer to that question is almost certainly 'yes', but Pushkin's manner seems especially manic as he hurls himself around the place, which is invariably followed by his coming to a complete dead stop, whereupon he falls into a deep sleep. Once asleep he is curiously hard to waken. At these moments he seems to possess the characteristics of the narcoleptic.

It is very clear that both Titus and Fannie are frequently disturbed by Pushkin's disruptive behaviour and in our different ways John, Michael and I all find ourselves attempting to comfort and reassure them. Sometimes, however, peace reigns supreme. This morning I watched the two girls fall fast asleep on the bed behind me, with Pushkin lying quietly behind them in the little hammock by the wall (he got sent there by them because they were cross with him, but he was so tired that he just curled up and slept anyway).

CHAPTER 7

Early Summer

Slowly the relationship between the three cats is changing, although it continues to have its volatile and complex moments. Every day Titus and Fannie spend some time grooming Pushkin in a comforting, older-sister sort of way. They are mildly attracted to him and I think possibly won over by his babyhood, when he tries to sleep near them, which he does a great deal. He seems to like curling back to back, especially with Titus, and earlier today I found them like spoons around each other.

At the point when first he wakes up and is sleepy and stretchy and still yawny, and wants to go closer to them and bury his head in them, they are very sweet with him to begin with, but unfailingly he goes too far by boorishly head butting them. He means it as a great token of friendliness, but they stubbornly resist it. And the moment he has fully woken up and jumps up, Tigger-like, and wants to bounce, which he does a lot, they leap off the bed and run away. Their own relationship with each other has changed too. They do still groom each other, but much more

235

spasmodically, and when one of the sisters leaps at the other, where before Pushkin's arrival it would have been seen merely as an invitation to play and never refused, now there seems to be real suspicion and avoidance of play. Most surprisingly of all, the night-time chases between the girls seem to have stopped. Titus and Fannie will each, separately, chase Pushkin, and Pushkin will chase each of them, but never all three together.

Two or three days ago Titus was exhibiting being on heat in the most pronounced manner, putting her rear end uppermost and very emphatically 'displaying', and Michael and I speculate that it might be the maleness, although not matured, of Pushkin that is generating the flamboyance of her presentation. However, the downside of all this excitement is that Titus is offering her rear end to Michael, John, me and even, finally, dear Fannie in clear preference to Pushkin. Certainly both the girls take every opportunity to smell Pushkin, but they also use it as a way of 'putting him down' when he is getting too bumptious. In the cat world a wet nose up the bottom appears to do wonders for countering the opposition's confidence.

Titus, tonight, tries to leave home again. I'm opening the gate to get to the freezer in the shed and she comes out through the tiny gap I have left like a hare being coursed by hounds. She moves so fast I cannot believe my eyes. She runs up to the shed and then panics and stops dead. I run up the steps and scoop her up in my arms, and with the reassurance of my presence she finds new confidence and begins to struggle in order to continue with her quest. As I hold her I can feel her heart pounding. I gently put her back inside the yard. She slumps down on to the ground and looks desolate. She opens her mouth and no sound comes out. Since the invasion of the black cat into their yard and the possible fight that Oliver witnessed, Titus has had no discernible miaow at all. Did something happen in that yard that accounts for why she was so frightened?

The strangulated little moan coming from Titus when she tries to miaow has finally got to me and I decide that I must, somewhat belatedly, take her to the vet, so we go to see Kate who examines her carefully and concludes that she has got a damaged throat, which she believes has been caused by an object such as a stick. She injects Titus with antibiotics and an anti-inflammatory and poor long-suffering Titus very quickly starts to perk up again and within a few days her voice returns. So what caused that, I wonder? She does have a toy, which she is fond of and carries around with her from time to time, a stick with a feather on the end of it, so I now seek it out and quietly dispose of it.

Pushkin is growing up quickly but he still displays youthful errors in judgment from time to time, which are disarmingly lovable. Today I am sitting in an armchair in our bedroom, quietly reading, and I look up as Fannie trots into the room and leaps with sublime grace and deliberation a distance of about four feet up on to our very high bed. Pushkin, who has been lying outside the door on the landing watching, stretches, runs across the room, and springs up in a perfect imitation of the same jump and lands heavily on top of her. This produces huge squawks of protest, a long spitting hiss, a thump as Fannie hits the floor at speed, and a thunderous running downstairs.

'Now look what you've done,' I laugh. He beams seraphically. Perhaps it was not a mistake.

~

It is now mid-June and the day promises to be glorious and hot although first thing some intermittent banks of cloud produce sudden cool intervals. The garden is ablaze with colour. The crimson of the overblown peonies vies with the pink and lilac of the foxgloves that are standing shoulder high amid the clumps of wild blue geraniums and pink and purple lupins; and the climbing roses tumbling over the pergolas seem somehow more wonderful than I ever remember them. I walk back to the cottage yard, absorbing the background sounds of busy bees bumbling around and nervous birds calling out raucously to each other and their growing young. Inside the yard the cats are lying around in long, lazy, stretched-out heaps. Earlier on in the morning they had jostled about for the patches of sun, but as it ascends the sky and the clouds burn off and the sunlight floods the yard, they settle down contentedly, each in their own space. But even as I enter this languid paradise, Pushkin leggily stands up, yawns with jaw-dislocating abandon, and looks about him with the undisguised intent of one who needs to disrupt the status quo. He has grown rapidly and is now sleek, muscular, long bodied and foxy-faced. His angular muzzle gives him a typically elongated profile, as opposed to the rounder, more delicate but shorter silhouette of the girls, and I feel a pang of disloyalty as I find myself unconditionally admiring him. He stretches out his long neck and front legs and then rocks back to stretch out and jiggle each hind leg in turn, he then shakes himself all over, dog-like, and springs high up off the ground into the air and lands four square on top of Titus, whom he proceeds to beat up; there is a certain amount of squawking at the end of which he, not Titus, retires hurt.

He then repeats the performance with Fannie, sinking his teeth into her throat for good measure. Much scuffling and a series of loud squeaks follow this, which ends, as always, with Fannie retiring – this time into the calm depths of the cottage. Boy cats seem to be quite different from girl cats.

Shortly after this Michael and I are away from the cottage for two nights at a conference and John is in charge. He is made desperately late for work on the Friday morning as he is completely unable to find Pushkin. The latter is very laid back, the nature of the Russian Blue, and lies under beds and similar places and does not come out at all when called, as the other two do. In the end, poor John has to go to work not knowing where Pushkin is. On his return, Pushkin comes down to greet him from wherever it was that he had hidden with nary a word of explanation nor a hair out of place.

All three of them have recently frightened the life out of me. Titus and Pushkin have both charged out of the back gate and across the garden as if 'Old Nick' was after them, and only when they have gained the extremity of the garden have they stopped and allowed themselves to be caught; probably by then truly fearful but, in that cat-way of not losing face, not showing it. And Fannie, today, makes her own notable contribution to the escape-log with a calmness that belies the sounds around her.

At 8.30 this morning, as the rush-hour traffic is whoosh-ing along the road in both directions, I open the door to a man who is collecting my car for servicing, and as I am holding it ajar to hand him the keys, Fannie squeezes herself around it and calmly walks across the pavement, to the very edge of the road ten yards east of the place where her mother, her doppelganger, Otto, was killed. I lunge out through the door, wincing at the prick of the stones on the soles of my bare feet, and grab her unceremoniously by the scruff of her neck and fling her back into the safety of the cottage. After the man has left, while I am making some coffee, I am haunted by a thought. I come upstairs and look in my diary. Today it is 18 June and I reconfirm in my diary that it was 21 June that Otto was killed two years ago. Only a coincidence?

∾

I live too much under the fear of the cats disappearing. I am haunted by the concept of them going astray even though I am well aware that the vet says that they should take their chance. It is the demon roads that frighten me most, but they are not the only dangers out there.

There is a remarkable story told by Deric Longden* about his kitten Thermal who – having gone missing for a month and who is thin to the point of starvation when he finally returns home, in spite of having been tenderly fed and watered by his overjoyed humans – wakes from sleep and, on some sort of auto-pilot, begins systematically to lick the stonework around their fireplace:

'We watched in fascinated horror as his tongue covered stone after stone, his head angling so that he could take the horizontal mortar in one long sweep. He was still in his garage, or wherever he had been imprisoned – this was how he had survived, licking the moisture from the walls and harvesting protein as he went.'

Before Thermal returns home, Deric and his partner Aileen go to enormous lengths to find the little thing, and have all but given up hope when Deric's son Nick finally finds him close to home, but collapsed in exhaustion to the point of near death. It is that tenacity and belief that finding a lost kitten or cat against all odds is possible that I find so inspiring. Would I have the same determination?

~

Around this time my friend Trish, a lifelong cat lover, tells me a story of single-minded resolution that brings tears to my eyes. This story takes place some fourteen years ago when Trish lived in Nottingham, and is at this time sharing her life with two kittens who are four months old and the offspring of her cat Misty, a pretty tortie queen. The kittens

---

* From *The Cat Who Came in from the Cold* (Corgi, 1992).

are red and white tabbies and are called Baby and Sammy. The girl, Baby, is a smaller but identically coloured version of her much beefier brother Sammy, who has enormous paws like a miniature tiger. One Friday Trish decides to drive down to Bristol to see her sister and family. She arranges for a neighbour to come in to feed Misty, but decides to take the kittens along with her.

The journey to Bristol goes without a hitch and a splendid weekend is enjoyed by all, but by early evening on the Sunday Trish decides that leave she must, and with that Monday-morning-back-to-school feeling she sadly bundles the kittens up into the back of the car to make her tortuous cross-country run up to Nottingham. She has found on the journey down that the kittens travel more happily unconfined, and so on the return journey they are left at large to walk around the car freely. No sooner has she joined the M4 motorway than her old Ford Escort develops some minor engine trouble and she has to pull over on to the hard shoulder. With no especial talent as a car mechanic and this being long before the days of the now ubiquitous mobile phone, Trish gets out of the car and apprehensively flogs her way along the hard shoulder until she reaches an emergency phone where she is able to summon assistance. She returns to the car and checks that all is well with the kittens. She waits and waits and eventually an AA mechanic turns up who is able to sort out her problem. By the time he has fixed her car it has grown dark but, after duly tipping her 'knight of the road', she gratefully sets out on her journey again in some haste.

Soon she leaves the motorway and starts the meandering

journey through the country lanes of the Cotswolds. After travelling for some miles without seeing a signpost of any kind, she realises with an increasing sense of gloom that she is utterly lost. She comes to a crossroads and does not recognise any of the place names, so she stops and finds that the internal lights of the car are not working. Cursing mildly, she gets out and holds the flapping road map in front of the headlights. She makes a decision on which route to take, gets back into the car, slamming the door shut, and just before driving off feels behind the driver's seat. Her fingers grope soft furry kittens and so, without more ado, and singing the while to keep all of their spirits up, she continues on her journey towards Nottingham.

Late and feeling very tired, she reaches her street and, now happy to be home, parks the car outside her flat. She turns round to lift out the kittens and finds only Baby. There is absolutely no sign of Sammy with the big paws. She looks high and low, under seats, in pockets, even in the boot, but there is no trace of him. She races out of the car and runs down the street with a handful of 10 pences and phones her sister. She sobs to her sister that she is sure that Sammy got out of the car after the AA man had finished his repairs and that he, Sammy, will be sitting in some field scared and frightened and miles from anywhere. Neither she, nor her sister, voice the possibility that he might be squashed flat on the motorway. Her sister tells her to hang on and that she will drive from Bristol and stop exactly where Trish stopped. But which emergency phone was it? Trish, between her sobs, stumblingly admits she cannot remember exactly. Her glamorous sister then nobly drives down the M4 in a large black Rover and, completely illegally and very riskily, stops at every emergency phone where she then proceeds to climb the adjacent embankment, with her waist-long hair the colour of burnt amber billowing out behind her, calling for Sammy. No sightings. She finally gives up her solitary quest and returns home, safe but immeasurably sad, and gets her long-suffering husband out of bed. Together they write postcards describing Sammy and giving their telephone number. They then get back into the car and drive to every nearby village bordering the motorway and shove the postcards through the letterboxes of all the post offices they can find and, after that, they simply post them through the doors of the residents of the M4 corridor.

While all this is happening Trish remembers that the place where she stopped for a second time, when she got out of the car and used the headlights to read the map, is somewhere near Banbury, so the following day she phones her work and pleads compassionate reasons for her leave of absence and gets back into her car and painstakingly retraces her steps. She has one photograph of Sammy with her and a large notepad. After several hours she finds what she thinks is the crossroads where she stopped to map read, and she then walks to every farm and house and building where there is any habitation in that area.

'I'll tell you, Marilyn, I'm not kidding, it was deeply rural; just fields, fields, fields for blimming miles. It was a real jackpot when I actually found a dwelling place. I just plodded on and on, to every farm I could find. I had this feeling that if I was a half-grown kitten who had somehow escaped from a car which then just drove off into the night and left me, I would probably try to find buildings for food and shelter, and a farm would have more hiding places for me, so that might be where I would go. I walked and walked and every time I found someone in I would show them the crumpled photo of Sammy and give them a piece of paper with my telephone number and address on it.'

'Didn't they all think you were bonkers?'

'I was genuinely touched at how kind most people were, they understood, I think.'

'But what about your sister?'

'She hadn't had a response from anyone at all when I phoned her after I got back from the Banbury trip. I just kept saying to her over and over again: "I have lost him, for ever. I know I have. I blame myself. I was a bloody fool." '

While Trish has been telling me this story, we have been sitting in her office, sharing a bottle of wine. As she reaches this point, her eyes fill up and I turn away so she can't see mine, and take a big swallow from my glass. She continues her tale. Three long days later she gets a telephone call.

'I think I've got your cat here. Well, I'm not sure, but it fits the description and he has started to make himself at home, so if you don't get here quick we might have to keep him.'

It is one of the farmers she called on in her earlier foray, so with her heart in her mouth she drives back down again. Just before she turns off the main road, she stops at a garden centre and buys a huge pot of gladioli to offer as a thank-you present.

She gets to the farm, almost unable to breathe with anticipation and fear of disappointment. The door opens and she is met by a big bluff smiling man who is holding in his large hands what looks like a tiny ginger kitten. A ginger kitten with huge feet. Trish grabs the kitten with both hands and her eyes flood.

'You nearly didn't get him back, I'll tell you,' the farmer chuckles, which he follows with this glorious non-sequitur, which is complete news to Trish:

'He don't half like chocolate, dunnee?'

He spent the first night in the barn, the farmer reckons. They find him the next day and he spends the second night in the kitchen, and the third night he makes it into their bedroom. That is when the farmer remembers Trish calling with her photograph and her piece of paper and decides that if he is going to return the wandering kitten, now is the moment, before he and his wife are too wedded to him.

Trish thanks him and his wife over and over again as she joyfully clutches her small wandering waif. She hands over her thank-you pot of gladioli and the farmer and his wife say their gracious thank-yous in return and offer their good wishes to them both for their return journey.

'And that was when I saw them,' Trish groans.

'What?'

'As I turned the car round and went along the driveway I could see fields with rows and rows of glistening glass covering more dahlias and gladioli and things like that than I have ever seen. I mean, he grew them on an industrial scale!'

The kitten, Sammy, sat on her knee under the steering wheel purring happily all the way home, and never once made a break for freedom.

CHAPTER 8

The Plague of Frogs

It has rained, unremittingly, for twenty-four hours, and everything for miles around is completely waterlogged. The night air is heavy with wonderful smells, as it has been very dry and warm for several weeks, and the scents wafting across the garden, up from the parched but now drenched lawns, off the bowed roses and the crushed peonies, from the slightly battered and therefore especially fragrant lavender, are intoxicating in their mix and intensity. The rain finally, drippily, stops, and the cats, who have forlornly watched the inundation all day long through the open back door, gratefully exit into their watery yard. Fannie immediately presses her nose to the fence. Every muscle in her body is tensed. She is in full hunt mode. Titus senses this and joins her on the cat platform, and the two of them, in parallel, stare fixedly in one direction. I peer over their shoulders and see a large green frog staring straight back. As he has complete freedom to get away and they are on one side of a fence and have no such freedom, I leave him be, to wander off in his own time.

I go inside and am amazed to hear a few minutes later the unmistakable, high-pitched scream of a frog in terror. I go back out to see what is happening and find that the frog has fallen down between the wall and the fence and is jammed and screaming as the cats in turn prod at him with their paws. In his agitation he has turned partially red, which gives him the appearance of bleeding. Feebly, I call for Michael. Why can I not be less squeamish at moments like this? We get the cats back in the house and Michael deftly rips the wire netting away, and together we manhandle the frog out – who is now anaesthetised with fear, and therefore conveniently still. We carry him gently up into the garden. His skin gradually returns to its greeny-brown colour and we establish that he is not bleeding, but he is unquestionably very frightened. We put him down and slowly he crawls, and then tentatively hops, away. We let the cats out again who are, of course, very disappointed to find him gone.

Later that night, from two rooms away, I hear a distant commotion in the kitchen; lots of crashing around and digging in the cat-litter tray as if whoever is in there is burying a haunch of venison. It all goes quiet for a while and then there is more hubbub. I go down to see what is happening and find Michael on all fours peering under the fridge.

'Look, look. You can see his back legs.' And sure enough, there, protruding, are the back legs of a small brown frog. While we are watching he crawls along under the entire width of the fridge and emerges from the other side. This time all three cats are in attendance and Pushkin, who is new to this splendid game, makes it significantly more frenzied than it would otherwise have been, as he jumps over and leaps on top of everything and everyone in sight, with his claws extended so he doesn't fall off whoever his unfortunate victim might be – which in turn makes the humans present squawk and the cats yowl, and of course the frog is making that high-pitched froggy screech which we can all hear above everything else.

After what seems like an unending commotion of human protests reinforced with the odd unfinished expletive, combined with miaows and squawks and squeals, we finally get the cats rounded up and locked in another room and pick up the frog who is now rigid and quite still – legs stretched out dramatically in death-mode, which is what Michael declares him to be. We go up to the end of the garden bearing yet another stiff frog and I notice that this one is covered in granules from the cat-litter tray which sadly forces me to conclude that the 'haunch of venison' I could hear being buried earlier in the evening was all of three and a half inches long and still alive, and amphibious to boot. We put him on the soil and I pour water over him, which seems to produce a form of recovery, and slowly he pulls his limbs together and crawls away under the plants.

'Please let it never rain a plague of frogs,' mumbles the long-suffering Michael, who is much braver than me.

Having had torrential rain for several days, which produced our earlier inundation of frogs, the summer overall has been very dry and the sun is now again shining, uninterruptedly, which has made for glorious hot days, but the nights are sweltering and oppressively close. The garden has begun to dry out quite markedly and for the last two days one or other of us has been on serious hosepipe duty in the evenings. This watering inevitably flushes out a small army of frogs of all shapes and sizes, some of whom come calling on the house, to the delight of the cats and to our consternation, and frog rescue continues to be our major domestic distraction. This last night I toss and turn in the heat, unable to sleep for more than half an hour at a time, and each time I wake I am aware that Fannie, who normally sleeps next to me, is missing. I wonder if it is my restlessness that has driven her away. At around 5.30 a.m. I am aware that she has gently lain down next to me and somehow, then, I'm able to sleep.

At 7 a.m. it is almost, deliciously, cool and it's really hard to rise, but Michael is long gone by this time and guilt drags me from my slumbers as I now have the luxury of a four-day instead of five-day working week so there is one precious day when I don't work and don't need to go into London, and I feel I mustn't waste a minute of it. During the day I become increasingly aware that Pushkin alone seems to be about, as he follows me around – obviously wanting some sort of company. I eventually find Titus staring, disconsolately, into a corner in the yard in a rather hunched-up, out-of-sorts-way and I can't find Fannie at all. To begin with I take no notice, but her sustained absence begins to nag at me. There's a call, which I use for the cats, which embarrasses all other members of our household and even me on occasion, but it's the one effective way of bringing all three cats together. It's a food call.

'Kitteeeeee Kitteeeeee Kitteeeeee' ever

252

more insistently. I open up a packet of food and rattle the plate. Titus and Pushkin come immediately and Pushkin winds himself round my legs and purrs ostentatiously, which he follows with a bit of token head butting for good measure. Titus sits, duchess-like, white bib to the fore, staring down her nose waiting for whatever might be on offer. No sign of Fannie. I call again, no longer trying to hide the note of desperation in my voice. Still no sign. I hurl myself upstairs and look under all the beds, open the cupboards and wardrobes, and even, foolishly, lift the loo seat lid. I crash downstairs again, really bellowing. Suddenly there is Fannie, with a grey roll of dusty cobwebs hanging off her ears, licking her mouth in a speculative manner. Strange. Anyway, I sigh gratefully and murmur a small prayer of thanks and return to work upstairs.

I go down later in the afternoon, and there lying slap bang in the middle of the mat leading to the yard is a small, delicate, chestnut-brown field mouse with a white tummy and wide-open, frightened, dead eyes. Pushkin is lying atop the cat platform, ears erect, head on one side, staring down at the small corpse with the detached manner that I fancy a certain type of feudal lord might easily adopt.

So who did kill Cock Robin then? I will never know for certain, but speculate Fannie, probably. As there are no discernible teeth marks on his body and no sign of blood, I presume the cats must have played with him until he died of fright, as is often the case with cats, although I would prefer to think that they exercised the instinctive skill that all cats possess, and administered the killing-bite, which would have broken his spinal cord. I bury him at the foot of Septi's grave, believing it to be as safe as any other place on earth for him now.

~

We are about to leave for our annual holiday in southern France and as usual I am in a complete state of unease about leaving the cats. John, as always, kindly offers to stay on full cat-alert for the fortnight that we are away, and we are really lucky to have him do this. My neurotic sense of foreboding this time is such that I feel compelled to leave my sister, Margot, a quite absurd email on how to deal with the cats in the event of our death on the French roads (this, I justify, will act as a magic mantra to ward away the evil eye). I adore going on holiday but, as always, at this stage, I wonder whether the pain of separation from the cats is worth it.

This time we are much comforted when we get down to Cabrières and find that a charming English couple, Alan and Valerie, have moved in next door and have with them a sweet-natured white West Highland terrier called Erin and the most beautiful female tortie moggy cat with the silkiest fur I have ever stroked. Her name is Blossom, and very handsome she is with her darker cap, saddle and tail of rich ginger, brown and black offset by the dazzling white of her face, chest, legs and belly. It is July and very hot and she spends her days lazing in the bed of lush periwinkle that carpets half of the backyard of our terraced cottage adjoining our new neighbours, and which is slightly damp and, I imagine, refreshingly cooling.

Blossom, who only moved in five weeks earlier, is still learning French, so appears to be pleased to hear our English, this may or may not be true of her humans; being English, I felt it would be too invasive to ask them. Blossom is the quintessence of friendly cat with an irresistible and emotionally blackmailing trill as she does her little spring up and gently head butts you to be stroked and/or fed. She utterly charms us both, but the trouble is she makes me yearn even more for my own clowder of cats back home.

Our holiday draws to a close and we make the long trek up the length of France on our 750-mile homeward journey and, to spare the springs of my car, we leave one of the most abundant wine regions in France with barely more than a case of wine on board, intending to stock up with bulk supplies at a French supermarket near Calais so that the laden car will only have a few miles to chug along on its compacted suspension. Wrong! Saturday 14 July is Bastille Day, which of course we knew, but what we did not know is how very seriously it is taken.

Every supermarket, large or small, English or French, is firmly fermé and the purchase of wine, other than from a restaurant or café, is completely out of the question. Michael and I, having driven incredulously all round Calais and surrounding district to no avail, exchange a few sentences that are too bleak to reproduce here but, suffice it to say, I think it is sad that two people should speak to each other thus at the end of such a wonderful holiday!

By the time we have bounced emptily through the Tunnel and along the M20 and on to the M25 and are nearing home, however, we have recovered our spirits and are both longing to see John and the cats again. I can barely wait. The contained joy of knowing they are all safe and at home, waiting for us, however cross and betrayed (the cats cross and betrayed that is, John will be nothing of the sort), is exquisite. We unfold ourselves, stiffly, from the car and prepare to enter the cottage. Michael goes in first, calling the cats and John, in one long, boisterous, happy greeting and he disappears from my sight, round the corner into the dining room where, judging from sounds off, he has found, variously, John, Titus and Pushkin.

As I walk in, I see and hear my tiny, slim, excited Fannie, who has dodged the gang in the dining room and is skipping towards me across the room, with her mouth wide open, repeatedly calling out her loud, plaintive miaow. I scoop her up in my arms and feel her whole body thrumming as she purrs, very physically, but in almost total silence. She is shaking with emotion. I feel my eyes fill with tears of joy. It is a shocking fact that I realise my heart is more full of love for this small female cat than any cat I have known, including even Otto, her mother. She crawls up to my shoulder and pulls gently on the hair near my neck with her claws; and then her tongue licks me, in her funny special way of saying hello, and she continues to groom me, forgivingly.

'Fannie, Fannie, Fannie, oh I *do* love you so!' I murmur quietly, almost at peace, but still I need to see the others. I walk through and join Michael and John. John looks fit and well, although tired – but I suspect it is not the cat watching that has done that to him. We tease him a little and he us. I spy Pushkin, who has truly lost his kittenish looks and is now definitely a young teenaged tom, long and lean and sleek. His ears do not look quite so battishly large any more as his head has now grown so much bigger. He is good-naturedly happy to be greeted by me, as by Michael, but gives us both the slightly bewildering feeling he is not quite sure who we really are, and although I stroke him in his special places, behind his ears and under his chin, I do not hear that wonderful purr yet. Oh well, time will heal that.

But Titus and me? That is another matter. Michael picks her up as soon as he sees her and flings her over his shoulder, the place where she is most comfortable. She happily snuffles in his ears and generally indicates pleasure at his homecoming by repeating her sharp little miaowing yap, and in fact it only comes to an abrupt halt when she jumps off him, because he is trying, surreptitiously, to cuddle Pushkin at the same time. When I now approach her, she stares back at me with her large orange eyes and I cannot tell what she feels, but distance is what her body language is saying to me. I ignore it and scoop her up, but although she accepts a bit of cuddling, she squirms to get down pretty quickly and it is a good hour before I am really allowed to communicate with her closely or physically. By now I have managed to get her to purr in her fashion and I hear myself sighing deeply and happily. I am now, properly, at peace.

The next day dawns and is of course one full of domestic chores involving the sorting out of clothes and other sundry tasks. We have unpacked a great deal but, as always, we took too much away. I am of course the culprit, and I still have a mountain of clothes to sort out. For much of the day, as I move from room to room, I am aware of all three cats shadowing me, and note that they are also keeping regular checks on Michael's movements. John went on some epic jaunt last night and is away for most of this day, so the cats have only the two of us to concentrate on. At one point in the middle of the afternoon I am busy sorting out yet another pile of clothes in the bedroom when Fannie, who has been missing for half an hour, comes into the room and starts to make the most extraordinary sound. She is wailing. I turn round to look at her. Her eyes are wide open and dark with fear, and her mouth is agape so I see the red of her tongue and her throat and her glistening white teeth

as she yowls deafeningly and long. I pick her up and try to comfort her, perplexed, but she continues to call out, and painfully slowly I suddenly realise what is upsetting her. I had moved the big black suitcase, which was the one remaining thing I needed to sort out from our holiday, up on to our bed to make it easier to unpack. When we had been getting ready to go, two weeks earlier, that was where I had put it in order to pack it, and Fannie, perhaps inspired by the trauma of missing us, must have remembered that – so that when she enters the room just now and is greeted by the familiar but alarming sight of an open suitcase, she seems to assume that it is about to start again. She takes a deal of comforting and in the end I have to empty the case quickly and put it away, and only then does she become calm again.

Titus, meanwhile, has been lying on the bed slowly thrashing her tail back and forth, but in complete silence. Pushkin is downstairs doing his own thing, which in his case is usually sleeping, and misses all the fuss.

This night all three cats sleep in our room as they did the night before, but they are not used to it, I think, and keep jostling for position and swapping around in a way that is different from their normal habit. Cats are creatures of supreme routine and we cruelly broke it.

On Monday, our third day home, Pushkin is all purrs and attention and at one point when he is on the bedroom windowsill, and I am indulgently playing with him, I look down into the yard below and see Titus staring up at me, unblinkingly, and I find I am disconcerted by the intensity of the appraisal – which is neither friendly nor unfriendly, but somehow other worldly. The breakthrough happens half an hour later when Titus comes upstairs to find me and miaows her squeaky, repetitive, greeting miaow, which is how she registers that she needs to be loved, immediately. She has therefore gone through what would appear to be a three-day period before she becomes close again. A three-day sulk? Now she will not leave my side and is sitting on my PC mouse mat making life difficult. When not sitting exactly where I want to put the mouse, she repeatedly walks backwards and forwards over the keyboard. I swear she knows that it drives me nuts, but I feel too flattered to stop her – in spite of the fact that I have to keep correcting her 'input'. (That form of nonsensical indulgence is endemic in cat lovers throughout the world. If a cat has chosen your knee or makes an equivalent gesture of affection, it is very hard to spurn them and get up, so you can find yourself spending considerable chunks of time not getting another drink, or not going to the loo. Indeed, in Moon Cottage I have seen other humans even unable to change television channels for the same reason – when no other creature would make one behave so irrationally.)

Oh, you three cats, it is so wonderful to be home with you again. I am so grateful to you for the extraordinary depth of affection and companionship we all share.

CHAPTER 9

As July draws to a close we have sweltered our way through a sustained heatwave and today, formidably hot by any standards, I have donned a long, floaty dress as opposed to my normal livery of tee-shirt and trousers. We have been taking tea with Caroline near St Albans, who has greatly amused us by introducing us to her newly acquired and disconcertingly enormous labrador called Ben. In the manner of most large amiable dogs he crawls all over me, licking my face and arms en route, and then proceeds to roll his body in my voluminous skirts. Eventually we take our leave and as soon as we're home I change my clothes for the second time this day, trying desperately to get more comfortable in the heat. I casually toss my dress on to the bed, intending to put it away later, and vaguely notice the two female cats enter the bedroom. As I look across at them I see that they are both sporting the 'maiden aunt' expression they frequently affect, mouths pursed tightly into a prim 'o', which always makes me laugh. Titus, ignoring me in that special and maddening way that only cats can, approaches the bed from which the dress, abandoned in such haste, is now cascading untidily and, standing upright on her hind legs, sniffs it fastidiously. She turns away and walks towards Fannie. As she is about to pass Fannie, she stops and they nose each other communicatively. I have no doubt at all that they share a 'language' and its transmission appears to operate through the channel of smell, body posture and especially the twitching of ears, whiskers, tails and direct eye contact, although – oddly enough, in such vocal animals – the sounds they emit seem almost exclusively reserved for communicating with humans except when they are hurt, frightened, trapped or courting. Following this exchange, Fannie now walks towards the dress and re-enacts Titus's performance of mannered sniffs. I smother my giggles and try to scoop one or other of them up to cuddle them, but they walk off, each in a different direction, each waving her long tail like a question mark. I put their grumpiness down to the heat – it is now 88° Fahrenheit – or exasperation at my untidiness (my mother would have pulled a moue like that); but most likely of all options, I conclude, they smell perfidy? Oh dear.

Pushkin is in very subtle ways now changing and is halfway between kittenhood and adulthood in his mental development, and in size he is three-quarters grown. He plays, but then suddenly he sits looking thoughtful and curiously mature. Experimentally, it would appear, he flaunts his backside at both of the female cats, but most usually at Titus who sniffs it. If she is feeling especially benign she gives it a lick; Fannie tends to do the same thing casually, almost sneakily, as he is passing, which causes him to have a semi-permanent expression of surprise, which you see on his face as he looks backwards at her over his shoulder. The girls both play with him and, although they do not like to show it, are in quite serious competition with each other. Fannie is losing weight and I am concerned that it is some form of insecurity about Pushkin, but equally it might just be the summer heat. I sternly remind myself that the cats always lose weight when it is hot.

Pushkin is growing daily in length, although in other respects his physical development is slow. He has metamorphosed from small kitten to young cat, with an innate grace and beauty. I had put catnip on the cat platform the other day and he sprang up on to the top, writhing ecstatically, while looking up appealingly, head on one side. His every movement was extraordinarily sensual and lithe. Cats on land and above can become as dolphins in the water, a perfect extension of the medium they are in. His immaturity, however, is still marked by the fact that he frequently overestimates the scale of the thing on which he has landed and either falls off it or knocks it over. He is particularly active in the evenings and often downstairs we exchange rueful grins as we hear the crashing and banging of Pushkin about his evening callisthenics. When we creep up to bed there is the nightly ritual of putting things upright again. He watches the places on to which the gazelle-like Fannie leaps and he attempts to follow with almost invariable tumblings. When he is not rolling around sensuously or sleeping, he has a tendency to move fast and jerkily. I wonder, sometimes, whether he is dyspraxic, but perhaps I am making him run before he can walk – and indeed perhaps this is 'teenage' hormonal adjustment. He does have one exceptionally unlovable habit, however. Whenever he hears the other two cats at their food bowls he leaps over and head butts them out of the way. I am sure this is contributing to Fannie's weight loss, as she just turns away forlornly and gives up.

This last weekend I decide I had better check whether he has got his second teeth yet and am somewhat disarmed to find that he has two sets of upper canines rather than one, making him look disarmingly like a cross between Jaws and the evil one in the Bond movie with a mouth full of spikes. By Monday I am reluctantly wondering whether a vet visit is impending when, as he is eating, I hear a chinking sound and find that the second of his 'baby' teeth has dropped out, rendering him now 'normal'.

The three of them chase each other round more and more frenetically as each day goes by and I wonder if it is a positive or negative development. The agony of not knowing whether my grand plan is a good idea after all is beginning to unnerve me.

Today Michael comes out into the yard where all three of them are mooching around. Pushkin is playing 'pebbles' with the gravel on his own in a rather focused way. Titus is sitting, hunched up in the corner, back to us, staring out into the garden-jungle on semi-permanent frog alert, and Fannie is lying on a cushion on a chair in her favourite lion-couchant position, looking delicate and pretty and removed from it all.

'Come on, Pushkin. When are you going to do your stuff?' he chides.

'Don't say that. Perhaps it is a sign. I mean a sign that it should not be, the fact that he has not matured yet or that they are not turning him on. I am especially worried about Fannie. Perhaps I should get him fixed now?' I agonise.

'No, no. Not after all this. You leave him be.' And he walks back into the kitchen with studied deliberation.

As an underlining of my fears tonight, they are particularly disruptive and strange with each other. I think that Fannie might be on heat. Certainly Titus is paying her the attention that she has in the past when this is the case and Fannie keeps turning over on her back, wanting her tummy rubbed. The three cats are involved in a mighty chasing routine. Or, more accurately, Pushkin chases Fannie and then chases Titus, and the one who is not being chased lurks about, consciously provoking him to make chase. But when he does and leaps on top of Fannie, they roll around, face to face, and I hear her crying out – mostly her, but sometimes him too – and, along with the flailing legs, claws and teeth are fully utilised. Sometimes, indeed often, it starts with gentle and playful boxing, but it always degenerates into a more savage 'fight', with Fannie usually squawking loudly and running away. During the 'bout' there is much hissing and, as far as I can determine, the voice is Fannie's. The same thing happens with Titus, but Titus is the one who generally beats off Pushkin, so they are quicker and quieter bouts with Pushkin running away at the end, or sometimes just moving away as if it had never happened. Cats are complete masters of the art of 'as I was saying, before I was so rudely interrupted'.

I worry terribly that they are not happy. Titus seems to sit around the place, hunched up in a disquieting way. Fannie seems in particular need of physical loving and, on top of that she is so thin; also, when she comes to me in the morning for the ritual cuddle she has started a recurring dribble which, when first I became aware of it, I had thought to be a bad sign, but I now conclude it is an indication of her pleasure as it only occurs when she is purrfully thrumming. When I am in the bedroom, writing or reading, both Fannie and Titus spend most of the day on the bed behind me, or sometimes Fannie climbs up high on to the top of the highest bookshelf and lies on a pile of scarves up there. Pushkin spends the bulk of his day on John's bed.

Pushkin has just come into the room and is now lying on the bed with the other two. The girls, who have both been in here for about two hours, are lying back-to-back, with the curve of their backs just touching like a pair of crescent moons. I go over to the bed to attempt to stroke them all.

But three is difficult with only two hands, so I kind of mumble into Pushkin's ear, and fondle him with my chin while stroking the other two. He purrs loudly, nevertheless, which transparently irritates the other two. Each of the girls opens just one eye a crack and both watch him, slittily. I am always slightly nonplussed at the way cats keep their eyes on everything that is happening around them, even when they appear to be sleeping. Again Fannie starts her little dribbling. Titus lolls her head over backwards in her lazy way towards the purring Pushkin in the hope that he might lick her. He doesn't, so she lolls even further back and licks one tiny bit of him in a desultory manner, but then it is always thus with her. The two girls get up and change their positions. I walk across the room, leaving them to it, and pick up a book. I casually glance across at them and register that they are both involved in a great deal of rather fierce-looking self-grooming, and now Pushkin's ostentatious purr, lacking any external stimuli, slowly peters out. There is silence and then there is one 'flump', and a second and a third, as all three animals jump off the bed and high-tail it out of the room.

On another occasion around this time I am sitting at my desk upstairs doing some office work and activate the printer to run off a spreadsheet. As the printer clatters into life, Fannie, who is hovering on the edge of the desk, leaps up in the air in fright and actually screams.

'Oh Fannie, what is happening to you?' I am deeply disturbed by the violence of her reaction and think about it long and hard. I have to conclude that it is the introduction of Pushkin into their lives that has caused this hypertension in this tiny, nervous, thin little cat. She has always been easily frightened, in a way that Titus never is, although her mother too could be very jumpy, but not of her own shadow as is little Fannie. Her mother was more independent and that gave her a confidence lacking in Fannie. I have unfairly indulged myself in an experiment to satisfy my own desires and this has resulted in a young full tomcat frightening the life out of at least one of my cats. Is this fair – surely not? Michael is away and I long to talk this over with him, but feel that I must have Pushkin castrated as soon as possible and also organise for hysterectomies for the girls.

I recorded my remorse above a few days ago. Now, however, it is 3 p.m. on August Bank Holiday Saturday and the three cats have, without my awareness, come in from outside and are lying in complete silence on the bed behind me. Fannie is curled up, on my abandoned bath towel, in a semi-circle, and Titus, larger in length and width, is lying curled around her protectively, so they look like little spoons. Both are soundly asleep. Pushkin is about six inches away from them, curled up in the mirror image of them, facing the other way, and he also appears to be serenely asleep. There is a tiny breeze coming through the open window, but the air around us feels like warm bathwater. I look at the thermometer and see that it registers 83° Fahrenheit. That is warm, but not unbearable, just lazy-making.

I rest back in my chair and listen to the faint swish-swish of the traffic outside, bound for Tesco's and the great weekly shop, and then over that and louder I become aware of the constant hum in the sky of the air traffic to-ing and fro-ing from Heathrow, and I feel a surge of joy as I recognise the sybaritic pleasure of simply being in this tranquil haven that is our cool dark bedroom, with its tiny cottage windows and its thick ancient walls over a foot deep; and that I am with three cats at peace, whom I love, and that I am not going anywhere at all on this lazy, hot Saturday, while all the world outside, it seems, is busy, busy, busy.

∾

The emotional mix of all that happens between humans and animals can be an ever-shifting canvas and all sorts of factors can have an effect on the behaviour and responses between those that cohabit. We all have our moods.

Today I go schmoozing up to Titus, and clearly she is not in the mood for love, but I persevere with stroking her for just a minute too long. I know that I am pushing my luck, but I suppose I want to see what she will do and my effort is rewarded. She proceeds, not penetratingly, but warningly, to bite me. My amour-propre is hurt rather more seriously than my hand of course. She does seem to have a problem about me and my relationship with Fannie; or am I imagining it? Often, however, she does want to be cuddled and will purr quietly while I stroke her or turn over for her tummy to be tickled, but she never meets me with the vociferous call she gives Michael and John. She seems to gravitate towards males of the human species more readily than females in general and is fondly referred to by many male visitors as 'the tart'. She has an endearing habit of responding to the phrase 'give us a kiss' by holding her nose towards you and bowing her head; her own version of a hands-off kiss. I wonder, sometimes, if she knows that I am unable to control how much I feel for Fannie. My friend Elspeth says that she, too, knows that her adoration of her cat Arthur is more intense than the love she feels for his mother Freya, and she is sure that Freya senses this. Cats have an extraordinary degree of insight into the emotions in the human heart.

By contrast, Fannie will go equally easily to women and men, but only if she is in the mood, and woe betide anyone who picks her up when she is not in the mood, as they will be in receipt of deep scratches from her hasty departure. Fannie, most of all of the three cats, chooses exactly when and with whom and how she bestows her favours, but it is a feline characteristic anyway.

Pushkin couldn't care less yet. That might all be to come. Pushkin does, however, have an engaging habit of joining us when we eat. He will come and inspect the table and loll seductively on one of the vacant chairs. He loves to eat real meat, which is how he first learnt this habit, but he does it too simply for companionability. He actively seeks human company in the early evening when he rises from his day's gruelling inertia.

The summer is drawing to a close and I can feel that pang of sadness that enters the soul at this time of year. It has been warm and humid for some days – although already the early mornings and late evenings have the unmistakable nip and sweet sharp – and somehow poignant – smell of early autumn. London and the Home Counties alone in Britain have been enjoying the last remnants of an Indian summer, while it has rained heavily and unremittingly elsewhere. But today the

rain is pouring down on us too in that
drenching heavy 'monsoony' way
it does after sustained heat.

In a brief dry spell I grab
hold of a large basket of damp
washing to take out to the
drier in the shed. I briefly
jam open the gate to
manoeuvre the basket
through and Titus, who has
been sitting quietly on
the platform in the
corner, makes an astonishingly
fast dive straight through the gate and into
the garden. She belts up the steps and three-quarters of the
way across the lawn. I pull the gate shut, as fast as possible,
in the face of Pushkin, who is seriously thinking of joining
in, and check that Fannie is still lying couchant on the
table. I run up the steps calling her softly.

At this point, in her newly found freedom in the wider
world beyond her enclosure, Titus breaks my heart. Out
there in the garden she loses her nerve and squats down in
the very long wet grass, unsure what to do next. Her pupils
dilate in fear and her ears droop down to half-mast, so that
she bears more than a passing resemblance to Yoda, the
ancient and revered Jedi Master from *Star Wars*. She is
crouched low on the grass and stares up at me forlornly. I
approach her gently and scoop her up into my arms. She
snuggles into my neck and purrs quietly as I carry her back
to the cottage. About half an hour later I am up at my desk

and realise that I have not seen her for a little while. Searching, I find her hunched up under John's bed, apparently out of sorts – at the failure of the great escape? At the lost opportunity? Poor little Titus.

Sometimes I think that I fail Titus and that perhaps I may not care enough for her. However, since her attempted break-out a few days ago, and because a double ear infection has got me in its thrall, I have been incarcerated in the cottage on my own, rather deafly, for nearly a week, during which time Michael has been away with his mother in Ireland and John has barely been here. During this short time Titus has become very clingy and attached to me, and has indeed been making those very sounds to me in greeting that she normally, so completely, reserves for John. So, for Titus, in this desert of affection, I finally pass muster. In spite of the fact that I am so clearly Hobson's Choice, I feel profoundly honoured. It has been observed by many that some animals, but cats especially, are sensitive to emotional and physical hurt in the humans with whom they cohabit, so perhaps this is really Dr Titus at work.

Tonight the girls are much exercised in seeking out Pushkin, with whom they both want to play. The cottage yet again resounds to the noise of stampeding cats. Because both Titus and Fannie are taking it in turns to be chased by him, he comes downstairs to the sitting room, panting and apparently exhausted, where he drinks and drinks. At this both the girls, in open displays of impatience, attempt to incite him to further chasing activities, but he firmly stands his ground at the water bowl. He is his own boy is young Pushkin.

I have now retired to the bedroom to turn in for the night and, as usual, Pushkin, who had jumped on to the bed, disruptively causing both the other cats to jump off, climbs heavily on top of me, head butts me, pushes his face into mine, his breath smelling strongly of cat food, and purrs loudly. Satisfied that the status is quo he now makes his way to someplace downstairs where he sleeps, and Titus and Fannie both sit on the floor, watching me, waiting for me to put out the light. Fannie no longer sleeps near the bed, but rather on top of the bookcase, which is post-Pushkin behaviour. It saddens me, and I worry about her nervousness. In some perverse way, however, the fact that the vet said torties are always the most highly strung of cats helps me to be philosophical about it. I also feel that she is essentially a happy cat, if jumpy, and she is putting on a little more weight, I think – I hope – now.

Some days later Fannie, who has been lying on the chair beside me quietly all morning, suddenly leaps across the room and joins Titus on the bed where, with a fierce intensity, she bestows lick after lick upon the face and ears of her sister. Titus puts her front leg round Fannie in an encouraging sort of way, and just leans back and lets it happen. This state of bliss does not last long. Pushkin, currently at the other end of the bed and apparently asleep, wakes up when he hears the subdued commotion and attempts to join in at the Titus end of the arrangement. Tetchily, Titus rises and jumps off the bed and, by cat standards, almost stamps out of the room. Fannie makes her eyes go big, and pulls her mouth into that little disapproving 'o' and turns away. Pushkin hangs about in a kind of limbo, not sure what to do now, and then sits down inelegantly with his two back legs spread wide apart in front of him like a demented frog, and sets about a meticulous grooming of his testicles. Fannie sighs an enormous sigh that almost blows me out of my chair and curls up in a tight ball, eyes firmly shut, with all the outward appearance of a cat in deep sleep. Eventually Pushkin comes to the end of his marathon preening session and, turning round twice, he too sinks into a slumbering and – soon – sleeping position. Titus quietly re-enters the room and climbs on to the windowsill in front of me and sits staring out of the open window, basking in the sunlight, looking contented; but I notice the end of her tail twitches back and forth enigmatically.

I am completely unable to second-guess whether the symbiosis existing among the three of them is antagonistic or harmonious, or a combination of both.

CHAPTER 10

Autumn

Michael and Geoffrey and I drive to northern France to replenish our wine stocks, which are running low, and we decide to make it a more leisurely trip than the normal day-return raid, so we stay overnight in a small town in the Pas-de-Calais before descending on the oft-visited Calais branch of Auchan, whose wine stocks are formidable indeed. We return to the cottage in the early evening, just as dusk is falling. Fannie greets us with a series of frantic miaows and rolls over to be stroked. She is hotly on heat and calling loudly. When she is in this state she amuses us greatly because she seems so scared that she might actually attract a real tomcat that she always goes upstairs into the safety of the bedroom and calls from that window and then comes downstairs to see if it has had any effect; but perhaps I misjudge her behaviour and in fact her tiny plaintive calls may actually travel further from the higher window when it is open. Pushkin seems completely indifferent to Fannie, or at any rate to her condition, although he is undoubtedly hungry for human attention and head butts us repeatedly and walks across the table to sniff the food, before Geoffrey shouts loudly:

'Boris, get off, dammit! Not near the food!'

He does get off immediately, but with an unmistakable air of surprise, as he is unaccustomed to being shouted at.

'Why do you call him Boris?' I enquire as a diversionary tactic.

'Because Pushkin wrote the play that became the opera *Boris Godunov*, of course!' he beams.

'Oh! Of course!' I reply emphatically.

Later on this same evening, Titus too begins to call and makes plaintive trilling sounds, looking up at me, and then repeatedly bending her head low to the ground and finally throwing over her whole body in a great sensual roll. And still Pushkin appears remote.

Now, the very next morning, I open the kitchen door into the yard as normal, but Fannie, contrary to her normal caution, calls so loudly and long and with such harshness and intensity that I shut the door, as now I am the one who is afraid that this might bring a tom a-calling. The rest of the day passes tranquilly enough, the cats sleep in their accustomed manner and places, and move around from time to time to check what I am up to, but all seems normal. Later on, the two girls engage in a sustained mutual face-

grooming session on the bed and then fall asleep wound around each other. Pushkin maintains his own space.

All three of them are eating more than they normally do, but this is probably because the days – and certainly the nights – are now much colder than they have been. Autumn is on the way.

One Sunday afternoon in early October, Michael and I are preparing a leisurely, late lunch when at my urging Michael goes out into the garden to retrieve some pitta bread out of the freezer in the shed. He races back into the cottage, superficially soaked and, shaking himself like a wet dog, observes that it is blowing a real gale. I lazily cobble the lunch together and we sit down. We eat our food, drink a little wine, and talk in a desultory fashion, surrounded by the Sunday mountain of newspapers. We are completely relaxed and enjoying the luxury of not caring what time the clock is saying to us. Eventually Michael stands up, stretches indulgently, bids me a fond farewell and disappears through the front door, bound for the local wine bar to watch a football match.

As a result of the ensuing through-draught one of the newspapers gets sucked up and flaps its way, boisterously, out through the back door with me in hot pursuit. It is pouring with rain and, as I bend down to scoop up the pages, from the corner of my eye I realise the gate out of the yard is wide open and blowing backwards and forwards in the wind. I am immobilised in horror. Where are the cats?

I slam the back door shut and race upstairs calling the 'kittee' call, where I find a bog-eyed and still sleepy Pushkin on our bed but no sign, anywhere, of Fannie or Titus. I hurl myself down the stairs and charge outside, again slamming the back door to keep Pushkin safe, and race through the yard gate and up the steps into the main garden. Not a sign anywhere of anything resembling a cat. I call repeatedly.

Suddenly from under a fuchsia bush there is a small commotion and Fannie hurtles past me, her tail fluffed out to three times its normal width, and she tries to get in through the now closed back door. I run back and let her in. I return to the garden to find Titus. I run up the gravel path under the pergola thick with dripping roses and find no trace of her anywhere. I run diagonally across the lawn and through the other end of the pergola burdened with soggy honeysuckle leaves, but still no trace of any cat. I am hoarse with calling. I drag the waterlogged garden table to one side and peer under the garden bench where I am met by a pair of dark amber eyes staring back at me. Slowly, with tail erect and bushed out in fear, Titus walks out into the rain, but is reluctant to be picked up. When I do finally grab her and nurse her in my arms, she purrs with what I imagine to be the recognition of security.

I shut them both firmly inside the cottage, where, soaked to the skin, they start to groom themselves with great fastidiousness. I sink down on a chair with a new understanding of the possibility of carrying one's heart in one's mouth.

I am appalled that it is possible to be so completely frightened by something so small. So the two cats went into the garden. That is all. But I feel physically sick with apprehension. How could such a small act engender such an overreaction? Every second that they were out represented another cat life lost to me. When Michael returns, although I speak to him, with some passion, on the subject of open gates, I forget to inquire, 'How went the football?'

～

The two girls are slowly coming out of their current heat, but are spasmodically vocal. Fannie is currently calling more insistently than Titus, and although her voice is not big her high-pitched cry is very penetrating. Titus restricts her vocalisation to her more lowly pitched miaow, miaow, miaows. Pushkin still studiously ignores their pleas. It has to be said, however, that they direct their cries rather pointedly through the outside fence and not, it seems, to him.

Although he remains completely calm about them he does seem to be growing more manic as he gets bigger. This morning, excited by the raucous chattering of four magpies, he hurls himself at the fence, really high up, from across the other side of the yard, and vigorously head butts the plastic overhang that is meant to contain him, before resignedly jumping down. Twice in the last week he has managed to get himself out through the gap at the very top where the gate meets the post, and although I have now taped it together, making opening the gate for us infuriatingly difficult, he continues to try. He sits on the ground and studies the gate and the fence for long periods of time. As I have watched him he has turned away, but when I look at his face I see on it a ruminative expression and I am sure at those moments he is still thinking about 'the great escape'. Shortly after I witness Pushkin considering ways of getting out of the yard, I read in a book by David Greene*

---

* *Incredible Cats* by David Greene (Methuen, 1984).

of some laboratory experiments carried out at the Wesleyan University in the United States by Dr Donald Adams to assess whether cats are capable of abstract reasoning. In these experiments, Dr Adams shows that cats can remember successful problem-solving strategies and employ insight to think their way out of unusual situations. Cats typically look at the 'problem' they must solve, and will then turn away from it and employ thought to seek a solution. He concludes that cats possess the same high level of problem-solving ability skills as are found in monkeys, and considerably greater than those found in dogs. On the one hand, I find this piece of intelligence extremely interesting, but now I have a further thing to worry about. Pushkin is going to work out how to get out dammit!

On the subject of feline intelligence, Judith, my friend and publisher, who cohabits with two beautiful Burmese siblings called Daisy and Freda, has always sensed that cats can never be fooled by human subterfuge and I share her view. They seem to possess from an early age an innate wisdom of what is truth. On the related matter of training, however, she is definite that cats can be trained, as she has taught her two to resist sharpening their claws on her furniture by being persistently firm in her 'No, do *not* do that!' and although she says Daisy, in particular, will sometimes look at her with an air of hesitant challenge, I imagine the same look that lions will give in circuses on occasion, on hearing the all-important 'no' they always do go elsewhere to do their crucial sharpening and scent marking. Oh how I wish I had pursued Judith's line and had her gentle determination – even the cover on my cover is in shreds on the chosen sofa of the cats that live with me.

Following my inclusion of the above anecdote I then received this email from Judith, which made me chuckle, so I include it now:

| From: | Judith |
| To: | Marilyn |

Marilyn
  Can I just point out that the 'no' rule only applied to my then new sofas. This is important as I would hate your readers to think that I am obsessively house proud or that my girls are leading repressed, 'inhibited' lives. They have exerted their authority with 95 per cent of my furniture! But it was odd how they did understand the rule. As kittens they would rush into the

room in a state of high exuberance, make for
the sofa, and then stop and think again.
Yes, I think you can train cats, but probably
only one rule . . .
  Love
  Judith

So, might one conclude that cats win game, set and match?
They comply when it suits them.

~

Today, the last day of October, following weeks of torrential
rain, we are overjoyed to open the door and find, at last, a
magnificent blue sky overhead and the garden bathed in
the rich golden sunlight of high autumn.

Indulgently, I brew up a large cup of especially strong
black coffee and potter happily out into the yard, cup in
hand, to seat myself at the little mosaic table, long ago put
together, piece by piece, by some painstaking unknown
artisan under the far more intense rays of a Moroccan sun.
Titus is on my shoulder, purring gently, and I rest contentedly, relishing the warmth of the slanting sunbeams and
wondering, a little sadly, how many days are left of this
particular pleasure before the onset of winter. Tonight the
clocks are to go back one hour, heralding the early darkness
that so depresses the homecoming of that huge army of
commuters of which I am one. As I lean back on the chair,
squinting through my eyelashes at the sky, I become aware
of the staccato, but gentle, passage of a brightly coloured
butterfly floating between my eyes and the sun. Titus, the

hunter, is fortunately facing the other way. I leap up, spilling the cat on to the table beside the abandoned coffee cup, and pursue the insect out into the garden, where it executes a full fluttering circuit, scaling the heights and delving the depths, apparently intent on making anyone foolish enough to follow it run and jump as much as possible. At the very moment that I am about to give up the chase, as is the way of butterflies it lands an arm's length away from where I am standing, on the finely dentate leaves of some late-flowering anemones that are spectacularly alight in the rays of the full sun. At last I am able to establish, as I had thought, that the subject of my ungainly pursuit is a very fine-looking male Red Admiral. I watch him for a good half-hour as he visits the few remaining bearers of nectar in the garden. He touches the fuchsias, but they don't render unto him what he seeks. He spends much time on the flowers of some climbing ivy, which although drab in their pale green livery appear to be very nectar rich as not only he but a myriad bees and other flying insects are humming around the same blooms. But how he yearns for the sun-light. Frequently he must pause, landing now on a large autumn-gold leaf and now on the mellow redbrick of the cottage wall and just spread out the full glory of his wings, which he trembles again and again in the warmth of the sun. Slowly he opens and closes his wings, showing off the rich black velvet with the broad red band cutting across the top third and bordering the bottom and the brave white rectangle and circle in the top corners. How glad I am that we do leave the nettles to grow at the bottom of the garden by the shed and the washing line, which is where he probably came from in his larval form, and how cross I am that our neighbours at the bottom of our garden, unbidden, cut them down when fixing their fence.

But I am fearful for the future of my Red Admiral. There is much debate as to whether the second brood, and he must surely be one such this late in the year (even possibly a third), hibernates, migrates or dies. It is widely believed that for most species, in their 'butterfly' state properly called imago (oh, delicious word, for it has the most heavenly plural – 'imagines' – imagine!), each one lives only two or three weeks, having mated and laid eggs, its biological objective complete and, beautiful fleeting creature that it is, it dies. But the Red Admiral is not as other butterflies. It is speculated that certainly the first brood, and possibly some lucky members of the second brood, migrate to the Baltic, Scandinavia, the Canary Islands, Madeira or even the Azores. However, this one seems to be taking his time.

Two days later I find Titus with her nose pressed to John's bedroom window and, peering over her shoulder to see what she is watching so intently, I spy him – the Red Admiral. He is sunning himself on the now-yellowing wisteria that winds itself, just below the window ledges, all around the cottage from the eastern side, along the warm sun-facing southern side and now, this year, along the western side above the cats' yard. Well, it looks like the same fellow and two days ago, when I was on full butterfly alert in the garden, I am sure he was the only one around. So although the nights are now getting much colder, he has survived thus far. I so long to know what will happen to him. Perhaps he will hibernate in some sheltered place in our garden?

Or perhaps he will migrate? How thrilling but utterly daunting to consider that such a small, fragile creature can cross those vast distances and remain intact.

'Just don't die from the cold, please. Live until next year.'

CHAPTER 11

It is early November, which means that Pushkin is now nine and a half months old, and this morning when I come back from the bathroom having had a shower, I am slightly disconcerted to find him lying on the bed with his legs apart, licking what – for lack of a better phrase – can only be called a 'stiffy'. Titus is lying with her back to him on the far corner of the bed and appears completely indifferent.

Later on, around lunchtime, I hear a rampaging around downstairs and on investigation find that Pushkin is chasing Fannie from room to room. Suddenly they both stop and very gently, too gently, he grabs the back of her neck in his mouth. Fannie immediately hisses at him and races away. After a short interval he tries to chase Titus. Just as Fannie had, Titus pauses and Pushkin grabs her by the scruff of her neck. She has seemed out of sorts all day and she immediately turns round and swats him one with her left foreleg. A friend of ours has suggested it might be better to shut Pushkin up with just one of them, but I resist the idea as it feels simply too restrictive and almost menacing somehow and besides, I reason, he is still half a kitten.

Tonight Titus stumbles as she comes into the cottage – her back legs seem to almost collapse – and then at the last minute she saves herself and I briefly contemplate whether I should get her looked over by the vet, but on balance have decided that it is a one-off and she will be fine.

Shortly after this, Pushkin starts to behave uncharacteristically badly. He is apparently sitting quietly on the cat platform and then suddenly, for no reason at all, he tries to rip the bougainvillea plant to pieces. It is very prickly and he goes at it with his claws and his teeth, very fiercely.

'Pushkin! Stoppit! Enough!' I bawl, crossly.

He leaps down on to the floor and races round the sitting room and then suddenly stops and glares up at me. To transpose human emotions on to animals can be to misunderstand them, but it is truly hard for me to say that the stare he gives me is anything other than challenging. As I return his gaze and recognise the defiance I see in his face, I have a total recall of the angst I used to feel when I was near the ten- and eleven-year-old boys in the school next to mine, and how bullying they were with their taunts and their snowballs down the front of our gym tunics. I remember the fear I felt of that young masculinity, the 'smell' of testosterone and how intimidating they could be, certainly en masse. I pull myself together and bend down to pick him up, but he runs away. I reckon his hormones are shot to pieces and he is only just developing his male awareness. There has been no sign of his spraying around the house yet, but it feels like any minute he might start.

Looking at Pushkin I realise that he is developing and changing subtly almost by the day. He is lean, but astonishingly muscular and remarkably solid. Pushkin flies at things and falls off things, but in the manner of a battering ram he can get through things. Fannie could do this only as a ghost passes through walls. He runs at me while I lie in bed and thunders across the floor and up on to the bed and straight on to my stomach and chest. He has absolutely no sense of foreplay, so when any of us is in bed, or at the computer or reading a newspaper, Pushkin just charges in and is there, on top of your keyboard, in your face, astride your body. But also as he lies on top of his chosen person he purrs his wonderful rumbling vibrating purr, which makes you forgive him all his impertinences. That purr, however, seems to irritate the other cats intensely. Possibly it is a declaration of ownership on his part.

He is such a boy too. He will try to eat anything at all and simply loves real meat (not so good on fish), especially underdone garlicky lamb and pink beef. He does have balls in all senses of the word and I am amused at the way John has bonded with him and they lie around in heaps being boys together. He remains ungracious in the way that he head butts the other cats away from food, even though there is more than enough to go round, just for the sake of having ascendancy over the food bowl; but he is forgiving when, at other times, they both strike out at him and beat him down for nothing worse than coming alongside them and licking them. He merely looks perplexed, but not offended. I believe him to be generous of spirit in all but food, in spite of his jangled hormones.

This morning, when I let Pushkin outside, he stops sharply and scents the wind with his nose held high, almost vertically, much as on film I have seen wolves scent the wind – nose pointed far higher than is usual for most cats. He has always held his head this way when scenting the air, even from tiny kittenhood. A boisterous wind is agitating the full battery of assorted neighbours' wind chimes into a strident chorus. Pushkin dexterously rotates his large pointy ears back and forth registering the cacophony, and at the same time he ingests the smells of the first autumn of his life. I remember one blustery autumn day much like this one, meeting a Dales farmer, and as we stood, quietly gossiping and watching his two dogs running back and forth, covering the same ground again and again, scenting the air and snuffling the grass while trembling with excitement as they quartered the trail-rich verge, he observed gruffly:

'Aye – it's another world they live in – a world of smell, smell, smell. Thee and me couldn't even dream about it', and I remember then longing to know exactly what information animals that are scent-driven can glean from the smells they are monitoring.

Today the unusually animated wind, coming from all directions, is flapping the leaves upside down and revealing their pale undersides. Dalesmen say that if you see the 'secret' side of the leaves uppermost there will be rain before the day is through.

The messages borne on the breeze are clearly getting to Pushkin. He hurls himself at the fence twice and shoots up to the top of it, bashes his head against the overhang and flops back, frustrated in his escape attempt, on to the gravel at the bottom. This performance follows one an hour earlier, which displayed rather more physical endurance. I am now standing in the kitchen waiting for the coffee to percolate, and above the cheery gurgling of the coffee-machine I suddenly discern an ominous metronomic clanking in the yard. I glance through the open door and notice a couple of large sleepy bees erratically flying away from the unrewarding remains of a last summer's geranium left hanging on the wall. The sound that has arrested my attention is the creaking of the wrought-iron bracket containing the flower pot, from which is hanging, by one front leg, a long-bodied, sleek, glistening blue tomcat. As I watch him, he is, by dint of this one foreleg, slowly revolving one way and then the other. The bracket on the wall is one and a half times my own height. I pause, wondering how long he can hold this impossible position. Pushkin, for of course it is he, turns and looks at me with an expression that contains within it an element of anguish and even concern, mingled with annoyance and, just as I am about to ask him, inanely, what his intention might be, I recall Eeyore's gloomy response as floating helplessly on his back he also turns round first one way and then the other while the ever officious Rabbit asks him whatever is he doing:

'I'll give you three guesses, Rabbit. Digging holes in the ground? Wrong. Leaping from branch to branch of a young oak tree? Wrong. Waiting for somebody to help me out of the river? Right.'*

As I stride across, intending to rescue him, he twists himself around, yanks his claws free of the bracket and jumps down and, cat-like to cover his embarrassment, saunters over to a plant-pot holder and, in the time-honoured convention of displacement activity, drinks long and hard without giving me so much as a glance. He reminds me, suddenly, of how naughty young schoolchildren can be. A primary schoolteacher I know says she particularly dreads windy weather because her children in class are always especially badly behaved then.

As Pushkin slowly grows up and his hormones have him

---

* From *The House at Pooh Corner* by A. A. Milne (Methuen, 1928).

climbing up walls, his companion queens are now, in reproductive terms, fully mature.

Fannie, although she is physically tiny is now in her prime. She is the prettiest cat I have ever seen. I am of course hopelessly biased. But her tiny triangular face and her enormous eyes with their dramatic markings and her little dark pink nose outlined in fine chocolate brown and the elegant way she trots about, on the very tips of her toes, pulls at my heart strings whenever I look at her, or even think about her. She is hopelessly nervous and neurotic, however, and she gets worse not better as she gets older. I have no idea what has happened in her apparently uneventful life to cause her such concerns, but whenever I am near her, I am aware of the constant pounding of her heart. I sadly conclude that Pushkin joining the household has not helped. On the other hand, whenever I hold her in my arms, or on my chest or lap, as in our precious ritual of the early morning after my shower, the comfort and strength I receive from this tiny creature is beyond description. She has the ability to heal and to bestow love in a most remarkable way. She has this effect on many people, but especially Damian, Michael's eldest son, who, when she developed a lump on her back in reaction to the first lot of injections and which had made us speculate about all sorts of dark possibilities of the significance of said lump, declared with a passion that shocked me by its partisan nature:

'No – not Fannie. Not this one. The other one OK, but not Fannie.' Poor Titus to be so summarily dismissed. But, thank goodness, the lump was simply an initial reaction to the injection and disappeared after ten days or so.

In the way she moves, Fannie is precise and sure-footed and exceptionally graceful. She regularly balances on the top of the old timbered door of our bedroom with effortless ease, from which precarious perch she leaps up on to the top of the bookcase, where she lies and surveys all that happens below her. She jumps up on to the door top, which is less than two inches wide, from the back of an armchair. None of the other cats is able to do this. She would, if she were allowed, walk the roof as her mother did, but I cannot and dare not allow her that freedom, which would surely render her dead. Fannie has a lightness to her body that is both actual, yet somehow ethereal. I had never before understood the otherworldliness that many people associate with cats but, even though it is hard to explain and one sounds very strange attempting it, there is a completely different element within cats. They seem to me to be more airborne creatures than earthbound, as are dogs. Fannie is exquisitely delicate, but she also has more than a hint of wild spirit about her. When she gives her love to you, which she does with intensity, it is heady stuff because of this very wildness in her nature. My vet friend, Kate, told me once that vets are taught in college to classify dogs as domestic animals, and as such a vet should expect a dog's owner to have it under control during examination, but that cats are classified as 'wild' animals and therefore are exempt from expected forms of disciplined behaviour. All cats I have known, however apparently domesticated, seem to me to be only just this side of wild, and for that reason their relationship with us humans holds for me the same magic – that extraordinary cross-species bond – that developed between Gos and T. H. White and which he examined in his beautifully written and fiercely intense study of how to become a hawk-master:

> I had lived with this hawk, having been its slave, butcher, nursemaid and flunkey. What clothes it wore were made by me, what house it had was swept out and kept sweet by me, what food it ate was killed and eviscerated and hacked into pieces and served by me, what excursions it made were taken on my fist. For six weeks I had thought about it long into the night and risen early to execute my thoughts. I had gone half bird myself, transferring my love and interest and livelihood into its future, giving hostages to fortune as madly as in marriage and family cares. If the hawk were to die, almost all my present me would die with it.*

And yes, if Fannie were to die, almost all my present me would die with her.

---

* *The Goshawk* by T. H. White (Jonathan Cape, 1953).

The disparity between the three cats is as strong as it is possible to imagine. Both physically and emotionally they are markedly different from one another. Titus, physically, is a fluffy, round, light ginger-coloured red mackerel tabby with orange eyes. She is warm, cuddly, leisure loving and a complete foodie, albeit dried food only. She can be an active hunter when she believes that it might truly produce real game, but she is very lazy and the thing she enjoys most is simply lying around the place and especially on top of people. Her preferred victim for this form of schmoozing is male, ideally one watching a television. Perfect. Experience seems to have taught her that a man in this position is the most likely to stay put and to tolerate both her weight and her fur up their nose and, importantly, to stay still. She likes to lie on the left shoulder of said victim. There is also an element of flirtation involved in her choice, however. She responds much more strongly to male pheromones than to female in the human species, so when any number of people are gathered together in one room she will usually select a man in preference to a woman, but not *quite* always. Of the three cats she is the most conversational and she seems to seek and need human company more constantly than the other two. When Michael or John comes home after work she meets them at the door and squawks and squeaks in a series of clear but modulated greetings, which become louder when the homecomer bends down to stroke her back.

Recently she has started to greet me also in this way, but only if there is no man around. Much, however, seems to go on in her mind and she has a way of watching you that is quite unnerving.

An example of the workings of her mind and its inscrutability occurs tonight. I am sitting at my desk, and it's late and quiet. I'm alone but for the cats. Titus is curled up, asleep, on the bed behind me. In the silence I become aware of a small moaning sound, which accelerates very slowly, increasing in volume, until, as I turn round, it resembles a controlled near-scream. Titus is still deeply asleep, and evidently dreaming. Before the scream has reached its peak, I look up to the top of the bookcase where Fannie has been lying on a pile of my scarves and where she is now, sitting bolt upright, staring down at Titus with her beautiful, neurotic, penetrating eyes with their dark dilated pupils and an enormously concerned expression on her face. She leaps down to the floor and up on to the bed with Titus, whose face she starts to lick in a consoling kind of way. By this time, Titus is slowly waking up. She doesn't in any way look alarmed. She pays no attention to Fannie's gestures of solace, but instead yawns widely and long, swallows, stretches and, in no particular hurry, jumps down off the bed.

'Good dream – did you kill?' I inquire.

She ignores me, as she has Fannie. Fannie sighs.

'Suit yourself,' I call to her retreating bottom.

She continues, purposefully, on her way. I would lay considerable odds that she is just checking out the food bowls below, with the intention of sampling a little this and a little that.

Sweet things about Titus. She has a perfect, delicate and deliciously complex little pink nose and matching pale pink lips and pink pads. On her lower lip, visible only when she opens her mouth, she has a circle of freckles that are somehow completely adorable and make her very darling.

Last night I had accidentally left Titus out in the yard for about an hour and a half. It was bitterly cold, although not quite freezing, and I had shut the door while I was cooking supper. After we had eaten, Michael, fortunately, opened the back door to take some bags of vegetables out to the freezer and found a fluffed-out and rather cross Titus outside.

'Aagh – so it isn't only me who shuts you out. Poor old Tites. Bit cold are you?' Michael teased.

Guiltily I watched her come in and, to my consternation, as she walked through the door, her back legs seemed to collapse and then as I looked at her I saw that her left hind leg was sticking out at an odd angle.

'Michael, I am going to have to take her to the vet – there is something wrong.'

And to the vet we have just been. She has a luxating patella, I learn. Her left hind leg is the culprit. Could be the result of injury, could be a congenital deformity. Very painful. Needs surgery, which will be major, and the aftermath of that will be painful. She will have to be restricted in her movements and the pain will have to be controlled with drugs. The vet who is to perform the operation tomorrow is a locum and will leave immediately after the operation – and the surgery will be empty at night and they will not let me bring Titus home until Friday morning. I am unhappy, but resigned.

But I now see that in my diary against 20 August, just over three months ago, I wrote:

'I worry terribly that they are not happy. Titus seems to sit around the place, hunched up in a disquieting way.' So it was pain, not Pushkin, that was making her out of sorts. When will I ever learn to read cats properly?

CHAPTER 12

Thursday, 9.00 a.m.
A dark, rainy November day – and I feel sick with worry.
I passed a fitful night, being haunted by nightmares about
the operation that Titus is to endure today. I had several
strange dreams, but one in particular haunts me. In this
dream Titus, apparently because of her hunger, was compelled to eat a small brown frog, who remained wriggling
and screaming in her mouth while she ate him. I heard
the cats walking about all night – on instruction from the
vet I had had to withhold all food from Titus from 11 p.m.
when we went to bed. I could not bear to feed the other
two with Titus the only one on starvation rations, so
decided they must all suffer. This made them all very
restless and both Titus and Pushkin jumped on to the
bed in the early hours and thrust their faces into mine,
but inquiringly rather than affectionately, and quickly
jumped off again.

This morning, when I descend first thing, all three of
them are sitting in a line where the food bowls are normally

ranked, and they all look at me expectantly, each with his or her head on one side. Guilt, guilt, guilt.

Michael has been working all morning in the little study/bedroom, where he keeps his computer, and I have heard him, at regular intervals, whispering especially fond sweet-nothings to Titus – although I am not sure that he should have told her he was going to send her a get-well card, as he will almost certainly not keep this particular promise. I am glad that he is soothing her and much comforted that he cares too, not that I thought otherwise, but my getting upset gets on his nerves, as I suspect he considers it cowardly, which it is, so he doesn't show his own feelings about the cats to me in the same way, probably as a counter-balance.

11.45 a.m.
Am about to take Titus to the vet now, and once I am gone Michael will be able to put food down for the other two.

Midday
At the surgery I ask, a little boorishly perhaps, which part of the operation will be most dangerous and Alison, the vet who diagnosed the problem yesterday, but who is not operating on Titus, asks:

'What on earth do you mean?'

As I open my mouth to elaborate, I suddenly and embarrassingly feel a couple of large tears roll down either side of my nose.

'What I am trying to ask is at which point in the procedure is she most likely to die?' I gulp.

'Aagh. Well the procedure itself is not dangerous. With

cats it is always the anaesthetic. The anaesthetic can just be too much for them.' She gives me a small reassuring smile, but I am launched.

'So does that mean on the operating table or in the recovery room?'

'The difficult time can be as they regain consciousness and the tubes are removed, but we will have a fully trained veterinary nurse monitoring her at that time. By 5 p.m. she will be fully awake.'

Reassured thus far, but unable to stop myself, I continue:

'Last night, Alice [the surgeon] told me on the phone that no one will be in the surgery at night, and I just cannot bear it that Titus will be on her own and frightened.'

'But I am on duty tonight and I will be visiting at 10 p.m., and if she is in pain then I will be able to administer an opiate that will keep her pain at bay. If you took her home, you would not be able to do this,' Alison interjects.

I incline my head in acceptance.

'Listen – phone at 3 p.m. and we will tell you how it is going then. She should be beginning her recovery by then.'

1.50 p.m.

Have been feeling strangely calm since returning from the vet empty handed, perhaps because having handed Titus over to them this is now the point of no return. Now, though, I feel tense, as the hands of the clock have passed the point at which they said they would be starting to operate.

3 p.m.

I phone the surgery and, after being kept waiting for what seems an eternity, the receptionist says:

'Alice is scrubbing up now. She is just about to start – tell you what, we will ring you, rather than you ring us, when it is all over.'

I stammer and stutter and then say 'Fine'. Why are they running late? Does that mean something went wrong in the op before Titus? Does that mean that Alice is tired and frazzled? Depressed and needing displacement activity, I play a game of solitaire on the computer and do that so dangerous childlike thing: if I win then Titus will be OK. I win in record time first go. But then I am ashamed of my naivety, so am not sure whether it counts because of that.

4.20 p.m.

Michael has gone out to the post and, I suspect, for a beer. It has been very quiet since he left and this second waiting period has seemed interminable.

The phone finally goes and it is Alice, the locum, who says in her rich Aussie accent:

'Well – it's pretty much good news. I have just finished the operation and Titus is now in the recovery room. She has not regained consciousness yet. But the operation went very well and there were no complications, and I am very pleased with what I was able to achieve. We are now through the big hurdle.'

As she talks and I listen, I doodle on a notepad and find that I have written:

Through the big hurdle
Through the big hurdle
Through the big hurdle
Antibiotics
Anti-inflammatories
Extra groove in bone
Internal sutures
Cage from the surgery

Slowly I hear, with a newly heightened awareness, that she is now saying:

'Titus must under no circumstances jump down from any height for at least a fortnight – and depending upon your house that might be impossible to arrange. Therefore we will lend you a cage and you must keep her in that.'

Oh Titus. You will go mad and you will hate us all and you will think that we are torturing you – even more than you already do. There must be an alternative. Remove all the furniture from the sitting room – but where to put it? Must find a solution.

We finish the phone call, although she urges me to phone back at 6.30 by which time they hope to be able to tell me that Titus has regained consciousness and is on the road to recovery. I thank her abundantly for utilising her not inconsiderable surgical skills to maximum effect. She laughs and says it is she who should thank me for saving her from a final consultation, which she never enjoys. So this is a woman who prefers the challenge of surgery to the more, to her, onerous challenge of human interface.

6.20 p.m.

Can't wait any longer so I just dial the number. Speak to Vicky, the duty nurse, who says that Titus is doing really well and is beginning to sit up and look around her. She says that she cannot be fed yet, but she will give her some Hill's dried food just before she leaves tonight and she will also give her some water then too. She confirms that she must be left in a cage for at least a fortnight, and that if she is she will sleep mostly. She asks me to phone early in the morning and speak to Leanne who will be the duty ward nurse and she will tell me how Titus has fared overnight. All the time she is talking to me I can hear a confined dog barking persistently and mournfully in the background and wonder how Titus likes that sound. Feel such a rat leaving her there overnight, but feel it is best for her.

I utter an intense prayer of gratitude for her deliverance thus far.

Friday

I phone to speak to Leanne, the duty nurse, and am told, disconcertingly, that she cannot be interrupted as she is doing a ward round. More like a cage round, but I take their point anyway. She returns my call and says they have some concerns over Titus. The good news is that she is alert and looking around, and miaowing a lot. The bad news is that she wet her bed during the night and lay in her urine, not ideal with such a recent and deep wound, although there was a cat tray behind her. They are cleaning her up, but feel the sooner I can take her home the better, as they feel the environment is distressing her. I bet it is with all that barking going on, and anyway she has never been separated before from Fannie, who has called through the past night – I presume for her sister, although she may just be coming into heat.

I collect Titus and bring her home and murmur my apologies for what I have done to her, but reckon it will be a long time before I earn my forgiveness. I have been told that it is strictly impossible for her to be let out of the cage except for cuddling and pill administration, as rest is what she must have.

'Absolute confinement for two weeks. No messing!' the nurses and vets alike tell me sternly.

I tie the vet cage and our own cats' cage end to end with the openings facing each other so she has more space to sleep, given that she has to have a cat-litter tray in with her as well as everything else. She has eaten less than a teaspoon of food throughout the day, but has drunk a bowlful of water and slept a great deal. She has not, however, used the cat-litter tray.

Fannie's recurring response, from the moment I bring Titus back into the house, until early afternoon, has been to hiss and spit at her. I am shocked and Titus seems hurt, and she now turns her back on Fannie whenever she comes near her since her first spiteful attack. She is currently not hissing at her, but nor is she being friendly. I assume it is the horrid 'hospital' smells that surround Titus and the anaesthetic on her breath that make her seem an alien creature to her litter sister, and cat behaviourists always say that hissing is not purely aggression – it can also indicate fear and apprehension, which is more likely in Fannie's case. Pushkin, on the other hand, is being considerably friendlier, and licks her nose through the bars, although he did playfully try to swipe her with his paw just now.

I nervously hold Titus on my knee, as love and attention is important to her morale, and find she is tense and uncertain. In order to do the operation, which requires the surgeon to create a new and deeper groove in her tibia so that the cruciate ligaments will hold the knee joint stable, they have shaved her radically. They started shaving from just above the tarsal bones of her left rear leg and have gone right up to the pelvis and have also, for good measure, removed a large chunk of her tummy fur. This has created, rather strikingly, both a smooth and a hairy cat. The bottom part of her paw and ankle look like that of a ginger poodle, then there is a, relatively, huge expanse of shockingly white flesh, the shape of a very small delicate leg of mutton, and then up near her pelvis the fur begins again. She looks vulnerable and moth-eaten. The scar is neat and not leaking, but her flesh is very bruised in the immediate area around the scar. I hug her gently.

'Poor Titus. They wrecked your looks, but we all still love you, I promise.'

I feed both the antibiotic and, as importantly, the painkilling pills to her with some cat food pâté and because she takes them so easily, I persuade her to eat some more pâté. She does, and then ten minutes later is violently sick. I look for signs of the pills; it is hard to tell whether they have got into her system or whether she rejected them. I leave her in the cage downstairs overnight.

John comes in and gives her a big hug. I overhear him saying to her gently:

'Titus, you will get better soon. You will. You are my favourite cat, but shhhh, don't tell the others.'

Saturday
Today we are looking forward to a long arranged lunch party with Klaus and Joelle, who are dear friends, and because we had already postponed a lunch date a few weeks ago when I had my ear infection, we do not want, under any circumstances, to postpone it again, but I am fearful about how I shall attend to my nursing duties. At the outset I am concerned because I cannot get Titus to eat anything. I have moved her with her double cage up to our bedroom so that she will have some peace and quiet. This ploy seems to

have worked as the food in the bowl inside her cage is slowly disappearing. It is several hours later when I stay in the bedroom for a little while to give Titus some companionship that I spy Fannie, who having sufficiently conquered her previous distaste of the veterinary aromas clinging to Titus to get close to the cage, is systematically putting her paw through the bars and scooping piles of pellets out on to the carpet outside the cage and devouring them. Fannie the finicky, Fannie whose normal posture is to eat the bare minimum, and when upset to go on complete hunger strike, now, when confronted by her sick sister, becomes Fannie the thief. Titus, meanwhile, sits hunched up in a forlorn manner and is all too evidently eating nothing.

I phone the long-suffering nurse, Leanne, who suggests I cook chicken or fish and hand feed her, but that she will get the duty vet to phone me. I do cook some meat, but know in my heart of hearts it will not work as Titus eats only Hill's dried cat food and no other. I try to feed the meat in tiny pieces to her, but she rejects it. Even though there is a bowl of dried food within the cage and easily available to her, she has consistently ignored it.

I start to hand feed her little pellets of dried food and at last she eats one, and then, very slowly, another. I find that one way I can gain her interest is to 'rain' them one by one through the bars at the top of the cage so they plop down in front of her nose, which means that she has to half-heartedly 'hunt' for them. She eats about a dessert-spoonful before rounding her back in her 'go away' body language. I hasten downstairs and distractedly continue preparations for the lunch party.

Klaus and Joelle arrive and the sound of laughter and the pulling of corks from bottles fills the cottage. I become belatedly aware of just how hopelessly disorganised I am, as I have only just finished peeling vegetables, so cannot put the beef in the oven until the potatoes are under way – and at this point, of course, the phone rings and it is Leanne again.

She has talked to the duty vet who thinks that it may well be that Titus never absorbed the painkiller the night before and suggests that we continue with Titus at home today, making sure she does absorb today's painkiller, but take her back tomorrow, Sunday, if she has still eaten only meagre amounts of food. I am relieved to be able to report to Leanne that she is just starting to eat a little; and my hope is that now she has started, her natural gluttony will carry her through.

Leanne further speculates that Titus is likely to be depressed by the pure fact of her confinement – a condition that is bound to produce a depression in any animal, but especially a cat.

As the day progresses Titus appears to improve. Periodically I creep up from our lunch party to check her out and am hugely relieved to see that she has eaten some of her food and seems more alert than at any time since her op. I discover, however, that in spite of a small barricade I had created both Fannie and now Pushkin are still 'fishing' for her food through the bars, but because they cannot see where their paws are going they are considerably less successful than before.

However, Titus has turned a corner and is fighting her own. Over the next two days she continues to progress and eats small but regular helpings. She uses the cat-litter tray without any problems (but unfortunately the antibiotics have given her diarrhoea), she drinks copious amounts of water, and she is fantastically brave. She never miaows or complains. But she does appear deeply depressed, trapped in a lying position, ears only semi-erect, and eyes half closed – her only possible movement is to turn from one side to another or stand to eat and drink. She hates being given pills. I now have to give them whole by mouth as she no longer accepts them in pâté and she regards me with horror when she can tell that is why I am approaching her. But she makes not a sound in all of this, and although she looks at me with deep hurt in her eyes, she allows me to subject her to whatever is my will.

Michael has, only temporarily I am sure, lost his patience with Fannie, since Titus has been ill, because of Fannie's apparent self-centredness. And, to be honest, I too have to remind myself to avoid anthropomorphism, for what we perceive concerning their behaviour, and what actually happens in the cats' own world, may differ considerably. Fannie is moaning and lying on her back, and asking to be stroked. Michael grumpily complies:

'You are so selfish. All you want is things for you, you,

you. And what about your sister? If this had happened to you, we would hear non-stop miaow, miaow, miaow, and as for giving you pills, we would be scratched to pieces.'

Certainly I view with horror the thought of Fannie going through the mixed kennels at the vet's. Titus, you are one, brave, long-suffering girl and I have strongly learnt my lesson. You have courage, real courage, and I find that I love you greatly – and was so fearful that something terrible might happen to you when you were at the vet's.

CHAPTER 13

I reflect soulfully on why one crisis always has to follow
another. Michael and I had been looking forward to a rare
holiday at home for ages, and it started this Friday night.
Late on Monday afternoon, the first real day of our holiday,
Michael experiences a pain in his groin, a repetition of
something he suffered some weeks ago. I ask him if he
wants to see a doctor and initially he says no, but as the
evening progresses the pain becomes worse and finally I
call out a doctor in spite of Michael's protests. By this
time it is an unknown doctor on emergency call. The
doctor frightens the life out of me by saying that it might
be an arterial hernia, in which case it needs to be operated
on immediately.

We end up in our local General Hospital in the A & E
Department and, of course, we are there for hours. We see
a series of house doctors who do all that they can to help,
but suddenly, after taking X-rays, they conclude that it is a
crumbling hip and not the 5-star emergency we had thought.
I get Michael back home at 1.30 a.m. and we then have to
go back to the hospital the next day, Tuesday, to see an

orthopaedic surgeon who decides that he must have surgery pretty imminently, so on to a waiting list he goes.

On this same Tuesday night I take Titus back to the vet, to Alison, for her post-op check-up. Titus is progressing well, but I am told off for letting her out of the cage this afternoon, which I did with Michael to help me, to walk around a little bit. Alison says the confinement is absolutely essential to ensure the mending of the leg, while the leg heals itself internally. I try to argue that good morale and also muscle tone are important to her in the healing process, but Alison is very firm, and although Titus is a good patient, I can tell that I have less than the top score in brownie points as the patient's carer.

I find the fortnight's solid confinement of Titus almost unbearable and I have to say that poor little Titus finds it pretty terrible too! Finally, however, we are allowed to let her out, but to begin with she must be prevented from climbing at all costs, which is quite a challenge. As she walks round the cottage it is clear that her muscles are terribly weak from just a fortnight's confinement, and it is some time before she properly has the confidence to jump from floor to table as she would have done prior to the operation, but of the three cats she has always been the least athletic or inclined to exercise.

Throughout the rest of December her recovery is steady and her leg gets stronger as she uses it more, but she continues to lack self-assurance in movements that involve leaping across distances and up on to things. Although her muscles seem to be building well, the surface of her leg remains hairless for an astonishingly long time. Alison had told me that she would look 'normal' before the year was out, but by Christmas Day she is merely sporting the slightest hint of bum fluff. It has the inane charm of the first facial hair of an adolescent boy, who has neither enough whiskers to make a moustache nor even to shave them off.

By late January Titus is stronger and increasingly well recovered from her surgery, and she and Fannie have become ever closer. They now seem more and more to be blocking out Pushkin, who leaves them mainly to themselves, certainly during the daytime.

The days are getting longer and now Titus and Fannie both come on heat. Both of them are very attentive to and demanding of all the human members of the household, but it is restricted to people. Although Pushkin, at regular intervals, approaches them to scent their small discharges, they always bat him away with a paw or, at best, they will simply sit, uninvitingly, with their backs towards him, thrashing their tails. Poor

Pushkin, hungry for love and wanting to be accepted, but eternally rejected. All three continue to play tag at night, the girls taking turns and Pushkin always chasing, but the moment his chasing changes tack and he looks like his thoughts might have progressed to other things, he is again, emphatically, disdained. I have met many cat owners and also two different vets who are genuinely surprised at the way events are turning out, but it is more than likely that Pushkin's inexperience, which is shared by the female cats, is a hurdle too far for them all to jump. It is said that male cats learn the procedure involved in the act of mating in the wild by watching the neighbourhood alpha tomcat perform. On top of all this, Pushkin is, as are most Russian Blues, timid by nature and it is possible that he simply does not want to upset the status quo by asserting himself.

A friend of ours, Robert, who at any one time is likely to share his life with upward of seven dogs and three cats, says that he kept a full tom and queen in the same household for five years and they never consummated their relationship and his cats were outdoor cats.

Fannie, as she rolls on her back and cries out for attention while twisting and turning lasciviously, is so completely possessed that she becomes the quintessence of all female passion. All desire, all yearning, all sensuality is encapsulated in her tiny, flailing body as she rolls herself around, snagging the sheets with her claws, which extend and retract as if in spasm. She accompanies these ardent callisthenics with, alternately, sensual groans and mellifluous trills, which, one would have thought, might melt an iron fence.

Pushkin, if he pays any attention at all, merely looks on in a bored, uninterested kind of way.

Titus does not roll around so much. More, she demands to be picked up, when she immediately sets up a loud purring. Then she wants down. Then up again. Then down, and then on her back for her tummy to be rubbed. And all the while she makes a demanding, unceasing kind of squawky mewing. It is exceptionally repetitive and very penetrating, and if you dare to ignore her it will become louder and louder. She is at her most insistent with both Michael and John, and I can often hear Michael, who habitually conducts lengthy conversations with her, pleading for peace, as he peers at his computer screen. Sometimes they develop an astonishing duet, which is both funny and irritating at the same time:

'Hello, Tites.'

'Miaow.'

'Howyer doing, Tites?'

'Miaow.'

'It's time to open the bar, Tites.'

'Miaow.'

'First one today, Tites. In here, Tites.'

'Miaow.'

'Yes, Titus.'

'Miaow, miaow.'

'What, Tites?'

'Miaow, miaow.'

'I know, Titus. Who's Daddy's girl, then?'

'Miaow, miaow, miaow' loudly.

'Oh Titus, why don't you go and find Pushkin', quite crossly.

'Miaow, miaow, miaow, miaow.'

Silence. Tap tap tap on the keyboard. Michael, that is, not Titus.

'Miaow, miaow, miaow, miaow, miaow', very loudly indeed.

'Titus, push off. Go and see Pushkin. Push off. Push off.'

'Miaow, miaow, miaow, miaow, miaow, miaow, miaow, miaow.' And so on.

Pushkin's inhibitions concern me more than Titus, it would appear.

~

Pushkin has taken to lying on my shoulder quite often as I type, but now he is so heavy and so long that I cannot bear the weight for more than ten minutes at a time, although he will stay there for much longer periods if allowed. Just now, Fannie has come across and begged to be picked up, and as I put her on the same shoulder I am astonished at how light she is; there seems to be so little of her, and as she nestles into my neck and licks my hair I can feel my own hairs stand on end from the pure pleasure of the feel of her. But it is Titus who lies on the bed behind me for hours like the faithful dog. Fannie sometimes leaves the room if I play music. Titus and Pushkin stick it out.

Both Fannie and Titus have, to my way of thinking, some of the characteristics of small tigers, but Pushkin, perhaps because of his maleness and his wide neck and shoulders, seems to exude essence of lion instead. He has other qualities that are not especially leonine, nor altogether endearing either. Pushkin has always broken wind a great deal even when a small kitten. If you hold him in your arms and make him purr, his ecstasy is emphasised by a very smelly cushion-creeping sort of emission. Today as I'm stroking Titus, who is lying on the bed, Pushkin leaps up in his sudden way and flops down near her head. I hold them together in this position, stroking both of them, when Pushkin suddenly tries to move away, but because he is firmly under my grasp he is stuck and lets a silent one rip right in front of Titus's nose. They both look really shocked and, as I stand back laughing and let them go, they each scuttle off in a different direction. It would appear that there is strict feline etiquette, and by my unwitting pinioning of him I made the boy break the rules.

This reminds me of a Saturday some weeks ago when I am lying in bed and Pushkin comes and lies on top of me turning round, elaborately, finally presenting me with his rear end. Because of his silent but deadly habit, I shout out:

'Pushkin, if you fart, you are dead.'

I hear a hoot of laughter from the room across the corridor where Michael is tapping away on his computer.

'So wrong, Marilyn! If he farts, *you* are dead.'

∾

Gerard and Sandra, Michael's brother and sister-in-law, and their two boys, Ryan and Benjamin, come to stay for the weekend. Michael takes Gerard and Ryan all the way out to West Ham for a disastrous football match (i.e. their team, Blackburn Rovers, loses) and Sandra, Ben and I mess around in the house. For a lot of Saturday and most of Sunday, Ben chases all three of the cats. Titus is obligingly responsive and I have a photograph of Titus sitting meekly on Michael's knee while Ben makes his white rabbit ride on her back. In return for her tolerance, Ben adores her and he whispers to me in a confidential sort of way:

'Titus is a cat who is smiling.'

She does have a smiley mouth, he is quite right. It bends right up her face, just as her father's did. Children have wonderful, proper imaginations, untrammelled by adult inhibitions. Ben, for example, had asked his mother, just a few weeks earlier, when talking about their young, excitable, panting Border collie, Peggy:

'Why does Peggy have a tongue like a diving board?' A question of pure magical imagery.

So Titus earns her colours. She is after all a sweet, tolerant cat, who puts up with a great deal and can be deemed to be good with children. This cannot be said of the other two. Fannie, to begin with, is game, but very quickly backs off and Pushkin seems to disappear altogether within about ten minutes of Ben entering the cottage. There is a wonderful moment when I ask the four-year-old Ben to tell me how he has found the cats and he responds with his mouth wide open and makes a funny shushing noise. I query this with Sandra, and at this point she shrugs, also uncertain what

As the Cat said
To Ben
puss-off
Picture by
Ben

this means. We find out soon enough. We go upstairs and Ben finds Fannie in our bedroom and, sure enough, as soon as she sees him she opens her mouth as wide as wide can be and hisses long and hard. To my astonishment we then find that Pushkin is doing the same, but even more loudly and with his fur all fluffed out. This is after I have looked everywhere for him, and finally find him curled up in the bottom of our wardrobe, where he spends the rest of the time until Ben leaves. So although Ben enjoys his stay, I think in terms of its success in persuading him that cats are child-friendly it can only be considered a partial success.

Soon after Sandra and Gerard have returned home to the north we receive a very sweet thank-you card from Sandra in which there is this drawing that young Ben has done. It could be either Pushkin or Fannie, but the probability is that it is Fannie. In the card, Sandra has written of Ben:

'He just loved the cats. He's told everyone he meets about them, about the way they express themselves – as in "go away, Ben, I'm not your friend".'

~

There have been fierce gales blowing for some weeks through from the end of January right into the first week in February, bringing in their wake much storm damage. The rendering on the east-facing chimneystack fell down in the winds the other night, and if anyone had been passing it would have been very bad news indeed. The cat fencing has repeatedly been blown out of line, so it doesn't fit just as it should do, leaving a small gap visible between the fencing and the gate. For three days on the trot we have found Titus outside in the garden, fortunately too frightened to venture out on to the road. On one occasion she had been there for a good half-hour before I found her. On that particular occasion I was very disconcerted by it. I had wandered out to put some washing in the drier and suddenly felt this soft touch on my calf; when I looked down, there was Titus looking up forlornly and patting me gently with her foreleg. I had had no idea that she was missing from the house.

Shortly after these incursions into the great outdoors, I hear Titus directing her demanding squawks at Michael who is sitting in front of his computer, and I just know that she will be rolling wildly around waving her legs in the air. I can hear him solemnly addressing her.

'Tites, I know you want to go in the garden. But it will not be good for you out there in the garden. Do you know what will happen to you in the garden? You will call out. Yes?'

'Miaow, miaow, miaow.'

'Yes. And the next thing that will happen is that your dad will roll up. All ginger and fluffy and smiley and you will think him just gorgeous. And that would be a very bad idea.'

326

Silence.

'He was great, your dad. He was a very handsome cat and he looked like he'd enjoy a good laugh!'

'Miaow, miaow.'

I remember how passionately Michael had declared, when first he and I looked out of the window together and saw the ginger tom in full courtship with Otto, that if there were to be a kitten from this union that looked like him – Michael called him 'The Lion King' – he would want us to keep it, and keep her we did.

CHAPTER 14

Today is a 'snatched' day of holiday, which Michael and I have taken among some working days, and I am indulgently shmoozing with Fannie in the bathroom, for a longer time than we normally allow ourselves, while half listening to a natural history programme about the greatest of all the whales, the blue whale. The marine biologist is explaining that the 'song' of the blue whale is not audible to human ears as the frequency is so low, between 5 and 10 hertz, and that in order for it to be heard it must be speeded up ten times. They then play a few minutes of blue whale 'song' which has an extraordinary quality to it – a deep resonating booming sort of sound – and Fannie is transformed, as if electrified. Her ears quiver forward and become erect, she stands up. Her eyes are wide and I notice that her pupils are dilated. I am holding her, still, and can feel her entire body tense, trembling slightly. What interpretation is this small sensitive creature giving to this sound, for the impact of it is huge on her, and I am 100 per cent certain she has never heard blue whale sounds before? Often, when I am at my computer, I will play a favourite CD, which is a combination of flute and harp music mixed with dolphin and humpback calls. The cats seem to enjoy it, as they always stay in the room for that one, but is there some extraordinary 'message' to be gleaned from the different resonance detectable in the largest of all the cetaceans? The moment passes and no more whale sounds are forthcoming. Fannie jumps down and starts grooming nonchalantly, and I thus understand that both our cuddle and her appreciation of natural history are now at an end.

Shortly after this, however, I am sitting at my desk with my bath towel wrapped around my torso, kimono-style, when Fannie, who now wants a continuation of her bath-time love-in, and for whom the towel is a signal for such cuddlings, suddenly springs up at my bare back from across the room. She probably intends to land on the back of the swivel armchair, but instead embeds her claws into the skin of my right shoulder blade. The pain is excruciating and I, somewhat unstoically I admit, scream out loudly and at length. She releases her claw hold and drops down to the floor before my yell of protest has run its course.

Michael comes in to see what the fuss is about and observes blood dripping down my back. Not a lot, but enough for him to understand what the racket is about.

'Fannie, how could you do that to Mummy after all she does for you?' he asks, rhetorically. Fannie looks up at him from the bed across the room, where, with leg pointing skywards, she is busily licking her private parts. I moan theatrically and turn back to face my computer, feeling sore and abused. Michael shrugs, as I stubbornly ignore his offers of help in the form of bandages, sal volatile and other unctions, and leaves the room.

Alone now with Fannie I turn to look at her, filled with resentment and wanting her to know it. She looks back at me, and slowly her eyes close into slits and then open again. She barely opens her mouth and I hear the faintest, almost inaudible, miaow. As I look back at her she repeats the tiny sound, again without moving her lips. To interpret this action precisely – scientifically – is not possible, but because of the unambiguous effect of that infinitesimal miaow upon me, my instinct dictates to me that I have just been granted what passes for a feline apology. I would argue that this cat, and therefore probably all cats, has some knowledge of contrition and a wish to convey it. I walk across to the bed and bend down and give her a hug and I hear her long vibrant quiet deep purr. Our bond is secure again.

～

I wake very early this morning having had the strangest dream. In my dream Michael and I appear to have been moving house into what turns out to be an old, rambling, converted schoolhouse. We have travelled for hours and have, of course, brought all three cats with us. We have been met and welcomed by someone who seems to be uncannily like Gordon, a gentle, gruffly spoken farmer I knew when I lived in the Dales, who is now, sadly, dead. In the dream I keep checking that all the doors and windows are safely closed, in my neurotic need to keep the cats from traffic harm, and in this case, of course, they are total strangers to their surroundings. I am busy poking around the house, and am mystified by its layout as I pass through a labyrinth of doors and corridors. We turn a corner and suddenly I find myself entering a large room, which, Gordon announces loudly from behind me, was the largest of the classrooms when it was still a school. To my considerable consternation all the windows and two doors are wide open and, through them, beyond the road down to the village, I can see a line of undulating hills, an outlying farmhouse, and an unmade track with a tractor bobbing away in the distance.

Michael can be heard, laughing and calling, in some remote part of the house, helping unknown others, with luggage and furniture. I turn round and mumble to Gordon:

'Oh these open doors and windows! We must shut them quickly. The cats will get out. Quick, can you help me, please?'

'A cat, did thee say? A've just seen a cat outside. A dead'un. I reckoned I hadn't seen it around these parts before.'

'No. Gordon. Please no.'

'Aye, it were dead reet enough. Flat.'

'I can't bear it. No! No! No! What colour is it? What colour?'

There is a long silence during which he looks very uncomfortable. In desperation I shout:

'Is it tortoiseshell? Is it grey? Ginger! Is it ginger?'

Still no answer, but he makes a small shift in his position and I understand.

'It's ginger, isn't it?' I start to cry. I flow over. I cannot stop crying.

I wake up and although it is very dark, I know I am not in the schoolhouse, but instead in our old familiar cottage. My cheeks are wet and the pillow is damp. I stumble out of bed in the gloom and find my way to the chair where Titus normally spends the night. She is curled up, deeply asleep. I bury my face in her fur and inhale her sweet smell and feel her warmth.

'Hateful, naughty, bad dream,' I confide to her quietly, with feeling. She purrs softly.

~

It is late February and our friends John and Kathy come to stay with their cat Delilah, who is Fannie's and Titus's aunt. I collect them from their house in London and we drive out to the cottage, but rather sadly Delilah is sick in the car both going and returning, and when we arrive at the cottage she is met with a lot of huff and puff from the two resident girls the moment she gets inside, which is then subsequently augmented by Pushkin who, after awaking from a deep sleep, blinkingly joins the assembled company and immediately starts to sound disconcertingly like a pit viper in full aggression. The effect of these greetings ensures that Delilah stays in John's and Kathy's bedroom for the first part of the weekend even though the door is open, and the three resident cats leave her be in her newly acquired territory. Finally, curiosity and the need for company drive her downstairs to come and play. Titus attempts to seduce her, which is rather sad, but at least dear old sweet Titus gets on with anyone and everyone and is laid back and has no side, even if she cannot quite tell what is what in the gender department. Not true of poor Fannie, who hisses madly at Delilah, although by the Sunday is calming down. Pushkin is the one who is most upset. Delilah is the first unknown cat he has met (other than the two bossy ones with whom he cohabits and whom he has known since kittenhood), and for Delilah he is the first tom she has ever encountered, so it was probable that there would be some tension between them. After his own initial hiss and spit parade, he spends almost every minute of this weekend in the wardrobe as he did for the weekend with Ben.

After I take John and Kathy and Delilah back home, I return late through a torrential downpour. There has been heavy rain for several days. Although it's very wet it's surprisingly warm and muggy, so on my return, having opened a bottle of wine, I open the back door and all three cats leap outside with zeal. I can hear a lot of action and gravel flying so, wine glass in hand, I decide I had better investigate. Because the following day is Monday and Michael has a very early start and I am not working that day, Michael has gone to bed, so I am left to investigate on my own. I find what looks like an enormous frog, larger than any frog I have ever seen in our garden or indeed anywhere that I can remember. The cats are remorseless and hound him from place to place. He seems to be having a great deal of trouble getting about. The act of jumping, which is really necessary for him to get away from the cats, seems to be a huge effort for him. With some difficulty, as usual, I get the cats shut in and go to try to free the frog. I finally locate him, with the aid of the torch, in a corner and try to scoop him up. I then discover that what I am staring at is two frogs, one firmly clamped on top of the other. The lower frog, at about four inches long, is very much the larger of the two, and for her (being the female of the species I now realise), the combined weight of the two together has been what is making it so tough for her to leap out of trouble. Both pairs of eyes stare up at me in alarm, pupils widely dilated, black-spotted, greeny-brown skins glistening and pale throats throbbing from fear of me and of the cats. I gently coerce them out of the yard and into the garden, where, presumably, they continue the night and even the next day in their amplexus until the female is ready to lay her eggs. (Really rotten having to be the frog on the bottom. For years I have harboured a small resentment that being a woman should not mean that automatically, if one is sharing, one gets the tap end of the bath. Name me a man who chooses the tap end without it being suggested to him first.)

I subsequently discover from Michael that earlier on in the evening, when it was still light, he had found the very same pair of frogs at the front of the cottage. They had apparently crossed the cat-killing (and for that matter frog-killing) main road and landed by our front door where Michael had taken a magnificent photograph, and then, to save them from 'death alley', he had moved them into the garden, but somehow, in that froggy way they have, they had crawled through the guttering into the cat enclosure. Bad idea!

Seeing those two frogs clamped together and also thinking about the theme of the tap-end-of-the-bath reminds me of an extraordinary story told to me by my friend Thomas, who used to help me look after my hens when I lived in Yorkshire. When Thomas was in his late teens his father had repeatedly aired his concern at the lack of eggs from a particular flock of hens and reckoned that something or someone was taking them. One summer's day, very early in the morning, he and his son arrive at the henhouse to witness the most extraordinary scene. The tableau that unfolds before them consists of one large rat, turned over on its back, legs in the air, being slowly, and probably painfully, pulled along the grass by another rat, who has firmly gripped the tail of the inverted rat in its mouth, thus creating a tow-bar. The reason for this towing exercise is plain enough to see, as the towee is clasping a hen's egg between its front feet, the weight of which is resting on its stomach. The arrival of the two men disturbs the rats, who drop the egg and run. But the delicate question still haunts me now. How did they decide which one should be the haulier and which one the carter? (Probably if you're female, you get to be towed?) Thomas reckons that the rats took this amount of trouble in order to feed a nest of young nearby, who had developed a fondness for still warm hens' eggs.

CHAPTER 15

February has blown itself out and March has come stalking in. Recently we have had one small frog in the house and just a couple of weeks ago a fieldmouse came calling, but luckily escaped before he could be set upon by the cats. Tonight, as we have been getting together the rubbish for collection first thing in the morning, Fannie has been behaving very strangely. She keeps walking towards the back door and then round the kitchen and past the washing machine which is in the corner under the window. From time to time she sits down in front of the washing machine.

'Michael, I reckon there is a mouse or something there.'

'Oh, leave it, the cats will get it eventually.'

'But that's not fair to it, and anyway it will mean mouse droppings everywhere and it isn't hygienic and it's beastly on the mouse!'

It has been windy all evening and the gate outside has been banging open and closed when it should have been firmly fastened, so I decide to check on the other two cats. Pushkin is firmly asleep on a pile of newly ironed clothes on top of John's bed, looking pretty closed down for the night, but I cannot find Titus anywhere. I search and search. Panic stations. Major alert. Michael, John and I all go out into the garden and bawl and shout her name for minutes on end. No appearance in any form.

We all go back into the kitchen and Fannie is now sitting by a crack approximately one and a half inches wide between the washing machine and the cupboard. I begin to feel more and more certain there is a mouse in there, so I go and find the torch. I shine it down the tiny chink. Staring straight back into the torchlight, unblinkingly, are two large reflective red eyes, cat height.

'Titus, what in God's name are you doing in there?'

No reply.

'Come out, come on, come out at once.'

'Marilyn, how do you think she is going to get out of there? The crack is only a couple of inches wide!'

'Well, she got in there in the first place.'

The washing machine is in the corner at an angle, so in reality there are wide wedge-shaped gaps down the sides of it, but because it is plumbed into a tight corner, the space between it and the two cupboards is apparently minute from the outside. I try to work out a rescue strategy. I open the cupboard door, which has the boiler in it, and call her name. She must have wandered in there when the door was ajar for us to empty the rubbish bin which we also keep in there, squeezed herself along behind the oven which is red hot when it is on – so she was lucky I had not been using it – through the under-sink cupboard full of bleach, and powders and other domestic chemicals, and round to the side of the washing machine so she could communicate with Fannie through the small crack. Heaven knows how long she has been sitting in there. But will she come back the way she has gone in? No, she will not. She is, after all, a cat. We call repeatedly. In due course, with the three of us manhandling it, we manage to pull the reluctant washing machine forward from its tight fissure and Titus casually saunters out into the room, covered in cobwebs, apparently unconcerned, suggesting she would have been quite happy to have sat in there for another few hours if we had not discovered her. She walks into the dining room, sits down, and starts a thorough grooming of herself. As we attempt to push the washing machine back into its hole, to our horror we find that Fannie has now trotted in behind it, presumably to see what all the fuss was about and whether it was worth it after all.

'Oh no you don't, young madam,' says Michael firmly, grabbing her by her scruff and hauling her out. 'We have had quite enough excitement for one night around washing machines.'

Washing machines and cats can be a dangerous combination.

When Titus, Fannie and their brother Beetle were really tiny they would frequently crawl into the washing machine if I had lain a pile of dirty washing inside and been careless enough to leave the door ajar, so I lived in dread of setting the machine off with kittens on board. Jeanne Willis told me a story that made me ache with laughter about her tabby moggy Wilbur who, although a shorthair, has a coat on the long side. She had put a pile of woollen clothes in the drier together with conditioner, and as she set the cycle going after two revolutions she knew from the loud thumping noise that something was amiss and she stopped the machine and opened the door. Out shot Wilbur, not apparently any the worse for wear, but the conditioner had extravagantly worked its magic on his wildly erect fur.

'He looked exactly like a dandelion!' chuckled Jeanne merrily.

This was the very same Wilbur who, having disappeared for two days during which time the household assumed that he had gone off on his wanderings, was eventually discovered to be shut in a wardrobe in a spare room. The wardrobe had a round porthole-like window with a discreet curtain drawn across it and Wilbur, in his desperate attempts to attract the family's attention to his plight, had managed to skew the curtain to one side by climbing on to a coathanger and looping himself over the cross bar in order to get to the window from which he painfully semaphored for help.

Halfway through March our friends Geoff and Pat come to stay for the night. For a variety of reasons they have decided to emigrate to France and are upping sticks, selling their house, and moving lock, stock and barrel across the Channel. Michael and I are deeply envious although in our heart of hearts would probably opt for returning to our beloved North of England rather than tackling the complications of another culture, in spite of its huge advantages, but talking to them and poring over their photographs opens up the cross-Channel longing in us both again. France is such a civilised country and Geoff and Pat are the second couple from our circle of friends within only a few weeks to have made this decision.

Pat explains that she has had the dogs inoculated with their rabies injections, etc., but that they cannot be allowed back into the UK again until after July when they get their full passports, but for the cat they have taken a different route and will simply take him and he will stay in France, rather than journeying to and fro. In the meantime she is obviously worried about where he will live while they go through the disruptions of moving house and buying their French home. My heart goes out to him. He has had a tough life and he is a 'rescue' cat anyway, so I offer him temporary accommodation – wondering how the mad mix of that would be, if she takes me up on the offer. I wait until a few days later before telling Michael that I have made this commitment. He is sanguine in a resigned kind of way, good lad. In the event, however, the cat stays with their neighbours and all is resolved. Close one there, O cats of Moon Cottage!

Easter has just passed and with it some glorious mild weather promising spring, and even hinting of summer.

With the onset of the warm weather, Titus seems to be getting increasingly restless and she frightens the life out of us on Saturday as I return from a marathon Tesco's shopping spree. Having parked the car on the pavement, I am passing the bags in sequence from the car to Michael, who is standing in the open doorway of the cottage, when suddenly he shouts out:

'Titus. Under the car. Quick!'

I collapse down on to the road, face scraping the tarmac, and see her crouched under the car, with heavy traffic thundering past her. Michael, on the other side of the car, face also at pavement level, manages to entice her gently towards him and I watch him get his hand on the scruff of her neck and pull her out from the shadow of the car and back into the cottage.

As a regular thing now, Michael and I together let the cats out into the outer garden to investigate because it distracts and entertains them, but this may have been a bad decision as both Titus and Fannie now try to do a runner into the garden every time we open the gate and may have a stronger sense of imprisonment as a result. When they are in the garden they just run around on the ground and stand 'shivering' their tails, although neither of them has scent-marked the plants, fences or ground, it appears. Also, they have made no attempts to climb the pergola or trees, thank goodness, for then it would be very hard to catch them again. They are in sufficient awe of being outside to be easily caught. Interestingly, in spite of the insistent and very carrying whiny calls they make – Fannie especially – no tom has come visiting, so full toms are clearly in short supply. Pushkin remains his own cat completely and keeps himself to himself in the main, although he plays sometimes with Titus, who is less hung up than Fannie. Today, however, I was watching him with them both and when he is alone with either one of them he will give them 'little kisses' with his tongue on their nose and each one of them in turn reciprocates, so there is friendship between them.

~

Is it conceivable that cats play games with each other in the sense that they consciously deceive each other? It is certainly true that I have frequently observed instances when cats have appeared to 'save face' with each other, and even with the humans with whom they share their environment. Pushkin, for example, this evening turns over on the bed and slightly loses his balance. At the time Fannie and Titus are idly observing him, and so he starts to lick a small part of his chest that is very difficult for him to reach to make it seem that that is what he is aiming for. It is quite clear from his initial movement, however, that he had not intended to do this at all. And a commonplace observation is that a cat, having missed its step when it lands, starts to groom, exactly as if the grooming had been the original intention.

Earlier on this same evening, Fannie had, for no especially good reason except possibly inspired by some form of jealousy, suddenly leapt on the bed and bitten Titus who was lying there, asleep. Titus leapt up, making a yowling, snarling sort of complaint, and then briskly jumped down on to the bedroom floor and manifestly 'pretended' that something interesting had just leapt under the bed and that she was going to get it out, single pawed, at all costs. Fannie was completely taken in by this contrivance and looked on yearningly, and then tried to get under the bed too. At this point, Titus got up and walked away, erect tail waving graceful question marks, and I swear her swagger was triumphant.

Today it is 29 April, which is one day after the day that Titus and Fannie were born three years ago, and one day before it is my birthday and my father's death day. I record this information because of a curiously strange moment in the bathroom. Fannie is very insistent that she should come in, although I have not yet showered and normally she waits until the shower is over as she hates to be splashed by wayward droplets of water, but today she is in for the whole performance. I have been behind the glass screen washing my hair and not looking at her, but come out briefly to get some soap and look across and find her staring at me, with her mouth hanging slightly open, her eyes fixed in an intense, almost manic stare, and her body rigid with concentration.

'Hey, babe. Are you all right?' I murmur.

She holds the stare. I am suddenly deeply uncomfortable.

'Fannie, I haven't put on any more weight, so what gives?' I toss out, casually, over my shoulder, but she continues with the intense gaze.

What does go on in the mind of a cat and why do I sometimes discern this essence of something that is outside our world in them? It is not because she is staring, she does that constantly. I think it is the mouth agape. I sense that there is some essence of my dead father in her, but cannot explain how or why.

After I had written the above entry in my diary, exactly seven days later, on 5 May, there is a programme on Radio 4 on concepts of the afterlife, which gives me further food for thought. An eminent Buddhist commentator, a woman, talks about it being perfectly normal in the endless cycle of the wheel for a being to return to a form of life on earth again and again until Nirvana is finally achieved when they may no longer be compelled to return, but at last be free, and this is to be hugely desired. In the course of this programme she casually remarks that it is very likely that a

347

human being might, for example, come back as a cat or similar creature until by reliving their life they discover perfect harmony and may at last go to their rest. The programme was not so much on afterlife as on the mistaken use of language such as 'karma', etc. This was on the same day as an episode of *Start the Week* in which a novelist discusses her futile attempts to communicate with her dead husband and concludes, with an unusual intensity, that we are not meant to be able to speak to the dead, as they are not 'allowed' back. We are not meant to know anything. She admits to being brought up a Catholic and she believes this omission is intentional in order to strengthen our faith on our final journey. Both beliefs unnerve me in conflicting ways, and yet I find myself drawn to the idea, both in the context of the supernatural nature of cats and also in my deep yearning to find my father again.

CHAPTER 16

Summer

I return a telephone call to one of my customers. He is young, hip and irretrievably metropolitan. It is a warm summer's day and I have the window wide open. I am speaking to him from my mobile phone and although I have not paid it too much attention, I'm assuming he will think I am in my office in London. In the course of our conversation he says:

'Where on earth are you phoning from?'

'Hey – what do you mean?' I reply, wondering why I am getting the third degree.

'It sounds as if you are phoning from the middle of Kew Gardens. There is a deafening racket of birds and squawking things.'

At this point Fannie starts her insistent miaowing, which she does when she wants to be cuddled, and I lean down to try to quieten her.

'No – I got it wrong completely. You're phoning from the middle of London Zoo.'

The summer is promising to be near perfect. The sun,

day in day out, arcs its way across the sky without any interruption and there is just enough breeze to make it feel ideal. It is the sort of weather you just want to go on for ever. On a never-to-be-forgotten Wednesday in mid August, the day dawns brilliantly sunny and hot, without a cloud in the sky. Michael and I, unusually, have planned a day out working together, and leave home early in the morning. By late afternoon we have finished our business with our fellow colleague, Kate, and decide to potter off home and put in an hour's work on our individual computers. As I put the key in the lock and open the sitting room door, the sight that greets me makes my heart pound in fear and fills my head with pain. I hear Michael's incredulous gasp behind me as he follows me into the cottage.

The small windows in our low-ceilinged cottage make it dark on even the sunniest day, and yet before we switch on the prerequisite lights we can see that Michael's desk straight in front of us has been ransacked. Every drawer and compartment has been pulled out and its contents spilled. As we turn around, we see that the cupboards have been opened and their contents tossed randomly about. The television set is askew and wires are lying everywhere. The video recorder is missing.

'Did you leave the cottage like this?'

'You *are* joking?'

'Just checking,' he mumbles in horror.

I run through to the kitchen calling for the cats. As I rush through the dining room I dimly observe that again drawers are pulled out of the dresser and their contents spilled everywhere. The dining room table is covered in a medley of objects and it looks for all the world as if a jumble sale has been in full swing. I stop dead in the kitchen. The kitchen window is hanging open. A pane the size of a large book has been smashed and the intruders have unscrewed the bolt holding the window shut. There is a pool of glass fragments lying on the floor, glinting in the sun, and Titus is paddling her way backwards and forwards through them. I pick her up and call the other cats. No sign of them. The back door is shut, but the huge iron bolts have been drawn open.

Michael comes in and says: 'You go upstairs and I will go outside and try to find the cats.'

'Are you serious? The so-and-sos who did this might still be up there,' I suggest, less than bravely.

'Sorry, you're right, let's both go upstairs together.'

'Please just hang on for one minute.' I turn away, close to tears. I open the back door and run out into the back garden calling for the cats. After a few minutes Fannie runs across to me. She is trembling and very excited, but seems otherwise intact. I pick her up and nurse her in my arms.

I call Pushkin, but to no avail.

We walk up the stairs together, keenly aware that by blocking the staircase we are making a retreat difficult for any perpetrator with criminal intent, and in so doing are rendering ourselves vulnerable. We walk into our bedroom and I cannot believe the mayhem that lies within. They have, with evident violence, taken my laptop computer from my desk, which was attached to an adjacent printer, and in pulling it away have turned over the computer table and all the objects upon it, which are now sprawled across the room. The telephone is dangling upside down by its wire. The contents of the drawers and cupboards are, as in the dining room, spread everywhere and on my desk, where once sat my laptop, there are assorted jewellery boxes and cufflink boxes and all other manner of things that I have not set eyes on in ages. Box lids, assorted knickers, socks, earrings, hair combs, tights, shoes, paperclips, books – all are sprayed across the floor, and just by the door and out on to the landing is a trail of coins that appear to have been dropped in haste during a sudden departure.

We call for Pushkin and look inside the big wardrobe in our bedroom, which is his favourite hiding place, but cannot find him. I race downstairs again and out into the garden. I call him again and start to cry from shock and apprehension. My neighbour Shirley, who is in her garden, hears my sobs and calls out over the wall to find out if I am all right, and I shriek back some unrepeatable expletive about the thieves and the fact that they have stolen Pushkin. She tells me that she is coming round, and shortly after that I hear her at the front door.

I hear myself blubbering to Shirley: 'I know they have stolen him because he looks like a posh cat and he is so hopeless he will never find his way back here again and he has no collar and he isn't chipped.' In the middle of all this Michael suddenly calls down from upstairs:

'It's OK. Found him. He was in the back of the wardrobe buried under a pile of towels and he is shaking and seems very frightened. I pulled him out, but he has gone right back in again and burrowed further under.'

I am hugely relieved of course that he is at least

safe and am now more clearly able to take stock of what the thieves have actually taken. We all go upstairs and study John's room, which is in almost as bad a state as ours. I notice that a large brown bowl in which John always keeps change is completely empty, but that his television and video recorder are still intact. Bizarre.

Michael dials 999 and reports the 'incident', and we await the police visit. We are told to be careful not to touch anything as 'forensic' may well need to look for prints. Shirley returns to her home next door, anxious herself as she has left the door open and had come round to see us before John, her husband, has returned home. 'Forensic' duly arrives and sets to, finger dusting everywhere, but especially on and around the windowsill, where the entry was made.

'There's a large number of paw prints round here,' he sniffs, and continues, 'but no human ones of any kind that I can see, so I presume', he adds drily, 'it must have been a cat burglar.'

We groan loudly. However, he does find human fingerprints on other artefacts and has some optimism that the culprit might be apprehended.

I get home the next day, Thursday, to find a message on the answerphone, which appears to say: 'Good evening, my name is John Hall, from the Sins of Crime Office at North Watford Police Station. I have a crime reference number . . .' On replaying the message, I discover that rather more prosaically he had said 'Scenes of Crime Office'.

The burglar or burglars were never apprehended as far as we know, but at least their fingerprints are on file along with ours for elimination purposes. I wonder exactly what was done to Pushkin by them, however, as he remained traumatised for several days after this, as if he had been violated in some way. There was a chunk of the book I am in the middle of writing, not backed up, on my computer and numerous photographs and other things that I will never see or be able to recreate again, as is also true of the jewellery, some of which had been owned and worn by my parents and even grandparents; this had great significance for me, and it was the same for Michael and John. Crimes of this kind, on the Richter scale of seriousness considered 'petty', are far more harrowing to the victims than the perpetrators ever imagine.

~

The day after this, however, all thoughts of burglary are driven out by something so shocking and devastating for those involved that it is difficult to put into words.

At 6.30 a.m. on Friday morning I am slowly getting up, and Michael has just gone outside, intending to talk to a couple of lads who work across the road who have kindly volunteered to fix our broken back gate with iron support bars when, directly below our bedroom window, I hear him being addressed by a young-sounding female who is asking if he knows who owns the dog she is holding on a lead. Michael replies: 'Yes, he's John's dog, next door. But why? Has something happened?'

Then I hear the terrible words:

'Yes. I have some sad news.'

I cannot hear any more as their voices move away and, as

fear grips me, I stumble towards the bathroom. I hear
Michael calling up the stairs, as I dreaded I would. He
simply says:

'Shirley is crying, Mo. You must come.'

It was a policewoman outside our door with Dante, John's
and Shirley's labrador. I know no more, but my mind
imagines the worst. I go outside and knock at the door of
the adjoining cottage and enter, where I find Shirley,
devastated, with the policewoman's arms around her. A
jogger has found John's body on the bridge by the canal,
with Dante standing guard over him, barking his heart out.

Dante is in the room as I squat down by Shirley and hold
her. I cannot bear the pain for her. It is too awful. It is
unendurable even for me. As Shirley sobs, Dante paces
backwards and forwards and then, in some agitation, picks

up all of his bedding and shakes it, fiercely, up and down, growling loudly. I try to stroke him but, I then realise, he too is inconsolable.

I slowly piece together the events that led up to the policewoman being outside our cottage. John is returning from his morning walk when he simply has a massive heart attack and collapses dead. Dante refuses to leave him. When the police arrive the policewoman orders Dante home, with some difficulty, as he will not leave John initially. Dante finally leads her home, although as a slight deviation he stops at another house first, where the policewoman knocks on the door, and finds that the sleepy owners have a bitch on heat, but do not know Dante or where his home is. This is her reason for questioning Michael. She couldn't cope with another false trail in her unenviable task.

As I stand in Shirley's kitchen I realise with wretched clarity that I am witnessing a pain so intense that it is beyond bearing. To watch helplessly as Shirley struggles with the realisation of the ending of a partnership that was as special as hers was with John, a marriage in which I discover the couple have never slept away from each other for a single night, and in which no cross words were ever exchanged, is simply unspeakable. This pain is then replicated as the policewoman gets on the phone and breaks the terrible news to Shirley's and John's son, Stephen, and daughter, Karen, that their father is dead. And then Shirley, herself, has to break the news to John's mother, whose birthday this day is.

Shortly after this, I volunteer, as a small offering of help to Shirley, to identify John's body in the local hospital, which is a necessary requirement of the police. When I am taken to where he is lying, I am moved by the peacefulness of his face. He has already started his journey I feel, and has left his shell, but it was sadly definitely his shell. John was one of the kindest and most generous of neighbours it is possible to have, and no task was too much trouble for him. All over our cottage there is evidence of his generosity of spirit. Michael and I are hopeless at fixing things around the home and John's hand can be seen in the installation of an awkward antique gaslight fitting, which never was meant to be made into an electric light – but very handsome it looks now – assorted switches properly fitted to walls, plugs, window fastenings and all manner of other amazing things that he quietly screwed, plumbed or wired in. He was also fantastically kind and funny and warm, and the world is a much poorer place without him.

I return home with a heavy heart and, with an unusual intensity, find myself looking across at Michael that night on his return from work with warmth and love and gratitude, and think long and hard about the affliction that has hit that gentle family next door and ache for them. This August that had started out with such promise has become, instead, a dark place.

CHAPTER 17

Monday 23 September

Millions of Britons awoke late last night to the disorienting experience of the house shaking as a minor earthquake set off car alarms, broke windows and rattled nerves across England and Wales.

Thousands of people dialled 999 or rang their local police station after the quake struck at 12.54 a.m. No injuries or serious damage was reported.

The tremor measured 4.8 on the Richter scale – a minor shake in world terms, but the strongest quake to hit Britain in a decade. A much smaller aftershock, with a magnitude of 2.7, was recorded at 4.32 a.m.

The epicentres of both quakes were located about 9 km beneath the city of Birmingham, but the main quake was felt by people as far apart as south and west Wales, Northamptonshire, south Yorkshire, Oxfordshire and London. Glenn Ford of the British Geological Survey (BGS) said: 'We'd only classify it as a light earthquake. This would have been right under the city of Birmingham itself and we've already had reports of the fire brigade being called out to fallen chimneys.' The earthquake lasted for at least 10–15 seconds, he said.*

I record this event because many books by animal behaviourists and indeed other scientists make references to the responses engendered in animals by earthquakes and other phenomena of this kind, and as a close observer of cats this was a heaven-sent opportunity for me to log the cats' precognition of the earthquake that they were bound to know was coming. The trouble, of course, was that *I* didn't know it was coming. The night before the earthquake it is true that Fannie was especially lively, and kept darting round the house in her manic way, twitch-dancing sideways as if being pursued by ghosts, pounding up the stairs, lying behind doors and leaping out at more phantoms, but then she is often like that without the stimulation of an impending quake, and I merely log her behaviour with the benefit of hindsight – that all-knowing collaborator! The other two cats were not noticeably lively at all, but that too could have been a form of precognition – 'just keep your eyes closed and it'll go away'? Honesty compels me to say the jury is out on this one. I would like to say Fannie knew something, but am not sure.

The actual quake was, in a rather 'unearthquakey' way, quite dramatic, however. I had just gone to bed, Michael was fast asleep, when there was a tremendous sort of rumbling. All the windows rattled, exactly as if an enormous

---

*Extract from *Guardian Unlimited*.

and indescribably heavy lorry was passing the cottage too closely. It was emphatic enough for me to look through the window, but of course there was nothing unusual to be seen, so I shrugged and got back into bed. The cats seemed calm. They were awake and watchful, but then they normally are just before I turn out the light; there is an unfailing pre-extinguishing-the-light ritual of watching, so again nothing unusual, and I was genuinely surprised when I heard the news the following day, although aware of the rumbling at the time.

Children and animals know things that the rest of us either don't know or have lost the ability to know. We become desensitised and muffle our instinct. It is almost as if, in artistic terms, once we have the wisdom and knowledge to understand the concept of, let us say, perspective, we no longer have the courage and imagination that a four-year-old does to plonk an image in the mind's eye straight on to the paper, with brilliance and original creativity and no copying from others. There, square and in your face.

Earlier this summer Andrew, my stepson from Geoffrey, had visited us accompanied by his two daughters, Maddie and Bridie, and I became enchanted by their take on the cats and the originality of their way of thinking. Maddie had whispered to me in a confidential sort of way that she thought she was a little like Fannie:

'Because when Daddy has a party and there are people there that I don't know, I would rather just go and eat something, or keep my head down and not have to talk.'

'Is that what Fannie does?'

'Yes, I reckon that is what she does, till she knows you, that is.'

Bridie, Maddie's younger sister, had announced loudly and with pride that she liked and indeed was also like Titus:

'Because she has red hair and so do I, and did you know that all ginger cats that have three colours are female anyway?'

'I didn't, Bridie, else I would have given her a girl's name.'

'Well, I could've told you, if you'd asked me.'

They were an extraordinarily laid-back lot and it transmitted itself to the feline residents. Even scaredy-cat Pushkin and timid Fannie learnt to trust the girls and actually sought out their company, and Andrew, having painfully cracked open his head on our low door lintel bending down to tickle Pushkin's tummy, was gracious enough merely to laugh his rich self-deprecating chuckle. They share their lives with cats back in New Zealand, so that probably contributed hugely to the evident mutual sympathy that they seemed to share.

Just before the summer comes to an end, Damian, who is very strong on Fannie being his favourite cat, asks us all which cat is our favourite. I admit mine is probably Fannie because she is so girlie and vulnerable and clingy, but that I do love them all; and I add that I reckon that Pushkin is John's favourite, and then say that Titus is Michael's. Michael, who overhears this, firmly but gently replies:

'No. I am Titus's favourite. That is different. I have no favourites. I love them all equally.' Thus speaks the wise father who has made sure he loves all his sons in the same measure.

Today Damian and Jo, his girlfriend, have flown to South Africa to a new job and new challenges and both Michael and I have that slightly poignant sense of life speeding away as the birds flee the nest. Although sad for us, their impending new life with all its promise was exciting them as they chatted animatedly whiling away the hours until their flight, sitting out in the little cat yard, under umbrellas, as the sun burnt down and the temperature rose into the high seventies. At some point during the morning, Damian, Jo and John had all gone out for a walk and Michael and I were left on our own, so we decided to let all three cats out together into the bigger garden. They played together and ran around and it was wonderful to see them free, but then first one, then the other, and in the end all three of them, approached the back gate which leads to the killer main road and I lost my courage and took them back into their little yard again. All three of them sat on the table in the yard and stared out at the garden. I have noticed this before in cats. They think. They spend long periods of time pondering things. They were not communicating with each other as they were some distance apart, but each one exuded an air of concentrated contemplation.

The sweet sad smell of autumn is in the air and it is made the more melancholy by my little visits next door to see Shirley, and sometimes Stephen and Karen too. They feel the loss of John most terribly and the pain remains deep and sharp for all three of them, and grief is the cruellest mistress I know. She will never be denied and demands all the time that she requires, regardless of the hurt it causes the sufferer.

Meanwhile, within the feline fastness of Moon Cottage the cats continue their mysterious interaction with one another, sometimes fighting, sometimes loving; at times playing amicably, and at others being as distant as it is possible to be. Their emotions will at times be plainly discernible, but more often than not their feelings, or what causes them, remain inscrutable.

One warm evening, as dusk starts to fall, I am sitting outside at the little Moroccan table under the lamp which is wreathed by a horde of nocturnal insects. As I idly watch

Fannie I become aware that an expression of extreme concentration is etched upon her tiny face. Slowly, almost trance-like, she rears up vertically and stretches her forelegs high into the air. With great delicacy she catches a small moth between her paws and for one moment longer, as if supported by an invisible force, she remains upright. Her eyes, with their dramatic black eyeliner, are pure geisha. Her mask is Japanese. The gracefulness of her gesture, balletic in its poise, belies the violence of her act. In fact, as she finally lands gently, four feet to the ground, her front paws open slightly and the small moth flies free. Five seconds later, however, she pounces upon it again and, holding it in her upturned paw, she deftly spoons it, fluttering, into her mouth and swallows it.

September dwindles into October and Titus, who is on heat, is severely taxing the patience of both Fannie and Pushkin, and today she surpasses herself while I am involved in a consultation with Matthew G. from the builders about repairing some leak damage in the dining room from the bathroom above. We are standing in the dining room and he is periodically injecting the wall with his damp meter and tut-tutting about the amount of water the walls are holding when she not only rolls around, looking cute, but as he leans down to write some notes on a pad on the table, she struts across the table 'presenting' to him ostentatiously and unmistakably, to even a non-animal observer, front half well down and back half high in the air, tail on one side and making a harsh 'miaow, miaow, miaow' noise the while. He looks across at me with horror on his face and I lift her off the table and put her on the floor and gently shove her away with my foot. I hum a bit and pretend nothing at all is happening. For about three minutes all seems well until, out of the corner of my eye, I see Titus spring up on to the piano, walk across the covered keyboard, and from there it is only a small jump on to the table where she marches straight down to the builder and repeats her earlier performance of seduction in every detail. Oh Titus, do you have no shame?

This morning Titus lies down for Pushkin and flirts with him while lying on her back, and Michael is appalled to see Pushkin smack her away with his forepaw.

'Michael, I am sorry, but it really *is* sauce for the goose being sauce for the gander. He has been treated like that so many times by both Titus and Fannie that it is hardly surprising,' I protest.

'We have the only gay cat in Hertfordshire,' he retorts. I am sure he is wrong.

A couple of nights later, during a long, relaxed dinner in the cottage with our friends Hannah and Wendy, we enjoy the splendid diversion of John arriving home late – slightly the worse for wear – strolling in, with his jacket casually slung over one shoulder, finger through the loop, being terribly Mister Cool. Picking up a glass of wine, he immediately falls into full flirt mode, firing out quick-witted cracks at the two girls. At this point Titus, who has not seen him for at least five hours, throws herself on the floor in front of him and miaows fit to bust. She rolls over and groans and moans, her randy cries becoming ever louder. Wendy and Hannah collapse quietly in silent convulsions of laughter while John blithely carries on chatting away. Eventually

John, even though in full flow, is unable to compete with the unashamedly lusty performance being put on so noisily by madam, and realising now why the girls are laughing, he quickly gets up, makes his excuses, and withdraws to the upper floor. I turn round to find that the rejected Titus is sitting disconsolately at the bottom of the stairs looking yearningly upwards.

'Tough, Titus, that's life for you!' Michael volunteers.

We talk of many things this night, but among them there is inevitable cat talk as we all love cats and have many anecdotes between us. Wendy lives with two rescue cats called Oscar and Jemima, whom she has homed for nearly a year. When she first saw them they had been in the Rescue Cattery for eight months waiting for a home, and they had entered the home at the age of four months, already neutered. What sad story must there be behind their original abandonment?

'They were kept in the same cage together and the cattery wanted them to go to the same home, and we all assumed they were siblings, but of course we don't actually know. The extraordinary thing is that when I first got them home and gave them their freedom, Jemima would not come out from the bedroom, where I had first released her, to eat or drink. And the other surprising thing was that having been together in that cage for all that time, as soon as they had their freedom they spent hours away from each other, and when they did come near each other they fought. Even now, after all this time, they still have fights and scratch each other and strange surroundings really upset them.'

'Do you think they just got on each other's nerves all the

time they were locked up together and were waiting for their freedom to get even, or is this just an acute response to acute circumstances?'

'I guess it is just the overwhelming fact of freedom after such a long containment that made them enormously disoriented.'

On this evening Hannah tells us also the remarkable doings of Tiger, a cat who lived with her mother and herself in a flat in East Dulwich, when she was about sixteen years old.

'Tiger was a serious urban hunter. But I mean *serious*! He was always raiding food and bringing it back to the flat. We never knew where he got it from and always hoped he discovered it on some pile of rubbish somewhere.'

'What sort of things did he bring back?'

'Oh all sorts. Half-eaten chops, a bit of steak, some fish once. But his star performance was the night he brought back a kebab, in pitta bread, complete with chilli sauce and salad intact. The full works up three floors, all the way to the top, without spilling any as far as we could tell!' After we mop up our tears of laughter, Hannah looks down shyly and adds:

'I think I have to concede that he did steal that one off a plate somehow, but of course we never knew where he went for his raids, so we couldn't make it up to the hungry casualty who was now sadly minus his or her supper.'

CHAPTER 18

As the autumn draws in deeper and the days shorten, we decide to take the calculated risk of letting the cats out into the bigger garden more frequently during daylight hours. Although they remain quite intimidated by the smells and sounds around them in the outer garden, each cat takes up his or her own position, according to their individual natures. Fannie has a disarming faith that if she sits perfectly still for long enough on the bench under the bird-feeding station, the birds will eventually forget about her and come back to feed. This has happily not been the case thus far, but she is not discouraged. Titus spends her time in the garden nibbling grass more in the manner of those beloved Dales sheep of my dim distant past rather than the cat she really is, but she always comes indoors to be sick afterwards (both she and Fannie resolutely use the cat-litter trays inside, however long they are outside), and Pushkin patrols around the perimeter of the garden, 'scent' marking and also urinating, territorially, so he does know how to do it. However, it must be confessed that he does squat down in a rather girlie way. Pushkin is the biggest liability in the garden as he has a tendency to panic and run very fast in a manic way in whatever direction he thinks safety might lie, which is not always towards the house. I feel happier now that I am able to give them some freedom, but it is a severely curtailed one and I never can leave them out for more than half an hour as the enticing fence and the world of main roads beyond is too tempting for them.

'Michael, one day promise me that we will be able to let them out into the big world?'

'Marilyn, one day we will, I promise you.'

~

One lazy Saturday I find myself idly rummaging deep into the drawers of my desk when right at the back of the top drawer my fingers suddenly touch a once familiar object and impulsively I pull it out. What I realise I am clutching is the tiny pale green velvet collar with a small bell on it that was worn day and night by Otto, the mother of Titus and Fannie, who was killed in the road outside when they were small kittens and that has lain undisturbed in the back of the drawer since her death. I look at it for a long time filled with a powerful sense of love and loss. Eventually, and with no particular forethought, I toss it towards Fannie who is lying in the armchair to my side. I am not expecting her to react, or at most am anticipating some mild playfulness. I am surprised, therefore, when I find she is enraptured by it. She smells it intensely, again and again, and then, slowly, with apparent fascination, she starts to play with the little bell, patting it one way and the other. It stirs my heart watching her. Does she have a conscious memory that this belonged to her mother? Is the sound of the bell combined with the scent triggering something? But then her interest passes. A little later I repeat the exercise with Titus. She is also engrossed by the smell, but I wonder if it's now diluted by both Fannie's scent and my own. I pick it up and tinkle the bell and then drop it down in front of her. Titus looks at it in a very concentrated way. Her eyes glaze over slightly and she holds open her mouth about an inch wide. I never recall seeing her open her mouth in this manner before, although Fannie often does this, and I realise that what I am observing is Titus instinctively activating the *flehmen* response – in other words, she is 'taste-smelling' the collar. It is now four years since their mother died, so is it even possible that her scent is still on the collar? The response of the two cats before me suggests quite strongly that there is some residue still impregnated on it and although Fannie and Titus were only seven weeks old when Otto was killed, they could have held her scent in their earliest memory, as they also might have done with the omnipresent 'tinkle' of her bell as she trotted in and out of the room to feed them. When the kittens were first orphaned, although they visibly missed their mother, they learnt very quickly to fend for themselves (the ability of young animals to survive is supreme), so it was quite hard at the time to gauge what levels of grief they may have been experiencing. It is certainly true, however, that adult cats can experience quite astonishing depths of grief after the death of a close companion cat and will often come near to starvation in their suffering as they simply 'forget' to eat. I often wonder whether Septi's cancer, written of in *The Cats of Moon Cottage*, was triggered by grief after Otto's death. Jeffrey Masson and Susan McCarthy, in their profoundly moving book *When Elephants Weep*, discuss at length, and with convincing evidence, the hypothesis that animals experience acute grief, extending further Charles Darwin's observations in *The Expressions of the Emotions in Man and Animals*.

Looking at another grief, the grief felt by a human at the death of a beloved animal, is a topic that concerns me deeply as I believe it is one of the great underestimated emotions of pain that many humans experience and are frequently inhibited from discussing. On more than one occasion I have experienced an almost heightened consciousness of how privileged I am to be able to love these three cats as much as I know I do and, as all animal lovers are aware, there is a price to be exacted for that degree of passion. That does not mean that I do not love my own species greatly, it is simply that the human love of animals and possibly the animal love of humans is a different sort of love. There is often an intensity in the bond that is different from human interaction perhaps because of the mutual 'blind' faith that both parties allow each other, which maintains the cross-species communication. There is, in the relationship between animal and human a purity, a lack of ambivalence. That same look in the eye that can be exchanged between human and animal heavy with trust and love; that gentle touch of the paw rewarded by the light stroke of the hand; that fondle of an ear in just the right way and the returning tickle of a whisker against the skin; that affectionate dab of a wet cold nose and the ensuing shiver of pleasure, all combine to make the mutual love deep and binding. And there is too that lack of betrayal; no words can destroy this relationship, only death. So when the death comes – and by the nature of the short life expectancy of most animals with whom we share our lives, the death will come all too soon – the pain is profound and enduring.

There is a beautiful essay in an altogether remarkable book by Raimond Gaita* on why science needs the partner of philosophy to help deepen our understanding of animals. He argues that informed, rigorous, controlled observation is important, but it needs to be married to intelligent emotional responses and the all-important challenge is the use of the language of expressing those findings. He discusses a chapter entitled 'Death of a Dog' in a book called *Moral Questions* by Rush Rhees, in which the philosopher understands that his grief, which even after a passage of time is still excruciating, is distinct and different from grief for a human and that this is specifically for his dog, Danny (a dog where he knew that they both knew where they stood with each other); but the consciousness that it is grief *just* for a dog does not in any sense dilute the power of the pain. He expresses his loss at a distance of two years after the death in this way:

When I try to get on with working at (trying to understand) the philosophy of mathematics (mathematical induction, recursion), I realize how, in

---

* *The Philosopher's Dog* by Raimond Gaita (Routledge, 2003).

what I was reading and writing, I made no move
without him: how I brought him along in every move.
(He was sleeping in the corner or there in front.) And
if he is past – how am I supposed to move? – what do
I do here now?

In September 2003 the first book about this family of cats,
The Cats of Moon Cottage, was published, and Peter Warner,
the outstanding illustrator of that book (and also, magnificently, of this one), who had used his beautiful nineteen-
year-old red tabby Django as the model for Michael's
nineteen-year-old Septi in the first book, had organised local
press and television publicity. And as a strong visual prop
for this publicity, he had allowed the filming of the ever-
obliging Django by the local press photographers and a
television crew, who all took umpteen photographs and reels
of footage of him, which duly appeared in the press and on

television within the Kent region. Sadly, in early October, as all the local publicity peaked, Django's health deteriorated and Peter gently nursed him through the last stages of kidney failure. The following words are extracted from Peter's own, which he put down to be spoken as a memorial for Django at his burial on 12 October:

Django
Django died at 7 p.m. on Thursday 9 October, aged 19 years, 3 months and 9 days, after a blessedly short deterioration from kidney failure.

He was universally loved and loving, everybody's friend, never happier than on your lap and in raptures when his lower back was scratched, that upward gaze, eyes closed in bliss, telling you what paradise for him was like.

He it was who sat on the kitchen dresser in the old kitchen, with his brother Oliver, staring down aghast at the invasion by Solo's puppies.

So uncouth – but interesting!

Although large numbers of people don't know it, he has been the model for icons on millions of pet food labels, dressed in appropriate clothing. He appeared pretty much as himself as Go-Cat over many years, and as a semi-longhair, debonair new Whiskas cat, from 1986, until moving over for the recent new photographic upstart.

He was the choreographer for the Japanese calendar cats, later collected into the book *Perfect Cats*. And most recently he has modelled for Septi in *The Cats of Moon Cottage*. A veritable Walter Mitty.

Above all he has been the perfect cat companion, for the dogs as well as me; loving, uncomplaining, gentle, delighting the eye with his grace and equilibrium. His light-footed trot through grass and leaves was unique. He seemed to move without touching anything.

So our book *The Cats of Moon Cottage* has become a memorial for him. After several local press photo calls in recent weeks, on Tuesday 7 October he gave his first – and last – TV appearance, on *Meridian Tonight*. Over the last few nights the full moon seemed to find all the empty spaces of the kitchen as if searching for he who has been ever present, so warmly welcoming, these past 19 years. Blue, my Abyssinian, seems lost too. (*Peter Warner, 12 October 2003*)

So gently I draw these further cat tales from Moon Cottage to a conclusion. I am in awe at the pleasure I, and so many others like me, receive from the company of cats, and only hope that in part I may repay to my own companion cats particularly, and all cats as a species, the gift they give to me, to us all. I love most animals, I might even say all animals, and high up on that list are whales, dolphins, horses and dogs. Dogs were my first love in fact, and it is only much later that I have come to revere cats as I now do.

They are not better than other animals, they are simply their own creatures whose subtleties and intelligences continue to hold me in thrall, and of whose antics I shall never tire.

EPILOGUE

Giles Gordon, to whom I dedicate this book

A cat who has had great import in my life, but whom, sadly, I have never met, is a small Burmese called Harry. This cat belonged to a truly remarkable man called Giles Gordon, whom I have known for many years as a close friend, but who only recently became my literary agent. When Giles first agreed to read the manuscript that was to become *The Cats of Moon Cottage*, he sighed audibly – even to me – before putting the phone down, having firmly warned me that he was taking on no new authors. He told me afterwards that the night he read my book was an evening in which he had had to read three manuscripts, not untypical for an agent such as Giles I imagine, and that mine was the third, so it was late in the evening before he started it.

Shortly after he started reading my manuscript, his cat, Harry, jumped up into his lap, and Giles says that as he began to enjoy the book he relaxed and, as he did this, so Harry began to purr; and in that position of mutual comfort Giles read on, quietly stroking Harry's purring body, until he had finished it, certain that it had Harry's approval. The next day Giles took me on as one of his authors and the rest is history.

I have long wanted to meet Harry and shake him by the paw as I know I owe him, so I was extremely sorry to hear from Giles one day in October 2003 that Harry had gone walkabouts and had not returned, and that Giles's youngest son, Leo, was especially upset.

Because I felt I did not want to keep asking Giles whether there was any good news, I emailed his kind and ever-willing assistant, Joanna.

From:	Marilyn
To:	Joanna
Sent:	28 October 18:32
Subject:	Favour

Dear Joanna

So sorry to ask you this, but am so worried and upset for Giles about Harry going walkabouts and don't want to keep asking him if Harry has returned because if he hasn't, it is even more upsetting.

But if by a miracle he does come home again or there is any news, would you mind awfully letting me know. I am willing like mad that the little thing surfaces again and comes back home.

Aaagh!

Love

Marilyn

From: Joanna
To: Marilyn
Sent: Wednesday 29 October 9:58
Subject: RE: Favour

Dear Marilyn
  Of course I will let you know if the wee
thing returns home, it is worrying. My dad's
cat did the same and disappeared for over a
year, but came back when we thought we had
lost him - goodness knows where he had been,
if only he could talk.
  Joanna x

Following this email from Joanna, I received various emails from Giles himself, and then, on Monday morning, 3 November, I received the terrible phone call from Joanna telling me that Giles had had a fall at his home in Edinburgh on the Friday night which, I afterwards recall, was Hallowe'en. This was then followed by an official announcement from Giles's main office of Curtis Brown in London:

> As has been widely reported in the press, Giles suffered a serious head injury after a fall at his home in Edinburgh last Friday evening. He is being cared for at the Western General Hospital in Edinburgh where he is currently under drug sedation. A full assessment of his condition will not be known for several more days.

I began to be frightened as the bulletin sounded far from good and it was difficult to find out anything beyond the information contained in this statement – and all Giles's authors had been emphatically requested not to phone the hospital. Just over a week passed during which time I went into hospital to have a bi-lateral carpal tunnel release performed on my wrists. On the day I returned home, still heavily sedated, arms immobilised and confined to bed, I discovered via my sister, Margot, whose very first job was as Giles's secretary, that BBC Radio 4 had broadcast an announcement that Giles was dead. Michael had tried to censor her news from me, but I knew that something terrible must have occurred when I heard she had phoned twice. I begged him to let me know what was going on and when, with great reluctance, he told me Giles was dead, I heard my heart break.

My rock was no more. Giles, whose judgment of what was good or bad was considered by many to be impeccable, would never be able to make such a judgement again. Father, husband, brother, friend, colleague, agent, writer, man of letters, life force, wit, bon viveur was gone for ever. This man, who was to a fault considerate, outrageous, adorable, wise, anarchic, lovable, outspoken, compassionate, infuriating, encouraging, irreverent, amusing and oh, such good company, Giles was never going to bark out his impish laugh again.

That night I cried for a long time and in the days and nights to follow, but amid the selfishness of my own grief I did find time also to consider how his courageous wife Maggie, who worked in London and lived shuttling between London and Edinburgh, was going to hold herself and her brood together, the youngest of whom was just four years old, but I felt sure she would, as she is a remarkable and strong woman worthy of Giles. I ached too for his older children by his first marriage, who had now, prematurely, lost both of their parents. Hattie, his oldest daughter, had just published her first book and Giles told me at the very last lunch I had with him how very proud he was of her.

A week later Michael and I attended the beautiful but elegiac service to celebrate Giles's life held in the cathedral of the same name in Edinburgh. When I first heard where the funeral was to be held, I remembered Giles telling me years earlier that he bet he was the only person I knew who was named after a cathedral. I feel sure that that still holds true: Giles the only eponym in reverse I have ever known. At the reception following the funeral I discovered that Giles's cat, Harry, had never reappeared. A fellow mourner confided to me:

'They always know when bad stuff is about to happen, cats, and they get out while the going's good!'

Irrationally, I shuddered mildly as I remembered the night of Giles's fall was Hallowe'en and outlandish associations with cats and witches and all souls raced through my mind. To counteract these nonsensical thoughts, I protested:

'But something might have *happened* to Harry!'

'Well, in that case he's there, waiting to greet Giles.'

Giles, I offer from all your authors and those who love you and admire you, and know you for what you are, the last line of my first book that you so teased me about:

'For while we live you shall not die.'

Animal *Health* Trust

The Feline Unit at the Animal Health Trust

Cats are now the most popular domestic pet in the UK. Although our knowledge of feline diseases has increased over recent years, our level of understanding of many of these conditions is still relatively poor. The Animal Health Trust is an internationally renowned centre of excellence that seeks to improve the health and welfare of animals by studying the diseases that affect them so that better diagnosis, treatment, control and prevention can be achieved. The Feline Unit provides a full clinical referral service for cats with internal medical diseases, and is a part of the small animal hospital at the Trust. It is dedicated to promoting feline welfare by providing the highest quality of care for sick cats, and by contributing to studies that are concerned with broader aspects of feline health and welfare that can impact on the quality of life of all cats.

The contact details for the Feline Unit at the Animal Health Trust are:

Lanwades Park
Kentford
Newmarket
Suffolk CB8 7UU
UK

Tel: (44) 8700 502424
Fax: (44) 8700 502425

Dr Andy Sparkes BVetMed, PhD, DipECVIM, MRCVS
RCVS Specialist in Feline Medicine
Head of the Feline Unit, the Animal Health Trust

A percentage of all author are donated to the Animal Health Trust.

POSTSCRIPT

To contact Marilyn Edwards via email and for an update on the Moon Cottage cats please visit her website: www.thecatsofmooncottage.co.uk or write to –

The Coach House
Hutton Roof
Kirkby Lonsdale,
Cumbria, LA6 2PG

For more information on Peter Warner and his illustrations see his website www.peterwarner.com